METHODS OF CRITICAL DISCOURSE ANALYSIS

Edited by
Ruth Wodak and Michael Meyer

SAGE Publications
London • Thousand Oaks • New Delhi

First published 2001
Reprinted 2002

SAGE Publications Ltd
6 Bonhill Street
London EC2A 4PU

SAGE Publications Inc
2455 Teller Road
Thousand Oaks, California 91320

SAGE Publications India Pvt Ltd
32, M-Block Market
Greater Kailash – I
New Delhi 110 048

British Library Cataloguing in Publication data

A catalogue record for this book is
available from the British Library

ISBN 0 7619 6153 4
ISBN 0 7619 6154 2 (pbk)

Library of Congress catalog card record available

Typeset by Mayhew Typesetting, Rhayader, Powys
Printed in Great Britain by Biddles Ltd, *www.biddles.co.uk*

Contents

Acknowledgements

This book could not have been written without the help of many people. We wish to express our gratitude to them all.

In particular, we appreciate the discussion and work with the student participants at our seminar on Critical Discourse Analysis (CDA) which we organized at the Department of Linguistics of the University of Vienna in the summer of 1999. This panel provided an important stimulus for our plan to publish a book on CDA.

We appreciate the collaboration with the authors of the contributions to this book: Siegfried Jäger, Teun van Dijk, Norman Fairclough and Ron Scollon. Not only did they write interesting papers, but they submitted them (almost) on schedule, and accepted our criticism and comments with understanding and patience.

Bryan Jenner has been indispensable in helping to mould our badly structured non-native English in an acceptable form. Michael Carmichael and Lauren McAllister at Sage were very supportive editors who contributed positively to the final result.

Contributors

Norman Fairclough is Professor of Language in Social Life at Lancaster University in the UK. He has written extensively on critical discourse analysis. His main publications include: *Language and Power* (1989), *Discourse and Social Change* (1992), *Media Discourse* (1995), *Critical Discourse Analysis* (1995), *Discourse in Late Modernity* (1999) (with Lilie Chouliaraki) and *New Labour, New Language?* (2000). He is currently working on language in new capitalism, an introduction to text and interaction analysis for social researchers, and on the theorization of discourse within critical realism.

Siegfried Jäger is Professor of German Language at the Gerhard Mercator University in Duisburg, Germany. He is also head of the Institute of Language and Social Research (DISS), a member of the board of the International Association for the Study of Racism (IASR), and a co-editor of *Discourse and Society*. His main publications are: *BrandSätze. Rassismus im Alltag*, fourth edn, Duisburg 1996, *Kritische Diskursanalyse. Eine Einführung*, second edn, Duisburg 1999. His main areas of research are speech act theory, sociolinguistics, discourse theory and discourse analysis. His research is focused on right-wing extremism, racism, militarism and bio-power.

Michael Meyer is an Assistant Professor at the Department of Management and Organizational Behaviour at the Vienna University of Economics and Business Administration. His main areas of research are social systems theory, qualitative methods, and organization theory. His recent research concentrates upon careers and social capital in and between organizations. His main publications are: *Methods of Texts and Discourse Analysis* (with Stefan Titscher, Ruth Wodak and Eva Vetter, London: Sage 2000), *Text und Gegentext* (with Stefan Titscher, *Soziale Systeme* 2 1998).

Ron Scollon is Professor of Linguistics in the Department of Linguistics, Georgetown University in Washington, DC and editor of the journal *Visual Communication*. His interests include mediated discourse, multimodal discourse, the sociolinguistics of literacy, and the relationships among technologies of communication and sociolinguistic analysis. His two most recent books are *Mediated Discourse: The Nexus of Practice* and *Intercultural Communication: A Discourse Approach* (2nd edn) (with Suzanne Scollon).

Teun A. van Dijk is Professor of Discourse Studies at the University of Amsterdam, and Visiting Professor at the Universitat Pompeu Fabra, Barcelona. After earlier work in literary studies, text grammar and the psychology of text comprehension, his research in the 1980s focused on the study of news in the press and the reproduction of racism through various types of discourse. In each of these domains, he has published several books. His present research in critical discourse studies focuses on the relations between power, discourse and ideology. His latest book is *Ideology* (Sage, 1998). He founded the international journals *TEXT*, *Discourse and Society* and *Discourse Studies*, and still edits the latter two. He is editor of the four volume *Handbook of Discourse Analysis* (1985) and of the new two volume *Discourse Studies. A Multidisciplinary Introduction* (Sage, 1997). He has lectured widely in Europe and the Americas, and was visiting professor at several universities in Latin America.

Ruth Wodak is Professor of Applied Linguistics and Discourse Analysis at the Department of Linguistics, University of Vienna and also Research Professor and Director of the Research Centre on Discourse, Politics, Identity at the Austrian Academy of Sciences (www.oeaw.ac.at/ wittgenstein). She has received many awards including 1996 Wittgenstein Prize for Elite Researchers. She also holds many visiting professorships (Stanford, Minnesota, Georgetown, Uppsala). She is editor of *Language and Politics*, co-editor of *Discourse and Society*, editor of the series *Diskursforschung* (Passagenverlag), *Sprache und Kontext* (Lang Verlag), *Discourse in Politics, Culture and Society* (Benjamins). Her areas of research include discourse and politics, methodology in CDA, racism and anti-Semitism, gender, organizational discourse. Recent publications include *Racism at the Top*, 2000 (with Teun van Dijk), *Discursive Construction of National Identity*, 1999 (with Rudi de Cillia, Martin Reisigl, Karin Liebhart), *Disorders of Discourse*, 1996, *Discourses on Unemployment in the European Union*, 2000 (with Peter Muntigl and Gilbert Weiss), *Discourse and Discrimination*, 2001 (with Martin Reisigl), *Gender and Discourse*, 1997.

1

What CDA is about – a summary of its history, important concepts and its developments[1]

Ruth Wodak

CONTENTS

Beyond description or superficial application, critical science in each domain asks further questions, such as those of responsibility, interests, and ideology. Instead of focusing on purely academic or theoretical problems, it starts from prevailing social problems, and thereby chooses the perspective of those who suffer most, and critically analyses those in power, those who are responsible, and those who have the means and the opportunity to solve such problems. (van Dijk, 1986: 4)

To draw consequences for political action from critical theory is the aspiration of those who have serious intentions, and yet there is no general prescription unless it is the necessity for insight into one's own responsibility. (Horkheimer quoted in O'Neill, 1979)

Preliminary remarks

The terms *Critical Linguistics* (CL) and *Critical Discourse Analysis* (CDA) are often used interchangeably. In fact, in recent times it seems that the term CDA is preferred and is used to denote the theory formerly identified as CL. CDA regards 'language as social practice' (Fairclough and Wodak, 1997), and takes consideration of the context of language use to be crucial (Wodak, 2000c; Benke, 2000). Moreover, CDA takes a particular interest in the relation between language and power. The term CDA is used nowadays to refer more specifically to the critical linguistic approach of scholars who find the larger discursive unit of text to be the basic unit of communication. This research specifically considers institutional, political, gender and media discourses (in the broadest sense) which testify to more or less overt relations of struggle and conflict.

The passage quoted above from Teun van Dijk which I have used as an epigraph summarizes some of the aims and goals of CL and CDA, in particular those which indicate the interdependence between research interests and political commitments in what he describes as critical science, where van Dijk's non-theoretically exclusive notion of critical, as used in his programmatic statement, highlights the customary sense of 'critical that such scholarship embodies'. In this 'critical' spirit, I would like to provide an overview of some basic theoretical principles of CL and CDA[2] and brief descriptions of the most prominent schools which have emerged in CL and CDA. Indeed, heterogeneity of methodological and theoretical approaches represented in this field of linguistics would tend to confirm van Dijk's point that CDA and CL 'are at most a shared perspective on doing linguistic, semiotic or discourse analysis' (van Dijk, 1993: 131).

This shared perspective relates to the term 'critical' which in the work of some 'critical linguists' could be traced to the influence of the Frankfurt School or Jürgen Habermas (Thompson, 1988: 71ff.; Fay, 1987: 203; Anthonissen, 2001). Nowadays, however, it is conventionally used in a broader sense denoting, as Krings argues, the practical linking of 'social and political engagement' with 'a sociologically informed construction of society' (Krings et al., 1973: 808), while recognizing, in Fairclough's words 'that, in human matters, interconnections and chains of cause and effect may be distorted out of vision. Hence "critique" is essentially making visible the interconnectedness of things' (Fairclough, 1985: 747; see also Connerton, 1976: 11–39 and see below).

Thus, CL and CDA may be defined as fundamentally concerned with analysing opaque as well as transparent structural relationships of dominance, discrimination, power and control as manifested in language. In other words, CDA aims to investigate critically social inequality as it is expressed, signalled, constituted, legitimized and so on by language use (or in discourse). Most critical discourse analysts would thus endorse Habermas's claim that 'language is also a medium of domination and social force. It serves to legitimize relations of organized power. In so far as the legitimations of power relations, . . . are not articulated, . . . language is also ideological' (Habermas, 1977: 259 and see below).

In contrast to other paradigms in discourse analysis and text linguistics, CL and CDA focus not only on texts, spoken or written, as objects of inquiry. A fully 'critical' account of discourse would thus require a theorization and description of both the social processes and structures which give rise to the production of a text, and of the social structures and processes within which individuals or groups as social historical subjects, create meanings in their interaction with texts (Fairclough and Kress, 1993: 2ff.). Consequently, three concepts figure indispensably in all CDA: the concept of power, the concept of history, and the concept of ideology.[3]

Unlike some of the research in pragmatics and traditional socio-linguistics in which, according to critical linguists, context variables are somewhat naively correlated with an autonomous system of language (for example Kress and Hodge, 1979), CL and CDA try to avoid positing a simple deterministic relation between texts and the social. Taking into account the insights that discourse is structured by dominance;[4] that every discourse is historically produced and interpreted, that is, it is situated in time and space; and that dominance structures are legiti-mated by ideologies of powerful groups, the complex approach advo-cated by proponents of CL and CDA makes it possible to analyse pressures from above and possibilities of resistance to unequal power relationships that appear as societal conventions. According to this view, dominant structures stabilize conventions and naturalize them, that is, the effects of power and ideology in the production of meaning are obscured and acquire stable and natural forms: they are taken as 'given'. Resistance is then seen as the breaking of conventions, of stable dis-cursive practices, in acts of 'creativity' (Fairclough and Kress, 1993, 4ff.).

In CDA nowadays a huge continuity, of course, exists with CL (see, for example, Fairclough and Wodak, 1997; Blommaert and Bulcaen, 2000) which developed in the 1970s and 1980s, primarily at the University of East Anglia, with Roger Fowler, Tony Trew and Gunther Kress (see below). The continuity is visible mostly in the claim that discourses are ideological and that there is no arbitrariness of signs (see also Kress, 1993). Functional systemic linguistics proved to be most important for the text analysis undertaken by this school (see Halliday, 1978).

Other roots of CL and CDA lie in classical rhetoric, text linguistics and sociolinguistics, as well as in applied linguistics and pragmatics. The notions of ideology, power, hierarchy and gender, and static sociological variables were all seen as relevant for an interpretation or explanation of text. The subjects under investigation differ for the various departments and scholars who apply CDA. Gender issues, issues of racism, media discourses or dimensions of identity research have become very promin-ent (see Wodak et al., 1999; Blommaert and Verschueren, 1999; Martín-Rojo and van Dijk, 1997; Pedro 1977; Martín-Rojo and Whittaker, 1998; many editorials in *Discourse and Society* over the years, specifically the debate between Emanuel Schegloff and Michael Billig in issues 2–4, 1999/2–4, 2000). The methodologies also differ greatly: small qualitative case studies can be found as well as large data corpora, drawn from fieldwork and ethnographic research.

To begin with: a small story about the formation of a 'scientific peer group'

CDA as a network of scholars emerged in the early 1990s, following a small symposium in Amsterdam, in January 1991. By chance and through the support of the University of Amsterdam, Teun van Dijk, Norman Fairclough, Gunther Kress, Theo van Leeuwen and Ruth Wodak spent two days together, and had the wonderful opportunity to discuss theories and methods of discourse analysis and specifically CDA. The meeting made it possible for everyone to confront each other with the very distinct and different approaches, which still mark the different approaches today (see the papers in this book and related literature). In this process of group formation, differences and sameness were exposed; differences towards other theories and methodologies in discourse analysis (see Titscher et al., 2000), and sameness in a programmatic way which could frame the differing theoretical approaches of the various biographies and schools of the respective scholars.

Of course, the start of this CDA network is also marked by the launch of van Dijk's journal *Discourse and Society* (1990) as well as through several books, like *Language and Power* by Norman Fairclough (1989), *Language, Power and Ideology* by Ruth Wodak (1989) or Teun van Dijk's first book on racism, *Prejudice in Discourse* (1984). But the Amsterdam meeting determined an institutional beginning, an attempt both to start an exchange programme (ERASMUS for three years)[5] and multiple joint projects and collaborations between the different scholars and approaches as well as a special issue of *Discourse and Society* (1993), which brought the above mentioned approaches together. Since then, much has changed, the agenda as well as the scholars involved. New journals have been launched, multiple overviews have been written, and nowadays CDA is an established paradigm in linguistics.

Since this first meeting (of course, CDA and CL had existed before, but not as such an international, heterogeneous, closely knit group of scholars) annual symposia take place and have accompanied the emergence of this paradigm, which is bound together more by a research agenda and programme than by some common theory or methodology. More scholars have taken part in these conferences, and more researchers have started with research in CDA, like for example Ron Scollon. Scholars from the German-speaking world seldom took part because the conferences were always held in English. Nevertheless, Utz Maas as well as Siegfried Jäger and their approaches have been understood and acknowledged (see Fairclough and Wodak, 1997; Titscher et al., 2000). This explains the wide variety of different approaches in this book, both theoretically and empirically, and the range of linguistic tools used to analyse discourse. The criticism which is often advanced against CDA covers several dimensions, which are also discussed in our book: the hermeneutic approach to text analysis; the broad context which is used to interpret texts; the often very large theoretical framework which does not always fit the data; and mostly, the political stance taken explicitly by the researchers (see Titscher et al., 2000 for an overview of criticism towards CDA, and the contribution of Michael Meyer in this book).

The history of critical linguistics and critical discourse analysis

The 1970s saw the emergence of a form of discourse and text analysis that recognized the role of language in structuring power relations in society (see Anthonissen, 2001 for an extensive summary of this development). At that time, much linguistic research elsewhere was focused on formal aspects of language which constituted the linguistic competence of speakers and which could theoretically be isolated from specific instances of language use (Chomsky, 1957). Where the relation between language and context was considered, as in pragmatics (Levinson, 1983), with a focus on speakers' pragmatic/sociolinguistic competence, sentences and components of sentences were still regarded as the basic units. Much sociolinguistic research at the time was aimed at describing and explaining language variation, language change and the structures of communicative interaction, with limited attention to issues of social hierarchy and power (Labov, 1972; Hymes, 1972). In such a context, attention to texts, their production and interpretation and their relation to societal impulses and structures, signalled a very different kind of interest (de Beaugrande and Dressler, 1981; see Titscher et al., 2000 for an overview). The work of Kress and Hodge (1979), Fowler et al. (1979), van Dijk (1985), Fairclough (1989) and Wodak (ed.) (1989) serve to explain and illustrate the main assumptions, principles and procedures of what had then become known as CL.

Kress (1990: 84–97) gives an account of the theoretical foundations and sources of critical linguistics. He indicates that the term CL was 'quite self-consciously adapted' (1990: 88) from its social-philosophical counterpart, as a label by the group of scholars working at the University of East Anglia in the 1970s (see also Wodak, 1996a; Blommaert and Bulcaen, 2000). By the 1990s the label CDA came to be used more consistently with this particular approach to linguistic analysis. Kress (1990: 94) shows how CDA by that time was 'emerging as a distinct theory of language, a radically different kind of linguistics'. He lists the criteria that characterize work in the critical discourse analysis paradigm, illustrating how these distinguish such work from other politically engaged discourse analysis. Fairclough and Wodak (1997) took these criteria further and established ten basic principles of a CDA programme. In the contributions in this volume, we find an even more extensive elaboration of these programmatic claims and proposals.

Many of the basic assumptions of CL/CDA that were salient in the early stages, and were elaborated in later development of the theory, are articulated in Kress's work. These include assumptions such as:

- language is a social phenomenon;
- not only individuals, but also institutions and social groupings have specific meanings and values, that are expressed in language in systematic ways;
- texts are the relevant units of language in communication;
- readers/hearers are not passive recipients in their relationship to texts;
- there are similarities between the language of science and the language of institutions, and so on (Kress, 1989).

Kress concentrates on the 'political economy' of representational media: that is, an attempt to understand how various societies value different modes of representation, and how they use these different modes of representation. A central aspect of this work is the attempt to understand the formation of the individual human being as a social individual in response to available 'representational resources'.

His present position as part of an institute of educational research has meant that much of Kress's effort has gone into thinking about the content of educational curricula in terms of representational resources and their use by individuals in their constant transformation of their subjectivities, the process usually called 'learning'. One by-product of this research interest has been his increasing involvement in overtly political issues, including the politics of culture.

Fowler et al. (1979) has been referred to, in order to ascertain the early foundations of CL. Later work of Fowler (1991, 1996) shows how tools provided by standard linguistic theories (a 1965 version of Chomskyan grammar, and Halliday's theory of systemic functional grammar) can be used to uncover linguistic structures of power in texts. Not only in news discourses, but also in literary criticism Fowler illustrates that systematic grammatical devices function in establishing, manipulating and naturalizing social hierarchies.

Fairclough (1989) sets out the social theories underpinning CDA and, as in other early critical linguistic work, a variety of textual examples are analysed to illustrate the field, its aims and methods of analysis. Later Fairclough (1992, 1995) and Chouliariki and Fairclough (1999) explain and elaborate some advances in CDA, showing not only how the analytical framework for investigating language in relation to power and ideology developed, but also how CDA is useful in disclosing the discursive nature of much contemporary social and cultural change. Particularly the language of the mass media is scrutinized as a site of power, of struggle and also as a site where language is apparently transparent. Media institutions often purport to be neutral in that they provide space for public discourse, that they reflect states of affairs disinterestedly, and that they give the perceptions and arguments of the newsmakers. Fairclough shows the fallacy of such assumptions, and illustrates the mediating and constructing role of the media with a variety of examples.

Van Dijk's earlier work in text linguistics and discourse analysis (1977, 1981) already shows the interest he takes in texts and discourses as basic units and social practices. Like other critical linguistic theorists, he traces the origins of linguistic interest in units of language larger than sentences and in text- and context-dependency of meanings. Van Dijk and Kintsch (1983) considered the relevance of discourse to the study of language processing. Their development of a cognitive model of discourse understanding in individuals, gradually developed into cognitive models for explaining the construction of meaning on a societal level. In the *Handbook of Discourse Analysis* van Dijk (1985) collected the work of a variety of scholars for whom language and how it functions in discourse is variously the primary object of research, or a tool in the investigation of other social phenomena. This is in a way a documentation of the 'state of the art' of critical linguistics in the mid-1980s, which then led to the new handbook (1997). New questions have become salient which I shall discuss below.

Van Dijk turns specifically to media discourse, giving not only his own reflection on communication in the mass media (van Dijk, 1986), but also bringing together the theories and applications of a variety of scholars interested in the production, uses and functions of media discourses (van Dijk, 1985). In critically analysing various kinds of discourses that encode prejudice, van Dijk's interest is in developing a theoretical model that will explain cognitive discourse processing mechanisms (Wodak and van Dijk, 2000). Most recently, van Dijk has focused on issues of racism and ideology (van Dijk, 1998).

By the end of the 1980s CL was able to describe its aims, research interests, chosen perspective and methods of analysis much more specifically and rigidly than hitherto. Wodak (1989) lists, explains and illustrates the most important characteristics of critical linguistic research as they had become established in continued research. The relevance of investigating language use in institutional settings is reiterated, and a new focus on the necessity of a historical perspective is introduced (the discourse–historical approach). This was followed by a variety of research projects into discursive practices in institutional contexts that would assist in developing an integrated theory of critical discourse analysis (see Wodak's contribution in this book).

Wodak (1996a, b) shows how scholars who have engaged in linguistic, semiotic and discourse analysis from different scholarly backgrounds share a particular perspective in which the concepts of power, ideology and history figure centrally. In an overview of the development of a critical tradition in discourse analysis, she refers to the reliance on Hallidayan linguistics, on Bernsteinian sociolinguistics, and also on the work of literary critics and social philosophers such as Pêcheux, Foucault, Habermas, Bakhtin and Voloshinov. She supports the suggestion of other critical linguists who believe that relationships between language and society are so complex and multifaceted that interdisciplinary research is required.

Whether analysts with a critical approach prefer to focus on micro-linguistic features, macrolinguistic features, textual, discursive or contextual features, whether their angle is primarily philosophical, sociological or historical – in most studies there is reference to Hallidayan systemic functional grammar. This indicates that an understanding of the basic claims of Halliday's grammar and his approach to linguistic analysis is essential for a proper understanding of CDA. For an exposition of Halliday's contribution to the development of CL, one should consider the work of Halliday himself (1978, 1985), as well as the work of scholars who have worked very closely with Hallidayan grammar, and have not only applied the theory, but also elaborated it. I refer readers specifically to Kress (1976), Martin and Hasan (1989), Martin (1992) and Iedema (1997, 1999). As early as 1970 M.A.K. Halliday had stressed the relationship between the grammatical system and the social and personal needs that language is required to serve (Halliday, 1970: 142). Halliday distin-guished three metafunctions of language which are continuously interconnected: firstly, the ideational function through which language lends structure to experience (the ideational structure has a dialectical relationship with social structure, both reflecting and influencing it); secondly, the interpersonal function which constitutes relationships between the participants; and thirdly, the textual function which constitutes coherence and cohesion in texts.

Moreover, argumentation theory and rhetoric have been successfully combined with functional systemic linguistics (see Reisigl and Wodak, 2001; Muntigl et al., 2000; van Leeuwen and Wodak, 1999).

Recognition of the contribution of all the aspects of the commu-nicative context to text meaning, as well as a growing awareness in media studies generally of the importance of non-verbal aspects of texts, has turned attention to semiotic devices in discourse rather than the linguistic ones. Pioneering work on the interaction between the verbal and visual in texts and discourse, as well as on the meaning of images, has been done by Theo van Leeuwen. Particularly the theory put forward by Kress and van Leeuwen (1996) should be mentioned here, as this provides a useful framework for considering the communicative potential of visual devices in the media (see Anthonissen, 2001; R. Scollon, 2001). Unfortunately we could not include a contribution by van Leeuwen in this volume and have to refer to his most relevant 'actor's analysis' (van Leeuwen, 1996) which is a systematic way of analysing the protagonists and their semantic roles in discourses and various genres.

Van Leeuwen studied film and television production as well as Hallidayan linguistics. His principal publications are concerned with topics such as the intonation of disc jockeys and newsreaders, the language of television interviews and newspaper reporting, and more recently, the semiotics of visual communication and music. His approach has increasingly led him into the field of education. Van Leeuwen distinguishes two kinds of relations between discourses and social practices: 'discourse itself [as] social practice, discourse as a form of action, as something people do to, or for, or with each other. And there is discourse in the Foucaultian sense, discourse as a way of representing social practice(s), as a form of knowledge, as the things people say about social practice(es)' (1993a: 193). 'Critical discourse analysis', according to van Leeuwen, 'is, or should be, concerned with both these aspects, with discourse as the instrument of power and control as well as with discourse as the instrument of the social construction of reality' (ibid).

The Duisburg school is massively influenced by Michel Foucault's theories. Siegfried Jäger is concerned with linguistic and iconic characteristics of discourse, focusing on 'collective symbols' (topoi) which possess important cohesive functions in texts. Discourse is seen as the flow of text and speech through time (Jäger, 1993: 6). Discourses have historical roots and are interwoven (diskursives Gewimmel). Jäger developed a very explicit research programme and methodology which allows analysis in several steps. The main topics of research have been right-wing discourses in Germany, as well as the analysis of tabloids (Bildzeitung). (See also Titscher et al., 2000 for an extensive overview of the Lesarten approach and the Duisburg school.)

The notions of 'critical', 'ideology' and 'power'

The notion of 'critique' which is inherent in CDA's programme is also understood very differently: some adhere to the Frankfurt school, others to a notion of literary criticism, some to Marx's notions (see above and Reisigl and Wodak, 2001 for an overview). Basically, 'critical' is to be understood as having distance to the data, embedding the data in the social, taking a political stance explicitly, and a focus on self-reflection as scholars doing research. For all those concerned with CDA, application of the results is important, be it in practical seminars for teachers, doctors and civil servants, or in writing expert opinions or devising school books. This, of course, points to Horkheimer's opinion, which I have quoted as an epigraph at the outset of this article.

Max Horkheimer, Director of the Institute of Social Research in Frankfurt in 1930, saw the role of the theorist as that of articulating and helping to develop a latent class consciousness. The tasks of critical theory were to assist in 'remembering' a past that was in danger of being forgotten, to struggle for emancipation, to clarify the reasons for such a struggle and to define the nature of critical thinking itself. The relation between theory and practice was seen as dynamic: there is no unchanging system which fixes the way in which theory will guide human actions.

Horkheimer believed that no single method of research could produce final and reliable results about any given object of inquiry, that to take only one approach to a given question was to risk gaining a distorted picture. He suggested that several methods of inquiry should supplement one another. Although the value of empirical work was acknowledged, he emphasized that it was no substitute for theoretical analysis.

The reference to critical theory's contribution to the understanding of CDA and the notions of 'critical' and 'ideology' are important (see Anthonissen, 2001 for an extensive discussion of this issue).[6] Thompson (1990) discusses the concepts of ideology and culture and the relations between these concepts and certain aspects of mass communication. He points out that the concept of ideology first appeared in late eighteenth-century France and has thus been in use for about two centuries. The term has been given changing functions and meanings at different times. For Thompson, ideology refers to social forms and processes within which, and by means of which, symbolic forms circulate in the social world.

Ideology, for CDA, is seen as an important aspect of establishing and maintaining unequal power relations. CL takes a particular interest in the ways in which language mediates ideology in a variety of social institutions.

For Thompson (1990) the study of ideology is a study of 'the ways in which meaning is constructed and conveyed by symbolic forms of various kinds'. This kind of study will also investigate the social contexts within which symbolic forms are employed and deployed. The investigator has an interest in determining whether such forms establish or sustain relations of domination. For Eagleton (1994) the study of ideology has to consider the variety of theories and theorists that have examined the relation between thought and social reality. All the theories assume 'that there are specific historical reasons why people come to feel, reason, desire and imagine as they do' (1994: 15).[7]

Critical theories, thus also CL and CDA, are afforded special standing as guides for human action. They are aimed at producing enlightenment and emancipation. Such theories seek not only to describe and explain, but also to root out a particular kind of delusion. Even with differing concepts of ideology, critical theory intends to create awareness in agents of how they are deceived about their own needs and interests. This was, of course, also taken up by Pierre Bourdieu's concepts of 'violence symbolique' and 'méconnaissance.'. One of the aims of CDA is to 'demystify' discourses by deciphering ideologies.

For CDA, language is not powerful on its own – it gains power by the use powerful people make of it. This explains why CL often chooses the perspective of those who suffer, and critically analyses the language use of those in power, who are responsible for the existence of inequalities and who also have the means and opportunity to improve conditions.

In agreement with their critical theory predecessors, CDA emphasises the need for interdisciplinary work in order to gain a proper understanding of how language functions in, for example, constituting and transmitting knowledge, in organizing social institutions or in exercising power.

An important perspective in CDA is that it is very rare for a text to be the work of any one person. In texts discursive differences are negotiated; they are governed by differences in power which are themselves in part encoded in and determined by discourse and by genre. Therefore texts are often sites of struggle in that they show traces of differing discourses and ideologies contending and struggling for dominance. A defining feature of CDA is its concern with power as a central condition in social life, and its efforts to develop a theory of language which incorporates this as a major premise. Not only the notion of struggles for power and control, but also the intertextuality and recontextualization of competing discourses are closely attended to.

Power is about relations of difference, and particularly about the effects of differences in social structures. The constant unity of language and other social matters ensures that language is entwined in social power in a number of ways: language indexes power, expresses power, is involved where there is contention over and a challenge to power. Power does not derive from language, but language can be used to challenge power, to subvert it, to alter distributions of power in the short and long term. Language provides a finely articulated means for differences in power in social hierarchical structures. Very few linguistic forms have not at some stage been pressed into the service of the expression of power by a process of syntactic or textual metaphor. CDA takes an interest in the ways in which linguistic forms are used in various expressions and manipulations of power. Power is signalled not only by grammatical forms within a text, but also by a person's control of a social occasion by means of the genre of a text. It is often exactly within the genres associated with given social occasions that power is exercised or challenged.*

The ways in which some of CDA research is directly and indirectly related to the research produced in the tradition of critical theory are particularly evident when one considers central concepts with which the various areas work, and social phenomena on which they focus. Examples of these are pertinent in their approaches to questions such as:

- what constitutes knowledge;
- how discourses are constructed in and constructive of social institutions;

* The very recent and exciting research of Christine Anthonissen about modes to circumvent censorship in South Africa during Apartheid manifest a variety of linguistic and semiotic strategies of power and resistance (see Anthonissen, 2001 for an extensive discussion of the concept of power).

- how ideology functions in social institutions, and;
- how people obtain and maintain power within a given community.

The contributions in this book, specifically the analysis of example texts, provide some answers to these questions.

Open questions and perspectives

Over the years, several issues have arisen as important research agenda which have not yet been adequately discussed. We would like to mention a few which are also central for the contributions in this book and which are discussed by Michael Meyer in his chapter.

1 The problem of operationalizing theories and relating the linguistic dimension with the social dimensions (problem of mediation).
2 The linguistic theory to be applied: often, a whole mixed bag of linguistic indicators and variables are used to analyse texts with no theoretical notions and no grammar theory in the background.
3 The notion of 'context', which is often defined very broadly or very narrowly: how much information do we need to analyse texts, how much impact do theories have?
4 The accusation of being biased – how are certain readings of text justified and validated?
5 Inter- or transdisciplinarity have not yet been achieved as a really integral part of text analysis.

This list could, of course, be extended. The approaches presented in this book will help clarify some of the problems yet to be solved, and give some answers to the many questions encountered while analysing discourse.

Notes

1 This short summary is based on long and extensive discussions with my friends, colleagues and co-researchers as well as students. I would like to mention and thank Rudi De Cillia, Martin Reisigl, Gertraud Benke, Gilbert Weiss, Bernd Matouschek and Richard Mitten with all of whom I have worked over the years. Moreover, many ideas have developed in work with my students. I would like to thank Usama Suleiman, Alexander Pollak and Christine Anthonissen for their extensive insights and elaborations as well as far-sighted comments and criticism. Finally, I would like to thank my peer group, whom I have written about and the many other colleagues I have not been able to mention here.
2 The terms CL and CDA were coined independently of one another and some practitioners of either CL or CDA might find arcane points on which they

differ. For most purposes those whose work could be described by either category may be said to occupy the same 'paradigmatic' space. In the event, in this contribution, the terms as well as their derivatives such as 'critical linguists' or 'critical discourse analysts' will be used interchangeably.

3   The literature on CDA and CL is vast. Therefore I can only provide a very short and thus also much too simple summary (see Fairclough and Wodak, 1997; Reisigl and Wodak, 2001; Anthonissen, 2001 and Blommaert and Bulcaen, 2000 for extensive and detailed overviews).

4   We could postulate, in the Habermasian sense, that every speech situation is 'distorted' by power structures, especially in contrast to his utopia of the 'ideal speech situation' where rational discourse becomes possible (Habermas, 1969, 1971; Wodak, 1996a, b).

5   The Erasmus network consisted of a cooperation between Siegfried Jäger, Duisburg, Per Linell, Linköping, Norman Fairclough, Lancaster, Teun van Dijk, Amsterdam, Gunther Kress, London, Theo van Leeuwen, London, Ruth Wodak, Vienna.

6   In the 1960s, many scholars adopted a more critical perspective in language studies. Among the first was the French scholar Pêcheux (1982 [1975]), whose approach traced its roots to the work of Russian theorists Bakhtin (1981) and Volosinov (1973), both of whom had postulated an integration of language and social processes in the 1930s. The term itself was apparently coined by Jacob Mey (1974).

7   The differences between scientific theories and critical theories lie along three dimensions, following the Frankfurt school (see Anthonissen, 2001 for a discussion). Firstly, they differ in their aim or goal, and therefore also in the way they can be used. Scientific theories aim at successful manipulation of the external world: they have 'instrumental use'. Critical theories aim at making 'agents' aware of hidden coercion, thereby freeing them from that coercion and putting them in a position to determine where their true interests lie. Secondly, critical and scientific theories differ in their 'cognitive' structure. Scientific theories are 'objectifying' in that one can distinguish between the theory and the objects to which the theory refers. The theory is not part of the object domain which it describes. A critical theory, on the other hand, is 'reflective' in that it is always itself a part of the object-domain it describes. Such theories are in part about themselves. Thirdly, critical and scientific theories differ in the kind of evidence which would determine whether or not they are acceptable. Thus, these theories require different kinds of confirmation.

2

Between theory, method, and politics: positioning of the approaches to CDA

Michael Meyer

CONTENTS

CDA as a difference that makes a difference

Approaches to social research are not isolated in space. In simplified terms they can be understood as a certain set of explicitly or implicitly defined theoretical assumptions which are specifically linked with empirical data, permit specific ways of interpretation and thus reconnect the empirical with the theoretical field. Normally approaches obtain and maintain their identities by distinguishing themselves from other approaches.[1] It is generally agreed that CDA must not be understood as a single method but rather as an approach, which constitutes itself at different levels – and at each level a number of selections have to be made.

Firstly, at a programmatic level, a selection is made of (a) the phenomena under observation, (b) some explanation of the theoretical assumptions, and (c) the methods used to link theory and observation. Within this triangle, the methodical aspect often becomes the distinguishing feature, because research is regularly legitimized as scientific by means of intelligible methods. The term method[2] normally denotes research pathways: from the researcher's own standpoint or from point A (theoretical assumptions) another point B (observation) is reached by choosing a pathway that permits observations and facilitates the collection of experiences. If one proceeds systematically wrong turnings are avoidable. 'Methodical procedure can, like Ariadne's thread, guarantee the researcher a safe route back' (Titscher et al., 2000: 5). It can also help both the addressees of research findings to reconstruct the researchers' argumentation and other researchers to see the starting point differently, and even to decide not to go back, but to find other more interesting starting points. Methodical procedure will make it easier to record findings and to compile reports of experience. Secondly, at a social level, a specific peer group is formed as a distinctive part of a scientific community, and thirdly, at a historical level, each approach to social research is subject to fashions and expiry dates.

The differences between CDA and other sociolinguistic approaches may be most clearly established with regard to the general principles of CDA. First of all the nature of the problems with which CDA is concerned is different in principle from all those methods which do not determine their interest in advance. In general CDA asks different research questions. CDA scholars play an advocatory role for groups who suffer from social discrimination. If we look at the CDA contributions collected in this reader it becomes evident that the line drawn between social scientific research, which ought to be intelligible, and political argumentation is sometimes crossed. Whatever the case, in respect of the object of investigation, it is a fact that CDA follows a different and a critical approach to problems, since it endeavours to make explicit power relationships which are frequently hidden, and thereby to derive results which are of practical relevance.

One important characteristic arises from the assumption of CDA that all discourses are historical and can therefore only be understood with reference to their context. In accordance with this CDA refers to such extralinguistic factors as culture, society, and ideology. In any case, the notion of context is crucial for CDA, since this explicitly includes social-psychological, political and ideological components and thereby postulates an interdisciplinary procedure.

Beyond this, CDA, using the concepts of intertextuality and interdiscursivity, analyses relationships with other texts, and this is not pursued in other methods. From its basic understanding of the notion of discourse it may be concluded that CDA is open to the broadest range of factors that exert an influence on texts.

From the notion of context a further difference emerges concerning the assumption about the relationship between language and society. CDA does not take this relationship to be simply deterministic but invokes an idea of mediation. There is a difference between the various approaches to discourse. Norman Fairclough defines the relationship in accordance with Halliday's multifunctional linguistic theory and the concept of orders of discourse according to Foucault, while Ruth Wodak, like Teun van Dijk, introduces a sociocognitive level. This kind of mediation between language and society is absent from many other linguistic approaches, such as, for example, conversation analysis.

A further distinguishing feature of CDA is the specific incorporation of linguistic categories into its analyses. CDA in no way includes a very broad range of linguistic categories: one might therefore get the impression that only a small range of linguistic devices are central for CDA studies. For instance many CDA scholars regularly use actor analyses as a means of focusing upon pronouns, attributes and the verbal mode, time and tense.

In principle we may assume that categories such as deixis and pronouns can be analysed in any linguistic method, but that they are crucial for CDA. Explicitly or implicitly CDA makes use of a concept of the so-called linguistic surface. For instance Fairclough speaks of form and texture at the textual level, and Wodak of forms of linguistic realization.

As for the methods and procedures used for the analysis of discourses, CDA generally sees its procedure as a hermeneutic process, although this characteristic is not completely evident in the position taken by the various authors. Compared to the (causal) explanations of the natural sciences, hermeneutics can be understood as the method of grasping and producing meaning relations. The hermeneutic circle – which implies that the meaning of one part can only be understood in the context of the whole, but that this in turn is only accessible from its component parts – indicates the problem of intelligibility of hermeneutic interpretation. Therefore hermeneutic interpretation in particular urgently requires detailed documentation. Actually the specifics of the hermeneutic interpretation process are not made completely transparent by many CDA-orientated studies.[3] If a crude distinction has to be made between 'text-extending' and 'text-reducing' methods of analysis, then CDA, on account of its concentration on very clear formal properties and the associated compression of texts during analysis, may be characterized as 'text-reducing'. These findings disagree with the mainly hermeneutic impetus of most CDA approaches.

A further characteristic of CDA is its interdisciplinary claim and its description of the object of investigation from widely differing perspectives, as well as its continuous feedback between analysis and data collection. Compared with other linguistic methods of text analysis, CDA seems to be closest to sociological and socio-psychologial perspectives, although these interfaces are not well defined everywhere.

Criticism of CDA comes from conversation analysis – the 'reverse side' of the debate between conversation analysis (Schegloff, 1998) and CDA. Schegloff argues that CDA, even though it has different goals and interests than the local construction of interaction, should deal seriously with its material: 'If, however, they mean the issues of power, domination and the like to connect up with discursive material, it should be a serious rendering of that material'. This means it should at least be compatible with what is demonstrably relevant for the behaviour of participants in an interaction. Only when such categories as the gender of participants are made relevant – for instance by an explicit mention ('ladies last') – are they important for an analysis. If CDA is understood in this way it would not, in Schegloff's opinion, be an alternative to conversation analysis, but would require a conversation analysis to be carried out first, 'otherwise the critical analysis will not "bind" to the data, and risks ending up merely ideological'.

Alongside this general debate about the whole enterprise of CDA, a more specific discussion has developed between Norman Fairclough and Henry Widdowson. Widdowson criticizes the fact that the term discourse is as vague as it is fashionable: 'discourse is something everybody is talking about but without knowing with any certainty just what it is: in vogue and vague' (Widdowson, 1995: 158). He also criticizes the lack of a clear demarcation between text and discourse. Furthermore – and here his criticism approaches that of Schegloff – CDA is an ideological interpretation and therefore not an analysis. The term critical discourse analysis is a contradiction in terms. Widdowson believes that CDA is, in a dual sense, a biased interpretation: in the first place it is prejudiced on the basis of some ideological commitment, and then it selects for analysis such texts as will support the preferred interpretation (Widdowson, 1995: 169). Analysis ought to mean the examination of several interpretations, and in the case of CDA this is not possible because of prior judgements. Fairclough (1996), in reply to this criticism, draws attention to the open-endedness of results required in the principles of CDA. He also points out that CDA, unlike most other approaches, is always explicit about its own position and commitment.

Actually these controversies concretize two irreconcilable positions within the methodological debate in social research: is it possible to perform any research free of a priori value judgements[4] and is it possible to gain insight from purely empirical data without using any preframed categories of experience? As for the first question, CDA agrees even with dogmatic positivistic methodology which permits value judgements in the process of the selection of objects and questions under investigation ('context of discovery'), but forbids them in the 'context of justification'. As for the second question, the CDA position fits well with most epistemology in Kant's tradition which denies the possibility of 'pure' cognition.

Methodology of CDA

CDA in all of its various forms understands itself to be strongly based in theory. To which theories do the different methods refer? Here we find a wide variety of theories, ranging from microsociological perspectives (Ron Scollon) to theories on society and power in Michel Foucault's tradition (Siegfried Jäger, Norman Fairclough, Ruth Wodak), theories of social cognition (Teun van Dijk) and grammar, as well as individual concepts that are borrowed from larger theoretical traditions. As a first step, this section aims to systematize these different theoretical influences.

A second step relates to the problem of operationalizing theoretical concepts. The primary issue here is how the various methods of CDA are able to translate their theoretical claims into instruments and methods of analysis. In particular, the emphasis is on the mediation between grand theories as applied to society at large and concrete instances of social interaction, the foci of analysis for CDA. As far as methodology is concerned, there are several perspectives within CDA: in addition to those which can be described primarily as variations from hermeneutics, one finds interpretative perspectives with various emphases, among them even quantitative procedures.

In empirical social research a distinction can be made between elicitation and evaluation methods: between ways of collecting data (in the laboratory or by fieldwork) and procedures that have been developed for the analysis of collected data. Methodical procedures for the collection of data organize observation, while evaluation methods regulate the transformation of data into information and further restrict the opportunities for inference and interpretation. The distinction between these two tasks of data collection and analysis does not necessarily mean that there are two separate steps: CDA sees itself more in the tradition of Grounded Theory (Glaser and Strauss, 1967), where data collection is not a phase that must be finished before analysis starts but might be a permanently ongoing procedure.

Particularly worthy of discussion is the way in which sampling is conducted in CDA. Most studies analyse 'typical texts'. The possibilities and limits with regard to the units of analysis chosen will be illuminated within the context of the issue of theoretical sampling. Some of the authors explicitly refer to the ethnographic tradition of field research (Scollon, Wodak).

This connection between theory and discourse can be described in terms of the model for theoretical and methodological research procedures that is illustrated in Figure 2.1.

Theoretical grounding and objectives

Among the different positions within CDA presented in this book, theoretical components of very different origins have been adopted. Moreover there is no guiding theoretical viewpoint that is used consistently within CDA, nor do the CDA protagonists proceed consistently from the area of theory to the field of discourse and then back to theory.

Within the CDA approaches presented here the reader may find all the theoretical levels of sociological and socio-psychological theory (the

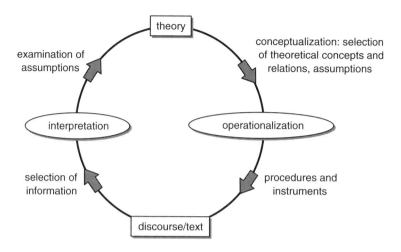

FIGURE 2.1 *Empirical research as a cirular process*

concept of different theoretical levels is in the tradition of Merton, 1967: 39–72; see also Ruth Wodak's contribution):

1 Epistemology covers theories which provide models of the conditions, contingencies and limits of human perception in general and scientific perception in particular.
2 General social theories, often called 'grand theories', try to conceptualize relations between social structure and social action and thus link micro- and macro-sociological phenomena. Within this level one can distinguish between the more structuralist and the more individualist approaches. To put it very simply, the former provide top-down explanations (structure→action), whereas the latter prefer bottom-up explanations (action→structure). Many modern theories try to reconcile these positions and imply some kind of circularity between social action and social structure.
3 Middle-range theories focus either upon specific social phenomena (such as conflict, cognition, social networks), or on specific subsystems of society (for example, economy, politics, religion).
4 Micro-sociological theories try to explain social interaction, for example the resolution of the double contingency problem (Parsons and Shils, 1951: 3–29) or the reconstruction of everyday procedures which members of a society use to create their own social order, which is the objective of ethnomethodology.
5 Socio-psychological theories concentrate upon the social conditions of emotion and cognition and, compared to micro-sociology, prefer causal explanations to hermeneutic understanding of meaning.
6 Discourse theories aim at the conceptualization of discourse as a social phenomenon and try to explain its genesis and its structure.

7 Linguistic theories, for example, theories of argumentation, of grammar, of rhetoric, try to describe and explain the pattern specific to language systems and verbal communication.

All these theoretical levels can be found in CDA. At first glance it seems that the unifying parentheses of CDA are rather the specifics of research questions than the theoretical positioning. In the following we want give a short outline of the theoretical positions and methodological objectives of CDA approaches.

Among the contributors to this book, Siegfried Jäger is closest to the origin of the notion of discourse, that is to Michel Foucault's structuralist explanations of discoursive phenomena. Jäger detects a blind spot in Foucault's theory, namely the mediation between subject and object, between discursive and non-discursive practices (activities) on the one hand and manifestations (objects) on the other. Here he strategically inserts Aleksej Leontjew's (for example, 1982) activity theory. The mediation between the triangle's corners is performed by work, activity and non-discursive practices. Thus the social acting subject becomes the link between discourse and reality, a theoretical movement which moderates the severeness of the Foucaultian structuralism. Jäger's epistemological position is based upon Ernesto Laclau's social constructivism, which denies any societal reality that is determined outside the discursive: 'If the discourse changes, the object not only changes its meaning, but it becomes a different object, it loses its previous identity' (Jäger, p. 43). That way Jäger introduces a dualism of discourse on reality, where the role of social actors is strongly reminiscent of Umberto Eco's (1985) *Lector in fabula*.

Jäger applies Jürgen Link's notion of 'discourse as a consolidated concept of speech' which determines and consolidates action and exercises power. He tries to reposition Foucault's definition of discourse which is too strongly caught up in the verbal. For this reason he reinvents Foucault's concept of the 'dispositive' as a shell which envelops both discursive and non-discursive practices and materializations. Jäger's method explicitly aims at the analysis of discourses and dispositives. Yet he admits difficulties with the determination of the dispositive which are connected to the lack of determination of the links between the triangle's corners.

Whereas Siegfried Jäger refers mainly to general social theories, Teun van Dijk is rather on the socio-psychological side of the CDA field. He sees theory not as the classical relationship of causal hypotheses but rather as a framework systematizing phenomena of social reality. His focal triad is construed between discourse, cognition and society. He defines discourse as a communicative event, including conversational interaction, written text, as well as associated gestures, facework, typographical layout, images and any other 'semiotic' or multimedia dimension of signification. Van Dijk relies on socio-cognitive theory splints and understands linguistics in a broad 'structural–functional' sense. He argues that CDA should be based on a sound theory of context. Within this he claims that the theory of social representations plays a main part.

Social actors involved in discourse do not exclusively make use of their individual experiences and strategies; they mainly rely upon collective frames of perceptions, called social representations. These socially shared perceptions form the link between social system and the individual cognitive system and perform the translation, homogenization and co-ordination between external requirements and subjective experience. This assumption is not new. Already in the first half of the nineteenth century Emile Durkheim (1933, for example) pointed out the significance of collective ideas which help societies to consciousness and reification of social norms. Serge Moscovici (1981) coined the notion of social representations as a bulk of concepts, opinions, attitudes, evaluations, images and explanations which result from daily life and are sustained by communication. Social representations are shared amongst members of a social group.[5] Thus they form a core element of the individual's social identity (Wagner, 1994: 132). Social representations are bound to specific social groups and not spanning society as a whole. They are dynamic constructs and subject to permanent change. Together they constitute a hierarchical order of mutual dependency (Duveen and Lloyd, 1990).

Van Dijk, however, does not explicitly refer to this tradition but rather to socio-psychological research: in line with current theorizing in cognitive psychology, such mental constructs have the form of a specific kind of mental model, as stored in episodic memory – the part of long-term memory in which people store their personal experiences (van Dijk, p. 112). He introduces the concept of context models, which are understood as mental representations of the structures of the communicative situation that are discursively relevant for a participant. These context models control the 'pragmatic' part of discourse, whereas event models do so with the 'semantic' part. Van Dijk names three forms of social representations relevant to the understanding of discourse: firstly knowledge (personal, group, cultural), secondly attitudes (not in the socio-psychological understanding), and thirdly ideologies. Discourses take place within society, and can only be understood in the interplay of social situation, action, actor and societal structures. Thus, unlike Jäger, he conceptualizes the influence of social structure via social representations.

Perhaps Ruth Wodak is the most linguistically orientated of the CDA scholars selected here. Unlike the others she, together with Martin Reisigl (Reisigl and Wodak, 2001), explicitly tries to establish a theory of discourse. They understand discourse as 'a complex bundle of simultaneous and sequential interrelated linguistic acts, which manifest themselves within and across the social fields of action as thematically interrelated semiotic, oral or written tokens, very often as "texts", that belong to specific semiotic types, i.e. genres' (Wodak, p. 66). In the discourse–historical approach the connection between fields of action (Girnth, 1996), genres, discourses and texts is described and modelled. Although the discourse–historical approach is indebted to critical theory, general social theory plays a negligible part compared with the discourse model mentioned above and historical analysis: context is understood mainly historically. To this extent Wodak agrees with Mouzelis's (1995) severe diagnosis of social research. She consistently follows his recommendations: not to exhaust oneself in theoretical labyrinths, not to invest too much in the operationalization of unoperationalizable 'grand theories', but rather to develop conceptual tools relevant for specific social problems. The discourse–historical approach finds its focal point in the field of politics, where it tries to develop conceptual frameworks for political discourse. Wodak tries to fit linguistic theories into her model of discourse, and in the example presented below she makes extensive use of argumentation theory (list of topoi). This does not necessarily mean that the concepts resulting from argumentation theory fit well with other research questions. Wodak seems strongly committed to a pragmatic approach.

Although this is not expressed explicitly, Norman Fairclough takes a specific middle-range theory position: he focuses upon social conflict in the Marxist tradition and tries to detect its linguistic manifestations in discourses, in particular elements of dominance, difference and resistance. According to Fairclough, every social practice has a semiotic element. Productive activity, the means of production, social relations, social identities, cultural values, consciousness, and semiosis are dialectically related elements of social practice. He understands CDA as the analysis of the dialectical relationships between semiosis (including language) and other elements of social practices. These semiotic aspects of social practice are responsible for the constitution of genres and styles. The semiotic aspect of social order is called the order of discourse. His approach to CDA oscillates between a focus on structure and a focus on action. Both strategies ought to be problem based: by all means CDA should pursue emancipatory objectives, and should be focused upon the problems confronting what can loosely be referred to as the 'losers' within particular forms of social life.

Fairclough draws upon a particular linguistic theory, systemic functional linguistics (Halliday, 1985), which analyses language as shaped (even in its grammar) by the social functions it has come to serve.

Ron Scollon can be seen as the micro-sociologist within the field of discourse analysis. He calls his approach mediated discourse analysis (MDA), which shares the goals of CDA but 'strategizes to reformulate the object of study from a focus on the discourses of social issues to a focus on the social actions through which social actors produce the histories and habitus of their daily lives which is the ground in which society is produced and reproduced' (Scollon, p. 140). MDA aims to establish the links between discourses and social actions where the focus of analysis overtly is upon action. Scollon emphasizes that all social actions are mediated by cultural tools or mediational means, whereby the most salient and perhaps most common of these mediational means is language or, to use the term Scollon prefers, discourse. Although this is only one of the mediational means in MDA, there remains a central interest in discourse mainly on empirical grounds.

Scollon theoretically links the micro level of action with the macro level of communities by means of six concepts:

1   mediated action;
2   site of engagement;
3   mediational means;
4   practices;
5   the nexus of practice;
6   the community of practice.

Using the concept of mediation and mediational means (cultural tools) Scollon not only explains the formation of practices out of singular actions but also builds his micro–macro link, meticulously avoiding the notion of social structure.

The methodical objective of MDA is

> to provide a set of heuristics by which the researcher can narrow the scope of what must be analysed to achieve an understanding of mediated actions even knowing that mediated actions occur in real time, are unique and unrepeatable and therefore must be 'caught' in action to be analysed. In a real sense it is a matter of structuring the research activities to be in the right place at the right time. (Ron Scollon, p. 152)

The more general goal of MDA is to explicate the link between broad social issues and the everyday talk and writing, and to arrive at a richer understanding of the history of the practice within the habitus of the participants in a particular social action.

Methodology in data collection

The conclusion made above that CDA does not constitute a well-defined empirical method but rather a cluster of approaches with a similar theoretical base and similar research questions becomes most obvious here: there is no typical CDA way of collecting data. Some authors do not even mention data collection methods and others rely strongly on traditions based outside the sociolinguistic field.[6] In any case, in a way similar to grounded theory (Glaser and Strauss, 1967), data collection is not considered to be a specific phase that must be completed before analysis begins: after the first collection exercise it is a matter of carrying out the first analyses, finding indicators for particular concepts, expanding concepts into categories and, on the basis of these results, collecting further data (theoretical sampling). In this mode of procedure, data collection is never completely excluded, and new questions always arise which can only be dealt with if new data are collected or earlier data are re-examined (Strauss, 1987: 56).

Whereas Siegfried Jäger at least suggests a concentration on texts extracted from television and press reports, no evidence can be found concerning data collection requirements in the contributions of Teun van Dijk and Norman Fairclough. Yet the text examples selected by these authors might indicate that they also prefer mass media coverage. This focus embodies specific strengths, in particular it provides non-reactive data (Webb, 1966), and certain weaknesses, for restrictions concerning the research questions have to be accommodated. Ruth Wodak postulates that CDA studies always incorporate fieldwork and ethnography in order to explore the object under investigation as a precondition for any further analysis and theorizing.

The most detailed discussion of this methodical step is provided by Ron Scollon. He argues that, at the least, participant observation is the primary research tool for eliciting the data needed for an MDA. This argument is in a strong ethnographic tradition. Even though observational methods play an important role in MDA, this does not mean that Scollon excludes the residual diversity of structured and unstructured methods:

1 To identify participants and mediational means relevant for the research question he even proposes surveys.
   a Scene surveys should narrow down the scope of the research to a few highly salient places or scenes, in which the actions we are interested in are taking place.
   b Event and action surveys aim to identify the specific social actions taking place within the scenes we have identified which are of relevance to the study of mediated action.
2 Focus groups should be identified and thoroughly analysed. The purpose of such groups at this stage is twofold:
   a 'The researcher wants to know to what extent the identification of specific scenes, media, and actions have reliability and validity for members of the group under study', and
   b 'the researcher wants to understand how important or salient the categories which have been identified are for the population being studied' (Scollon, p. 158).

These methods need not necessarily be applied stepwise but also simultaneously. Even media analysis has its place in Scollon's methodology, although 'media content surveys' and 'what's in the news' surveys do not play the crucial part that mass media coverage plays in other CDA approaches.

In a nutshell we might conclude that, with the exception of Ron Scollon's MDA, there is little discussion about statistical or theoretical representativeness of the material analysed.[7] Although there are no explicit statements about this issue, one might assume that many CDA studies (perhaps with the exception of Teun van Dijk and Ruth Wodak) mostly deal with only small corpora which are usually regarded as being typical of certain discourses.

Methodology in operationalization and analysis

As mentioned above CDA places its methodology rather in the hermeneutic than in the analytical-deductive tradition. As a consequence no clear line between data collection and analysis can be drawn. However, the linguistic character of CDA becomes evident in this section, because in contrast to other approaches to text and discourse analysis (for example, content analysis, grounded theory, conversation analysis; see Titscher et al., 2000) CDA strongly relies on linguistic categories. This does not mean that topics and contents play no role at all, but that the core operationalizations depend on linguistic concepts such as actors, mode, time, tense, argumentation, and so on. Nevertheless a definitive list of the linguistic devices relevant for CDA cannot be given, since their selection mainly depends on the specific research questions.

Siegfried Jäger distinguishes between firstly a more content oriented step of structure analysis and secondly a more language oriented step of fine analysis. Within structure analysis a characterization of the media and the general themes has to be made. Within the fine analysis he focuses upon context, text surface and rhetorical means. Examples of linguistic instruments are figurativeness, vocabulary and argumentation types. He takes into account both qualitative and quantitative aspects of these features: Jäger analyses

- the kind and form of argumentation;
- certain argumentation strategies;
- the intrinsic logic and composition of texts;
- implications and insinuations that are implicit in some way;
- the collective symbolism or 'figurativeness', symbolism, metaphorism, and so on both in language and in graphic contexts (statistics, photographs, pictures, caricatures and so on);
- idioms, sayings, clichés, vocabulary and style;
- actors (persons, pronominal structure);
- references, for example to (the) science(s);
- particulars on the sources of knowledge, and so on.

Teun van Dijk generally argues, that 'a complete discourse analysis of a large corpus of text or talk, as we often have in CDA research, is therefore totally out of the question' (van Dijk, p. 99). If the focus of research is on the ways in which some speakers or writers exercise power in or by their discourse, the focus of study will in practice be on those properties that can vary as a function of social power. Van Dijk therefore suggests that the analysis should concentrate upon the following linguistic markers:

- stress and intonation;
- word order;
- lexical style;
- coherence;
- local semantic moves such as disclaimers;
- topic choice;
- speech acts;
- schematic organization;
- rhetorical figures;
- syntactic structures;
- propositional structures;
- turn takings;
- repairs;
- hesitation.

He supposes that most of these are examples of forms of interaction which are in principle susceptible to speaker control, but less consciously controlled or controllable by the speakers. Other structures, such as the form of words and many sentence structures are grammatically obligatory and contextually invariant, and hence usually not subject to speaker control and social power. He further suggests six steps in an analysis:

1   analysis of semantic macrostructures: topics and macropropositions;
2   analysis of local meanings, where the many forms of implicit or indirect meanings, such as implications, presuppositions, allusions, vagueness, omissions and polarizations are especially interesting;
3   analysis of 'subtle' formal structures: here most of the linguistic markers mentioned are analysed;
4   analysis of global and local discourse forms or formats;
5   analysis of specific linguistic realizations, for example, hyperbolas, litotes;
6   analysis of context.

In their studies of racist and discriminatory discourse Ruth Wodak and Martin Reisigl (Reisigl and Wodak, 2001) developed a four-step strategy of analysis: after firstly having established the specific contents or topics of a specific discourse with racist, anti-semitic, nationalist or ethnicist ingredients, secondly, the discursive strategies (including argumentation strategies) were investigated. Then thirdly, the linguistic means (as types) and finally the specific, context-dependent linguistic realizations (as tokens) of the discriminatory stereotypes were examined.

In these studies the discourse–historical approach concentrates upon the following discursive strategies:

- referential strategy or strategy of nomination, where the linguistic devices of interest are membership categorization (Sacks, 1992; Bakker, 1997), metaphors and metonymies and synecdoches;
- strategies of predication which appear in stereotypical, evaluative attributions of positive or negative traits and implicit or explicit predicates;
- strategies of argumentation which are reflected in certain topoi used to justify political inclusion or exclusion;
- strategies of perspectivation, framing or discourse representation use means of reporting, description, narration or quotation of events and utterances;
- strategies of intensification and mitigation try to intensify or mitigate the illocutionary force of utterances (Ng and Bradac, 1993).

This methodology aims to be abductive and pragmatic, because the categories of analysis are first developed in line with the research questions, and a constant movement back and forth between theory and empirical data is suggested. The historical context is always analysed and integrated into the interpretation, although there exists no stringent procedure for this task.

In his MDA approach Ron Scollon focuses on four main types of data:

1 members' generalizations;
2 neutral ('objective') observations;
3 individual member's experience;
4 observer's interactions with members (participant observation).

Within the approaches selected, Scollon provides the most detailed and generalized analytical scheme, which is tightly linked to his theoretical frame. Thus he analyses firstly actions, secondly practices, thirdly mediational means, fourthly nexus of practice and finally community of practice:

1 Action: what is the action? What chain or chains of mediated actions are relevant? What is the 'funnel of commitment'? What narrative and anticipatory discourses provide a metadiscursive or reflective structure?
2 Practice: what are the practices which intersect to produce this site of engagement? What histories in habitus do these practices have, that is

what is their ontogenesis? In what other actions are these practices formative?

3   Mediational means: what mediational means are used in this action? What specific forms of analysis should be used in analysing the mediational means? How and when were those mediational means appropriated within practice/habitus? How are those mediational means used in this action? In what way are the semiotic characteristics of those mediational means constraints on action or affordances for action? To answer these question Scollon suggests methods of conversation analysis, rhetorical analysis and visual holophrastic discourse analysis.

4   Nexus of practice: what linkages among practices form a nexus of practice? How might the nexus of practice be recognized? To what extent is there a useful distinction between nexus of practice as group, as situation, and as genre?

5   Community of practice: to what extent has a nexus of practice become 'technologized'? What are the identities (both internal and external) which are produced by community of practice membership?

As outlined above, Scollon formulates a number of questions concerning each of these analytical levels, but – consistently with the ethnographic tradition – he does not provide any operationalizations or linguistic exponents which should be analysed.

Norman Fairclough suggests a stepwise procedure in preparation to analysis. Like Ruth Wodak he prefers a pragmatic, problem oriented approach, where the first step is to identify and describe the social problem to be analysed. His propositions are as follows:

1   focus upon a specific social problem which has a semiotic aspect; go outside the text and describe the problem and identify its semiotic aspect;

2   identify the dominant styles, genres, discourses constituting this semiotic aspect;

3   consider the range of difference and diversity in styles, genres, discourses within this aspect;

4   identify the resistance against the colonialization processes executed by the dominant styles, genres and discourses.

After these preparatory steps, which also help to select the material, he suggests first of all structural analysis of the context, and then secondly interactional analysis, which focuses on linguistic features such as:

• agents;
• time;
• tense;

- modality;
- syntax;

and finally analysis of interdiscursivity, which seeks to compare the dominant and resistant strands of discourse.

It was the goal of the preceding sections to give a brief outline of the core procedures applied in the different approaches to CDA. Finally it should be pointed out that, although there is no consistent CDA methodology, some features are common to most CDA approaches: firstly they are problem oriented and not focused on specific linguistic items. Yet linguistic expertise is obligatory for the selection of the items relevant to specific research objectives. Secondly theory as well as methodology is eclectic: both are integrated as far as it is helpful to understand the social problems under investigation.

Criteria for assessing quality

It seems to be beyond controversy now that qualitative social research also needs concepts and criteria to assess the quality of its findings. It is also indisputable that the classical concepts of validity and reliability used in quantitative research cannot be applied without modification. 'The real issue is how our research can be both intellectually challenging and rigorous and critical' (Silverman, 1993: 144; there he also provides a detailed discussion of these concepts and a reformulation for qualitative research). What about the criteria suggested and listed by CDA scholars?

Siegfried Jäger names the classical criteria of representativeness, reliability and validity. Beyond it he suggests 'completeness' as a criterion suited to CDA: the results of a study will be 'complete' if new data and the analysis of new linguistic devices reveal no new findings. Teun van Dijk suggests accessibility as a criterion which takes into account the practical targets of CDA: findings should at be least accessible and readable for the social groups under investigation.

Both Ruth Wodak and Ron Scollon suggest triangulation procedures to ensure validity – 'which is appropriate whatever one's theoretical orientation or use of quantitative or qualitative data' (Silverman, 1993: 156).[8] Wodak's triangulatory approach can be characterized as theoretical and is based on the concept of context which takes into account four levels:

1 the immediate language- or text-internal co-text;
2 the intertextual and interdiscursive relationship between utterances, texts, genres and discourses;
3 the extralinguistic (social) level which is called the 'context of situation' and explained by middle-range theories;
4 the broader socio-political and historical contexts.

Permanent switching between these levels and evaluation of the findings from these different perspectives should minimize the risk of being biased. Beyond this Wodak suggests methodical triangulation by using multimethodical designs on the basis of a variety of empirical data as well as background information.

Ron Scollon, too, is an advocate of triangulation: 'Because of the involvement of the researcher as a participant-observer, clear triangulation procedures are essential in drawing inferences about observations and in producing interpretations' (Scollon, p. 181).

Triangulation among different types of data, participants' definition of significance and issue based analysis to establish the significance of the sites of engagement and mediated actions under study, are suited to bringing the analyses back to participants in order to get their reactions and interpretations: to uncover divergences and contradictions between one's own analysis of the mediated actions one is studying and those of participants. Scollon claims that no study should rely on just one or two of these types of data for its interpretation.

Nevertheless strict 'objectivity' cannot be achieved by means of discourse analysis, for each 'technology' of research must itself be examined as potentially embedding the beliefs and ideologies of the analysts and therefore prejudicing the analysis toward the analysts' preconceptions.

Conclusion: CDA sitting on the fence

The goal of this brief chapter was to provide a short summary of CDA approaches, their similarities and differences. As the title of Teun van Dijk's article suggests, one of CDA's volitional characteristics is its diversity. Nevertheless a few landmarks should be pointed out within this diversity:

- concerning its theoretical background, CDA works eclectically in many respects; the whole range from grand theories to linguistic theories is touched, although each individual approach emphasizes different levels;
- there is no accepted canon of data collection;
- operationalization and analysis is problem oriented and implies linguistic expertise.

The similarity most evident is a shared interest in social processes of power, hierarchy building, exclusion and subordination. In the tradition of critical theory, CDA aims to make transparent the discursive aspects of societal disparities and inequalities. CDA in the majority of cases takes the part of the underprivileged and tries to show up the linguistic means used by the privileged to stabilize or even to intensify iniquities in society. Therefore critics like Widdowson (1995) object that CDA constantly sits on the fence between social research and political argumentation.

Notes

1 In her introductory contribution Ruth Wodak describes the social history of the process which has drawn the distinction between critical linguistics, CDA and traditional linguistic research.

2 See the criticism of this use of the term in Kriz and Lisch (1988: 176). They find 'model' a more appropriate term, since conventional methods actually depict information structures.

3 The question whether it is possible to make hermeneutic processes transparent and intelligible at all remains undecided, although Oevermann et al. (1979) developed a hermeneutically oriented method with well defined procedures and rules.

4 These conflict positions can be traced back to the 'Werturteilsstreit' (dispute on value judgements) in German sociology (see Albert, 1971).

5 Once again a reference to Emile Durkheim: 'The ideas of man or animal are not personal and are not restricted to me; I share them, to a large degree, with all the men who belong to the same social group that I do. Because they are held in common, concepts are the supreme instrument of all intellectual exchange' (Bellah, 1973: 52; excerpt from 'The dualism of human nature and its social conditions').

6 A general survey on sampling and the selection of texts is given by Titscher et al. (2000). The advantages and disadvantages of different methods of data collection are discussed from the point of view of the qualitative tradition by Silverman (1997), especially by Atkinson and Coffey (1997); Miller and Glassner (1997); Potter (1997) and Peräkylä (1997).

7 For discussion about the representativeness of qualitative data see again Titscher et al. (2000, 31ff.), Firestone (1993) and the articles in Ragin and Becker (1992).

8 An early proponent of the method of triangulation is Norman Denzin (1970). Further discussion of criteria for assessing interpretive validity in qualitative research is also provided by Altheide and Johnson (1994).

3

Discourse and knowledge: Theoretical and methodological aspects of a critical discourse and dispositive analysis

Siegfried Jäger

(Translated from the original German manuscript by Iris Bünger and Robert Tonks)[1]

CONTENTS

Preliminary remarks

Central to a critical discourse analysis (CDA) based on Michel Foucault's discourse theory are issues such as,

- what knowledge (valid at a certain place at a certain time) consists of;
- how this valid knowledge evolves;

- how it is passed on;
- what function it has for the constitution of subjects and the shaping of society and
- what impact this knowledge has on the overall development of society.[2]

Here 'knowledge' means all kinds of contents which make up a consciousness and/or all kinds of meanings used by respective historical persons to interpret and shape the surrounding reality. People derive this 'knowledge' from the respective discursive contexts into which they are born and in which they are involved for their entire existence. Discourse analysis, extended to include dispositive analysis, aims to identify the knowledge (valid at a certain place at a certain time) of discourses and/or dispositives, to explore the respective concrete context of knowledge/power and to subject it to critique. Discourse analysis pertains to both everyday knowledge that is conveyed via the media, everyday communication, school and family, and so on, and also to that particular knowledge (valid at a certain place at a certain time) which is produced by the various sciences. This applies to both the cultural and the natural sciences.

In this chapter, however, I will focus on the knowledge of the cultural sciences. Although transfers to the natural sciences would indeed be possible, they are not considered here.

My contribution will begin with a brief outline of the discourse-theoretical/methodological background to a critical discourse analysis.[3] Secondly, I will provide a sketch of what a dispositive is, that is to discuss the interplay of discursive practices (= speaking and thinking on the basis of knowledge), non-discursive practices (= acting on the basis of knowledge) and 'manifestations' and/or 'materializations' of knowledge (by acting/doing). Indeed, dispositives can be conceived of as 'aggregate works of art' which, being dovetailed and interwoven with one another in a variety of ways, constitute an all-encompassing societal dispositive.

Discourse theory

The notion of discourse

The most fertile cultural science oriented approach to a discourse analysis following Michel Foucault is that which has been developed by the literary and cultural scientist Jürgen Link and his team. Their concern, as well as mine, is the analysis of current discourses and the effects of their power, the illumination of the (language-based and iconographic) means by which they work – in particular by collective symbolism which contributes to the linking-up of the various discourse strands. The overriding concern of their work and mine is the function of discourses in the bourgeois-capitalist modern industrial society as techniques to legitimize and ensure government.[4]

In his most compressed version Link defines discourse as: 'an institutionally consolidated concept of speech inasmuch as it determines and consolidates action and thus already exercises power' (Link, 1983: 60).

This definition of discourse can be further illustrated by regarding discourse 'as the flow of knowledge – and/or all societal knowledge stored – throughout all time' (Jäger, 1993 and 1999), which determines individual and collective doing and/or formative action that shapes society, thus exercising power. As such, discourses can be understood as material realities sui generis.

At the same time, this implies that discourses are not interesting as mere expressions of social practice, but because they serve certain ends, namely to exercise power with all its effects. They do this because they are institutionalized and regulated, because they are linked to action.[5]

The (dominating) discourses can be criticized and problematized; this is done by analysing them, by revealing their contradictions and non-expression and/or the spectrum of what can be said and what can be done covered by them, and by making evident the means by which the acceptance of merely temporarily valid truths is to be achieved. Assumed truths are meant here, which are presented as being rational, sensible and beyond all doubt.

Any researcher conducting such an analysis must, moreover, see clearly that with his/her critique he/she is not situated outside the discourse he/she is analysing. If not, he/she places his/her own concept of discourse analysis in doubt. Apart from other critical aspects which discourse analysis also comprises, he/she can base his/her analysis on values and norms, laws and rights; he/she must not forget either that these are themselves the historical outcome of discourse, and that his/her possible bias is not based on truth, but represents a position that in turn is the result of a discursive process. Equipped with this position he/she is able to enter discursive contests and to defend or modify his/her position.

The context of linking discourse to power mentioned above is, however, very complex because: 'a discursive practice exercises power with all its effects in various respects. If a discursive formation can be described as a limited "positive" field of accumulations of utterances', as suggested by Link and Link-Heer to defend this connection, 'the opposite is true, that in this way possible other utterances, questions, points of view, problematic issues and so on are excluded. Such exclusions which necessarily result from the structure of a special discourse (which must in absolutely no way be misinterpreted as the manipulative intentions of any one subject), can be institutionally reinforced' (Link and Link-Heer, 1990: 90). Thus, power is also exercised over discourses, for example, in the form of easy access to the media, unlimited access to resources, and so on. What Link and Link-Heer relate to scientific discourses in my opinion also pertains to everyday discourse, educational discourse, political discourse, the media and so on.

Discourse analysis encompasses the respective spectrum of what can be said in its qualitative range and its accumulation and/or all utterances which in a certain society at a certain time are said or can be said. It also covers the strategies with which the spectrum of what can be said is extended on the one hand, but also restricted on the other, for instance, by denial strategies, relativizing strategies, strategies to remove taboos, and so on. Demonstration of the restrictions or lack of restrictions of the spectrum of what can be said is subsequently a further critical aspect of discourse analysis.

The emergence of such strategies points in turn to the fact that there are utterances which in a certain society at a certain point in time cannot yet, or can no longer, be said, unless special 'tricks' are used in order to express them without negative sanctions. The spectrum of what can be said can be restricted, or an attempt can be made to exceed its limits, via direct prohibitions and confinements, limits, implications, creation of explicit taboos, but also through conventions, internalizations, and regulation of consciousness. Discourse as a whole is a regulating body; it forms consciousness.

By functioning as the 'flow of "knowledge" – and/or the whole of stored societal knowledge – throughout all time' discourse creates the conditions for the formation of subjects and the structuring and shaping of societies.

The various discourses are intertwined or entangled with one another like vines or strands; moreover they are not static but in constant motion forming a 'discursive milling mass' which at the same time results in the 'constant rampant growth of discourses'. It is this mass that discourse analysis endeavours to untangle.

An important means of linking up discourses with one another is collective symbolism. Collective symbols are 'cultural stereotypes (frequently called "topoi"), which are handed down and used collectively' (Drews et al., 1985: 265).

In the store of the collective symbols that all the members of a society know, a repertoire of images is available with which we visualize a complete picture of societal reality and/or the political landscape of society, and through which we then interpret these and are provided with interpretations – in particular by the media.[6]

The most important rules regulating these links through which the image of such a societal or political context is produced are catachreses or image fractures. These function by creating connections between utterances and areas of experience, bridging contradictions, generating plausibilities and acceptances and so on, plus reinforcing the power of discourses. 'The locomotive of progress can be slowed down by floods of immigrants' is a so-called image fracture (catachresis) because the symbols 'locomotive' (meaning progress) and 'floods' (meaning a threat from outside) are derived from different sources of images, the first being taken from traffic and the second from nature. The analysis of collective symbolism including catachreses is consequently a further critical aspect of discourse analysis.

On the question of the power of discourses Foucault once said: 'It is the problem which determines nearly all my books: how in occidental societies is the production of discourses, which (at least for a certain time) are equipped with a truth value, linked to different power mechanisms and institutions?' (Foucault, 1983: 8).

To further illustrate the problem of power/knowledge it is necessary first to deal in more detail with the relationship between discourse and societal reality and second, to ask more precisely how power is anchored in this societal reality, who exercises it, over whom and by what means it is exercised, and so on.

It should be clear by now that in discourses reality is not simply reflected, but that discourses live a 'life of their own' in relation to reality, although they impact and shape and even enable societal reality. They are in themselves sui generis material realities. They are not, for instance, by character passive media of 'in-formation' (that is information and 'formative input') provided by reality, and they are not second-class material realities, nor are they 'less material' than the 'real' reality. Discourses are rather fully valid first-class material realities amidst others (Link, 1992).

This also means that discourses determine reality, always of course via intervening active subjects in their societal contexts as (co-)producers and (co-)agents of discourses and changes to reality. These active subjects conduct discursive and non-discursive practices. They can do this because as subjects 'knitted into' the discourses they have knowledge at their disposal.

Following this notion the discourse cannot be reduced to a mere 'distorted view of reality' or a 'necessarily false ideology' – as is frequently done by the concept of 'ideology critique' following orthodox Marxist approaches. In fact, a discourse represents a reality of its own which in relation to 'the real reality' is in no way 'much ado about nothing', distortion and lies, but has a material reality of its own and 'feeds on' past and (other) current discourses.

This characterization of discourses as being material means, at the same time, that discourse theory is strictly a materialistic theory. Discourses can also be regarded as societal means of production. Thus they are in no way 'merely ideology'; they produce subjects and – conveyed by these in terms of the 'population' – they produce societal realities.[7]

Subsequently, discourse analysis is not (only) about interpretations of something that already exists, thus not (only) about the analysis of the allocation of a meaning post festum, but about the analysis of the production of reality which is performed by discourse – conveyed by active people.

Yet, the simple question is: who makes the discourses and what status do they have?

The individual does not make the discourse but the opposite tends to be the case. The discourse is super-individual. Though everybody 'knits along' at producing discourse, no individual and no single group determines the discourse or has precisely intended what turns out to be the final result. As a rule discourses have evolved and become independent as the result of historical processes. They convey more knowledge than the individual subjects are aware of. Thus, if one wants to identify the knowledge of a society (for example, on certain topics) one has to reconstruct the history of its evolution or genesis. Foucault has attempted several experiments on this, not only with regard to the sciences, because he always included their 'surroundings', the institutions, everyday life (for example, in prison, in hospital).

Such an approach might well go against the grain for people who have the uniqueness of the individual in view. It also has to be considered that it is not so easy to follow the thoughts presented here because we have learnt that language as such does not change reality – which is in fact correct. Moreover, unlike notions which idealize language or even notions based on the magic of language that changes reality, we perhaps tend to allocate too strongly the idea of the material reality of the discourse to idealistic concepts. If, however, we regard human speech (and human activity in general) as activity in the broader frame of societal activity, being tied in with the historical discourse according to whose impact societies organize their practice, and regard societal reality as having emerged and emerging in connection with the 'raw material' of reality (matter), the notion ought to be more easily grasped that discourses exercise power, as power is exercised by the impact of tools and objects on reality. This impact can immediately be characterized as a non-discursive practice.

Discourse, knowledge, power, society, subject

As 'agents' of 'knowledge (valid at a certain place at a certain time)' discourses exercise power. They are themselves a power factor by being apt to induce behaviour and (other) discourses. Thus, they contribute to the structuring of the power relations in a society.

Yet what is the role played in this discursive interplay by the individual or subject? In this respect Foucault argues quite clearly:

> One has to liberate oneself from the constituting subject, from the subject itself, i.e. to arrive at an historical analysis which is capable of clarifying the constitution of the subject in the historical context. It is precisely this that I would call genealogy, i.e. a form of history which reports on the constitution of knowledge, discourses, fields of objects etc., without having to relate to a

subject which transcends the field of events and occupies it with its hollow identity throughout history. (Foucault, 1978: 32)

In contrast to what Foucault is frequently criticized for, he, or rather his discourse theory, does not deny the subject. He endeavours to arrive at an historical analysis which is capable of clarifying the constitution of the subject in the historical context, in the socio-historical context and thus from a synchronic and diachronic perspective. This is not directed against the subject but against subjectivism and individualism.

The acting individual is absolutely involved when we talk about the realization of power relations (practice). It thinks, plans, constructs, interacts and fabricates. As such it also faces the problem of having to prevail, i.e. to get its own way, to find its place in society. However, it does this in the frame of the rampant growth of the network of discursive relations and arguments, in the context of 'living discourses' insofar as it brings them to life, lives 'knitted into' them and contributes to their change.

The spectrum of all that can be said and the forms in which it emerges is covered by discourse analysis in its entire qualitative range, so that discourse analysis can make generally valid statements on one or several discourse strands.[8] However, quantitative aspects also emerge, since statements about accumulations and trends are also possible. These can be of importance when identifying, for example, thematic foci within a discourse strand.

I will summarize this first part in an hypothesis. Discourses exercise power as they transport knowledge on which the collective and individual consciousness feeds. This emerging knowledge is the basis of individual and collective action and the formative action that shapes reality.

From the discourse to the dispositive

Since knowledge is the basis of action and formative action that shapes reality, the opportunity arises not only to analyse discursive practices, but also non-discursive practices and so-called manifestations/ materializations as well as the relationship between these elements. The interplay of these elements I call, as does Foucault, dispositive. To explain this interplay more precisely I have to examine it in more depth.

As people – as actual individuals – we allocate meaning to reality in the present, in history and in the future for which we plan. Thus, we create reality in a certain way – both for the good and for the bad. Here, of course, it is not the world of natural things, the material side of reality, which is meant. The material side of reality only represents the raw material which is put to use by the active individual and which – frequently irrespective of societal reality – is researched by the natural sciences. For instance, even medical science regards people as if they were biological natural objects.

It is not reality that is reflected in consciousness, but consciousness that relates to reality, as discourses provide the application concepts and all the knowledge for the shaping of reality as well as further reality concepts. If the discourse withdraws from the reality 'on whose shoulders' it has been formed, or rather more precisely, if people for whatever reasons withdraw from a discourse which they have provided with a meaning, that part of reality which corresponds to it becomes meaningless in the truest sense of the word and returns to its natural state.

If the knowledge contained in a discourse changes, other meanings are allocated to it and it becomes another object. This happens, for example, when a beggar uses a bank which has become meaningless – its intended function having been removed – as a weekend house, or when steel works or nuclear power stations are converted into a leisure park. Here a withdrawal of meaning takes place. The well-trodden 'floor of meaning' is withdrawn from beneath the feet of the object in question and/or modified by allocating one or several other meanings to it.

In Foucault's *L'archéologie du savoir* ('archaeology of knowledge') he writes that discourses 'are to be treated as practices which systematically form the objects of which they speak' (Foucault, 1989: 74). Notwithstanding, Foucault also sees non-discursive societal practices which play a part in forming objects/manifestations. At the same time he stresses the importance of discursive 'relationships'. He guesses they are 'somehow at the edge of the discourse: they provide it [= the discourse, S.J.] with the objects about which it [= the discourse, S.J.] can talk, or rather . . . they [= the discursive relationships, S.J.] determine the package of relations which the discourse must induce in order to be able to speak of these or those objects, to treat them, to give them names, to analyse, to classify and explain them' (1988: 70). Thus, Foucault encircles the problem of the relationship between discourse and reality without solving it beyond doubt. It remains unclear what he actually understands to be 'objects'. One can only guess that he does not mean 'manifestations', but rather themes, theories, statements, in other words purely discursive 'objects'.

This circumnavigation of the problem is at its best, in my opinion, in his attempt to determine what he understands by 'dispositive'. In the collection of interviews and lectures *Dispositive der Macht* ('dispositives of power') (Foucault, 1978) he first defines dispositive somewhat daringly as follows:

> What I am endeavouring to establish with this terminology [namely dispositive, S.J.] is first a decisively heterogeneous ensemble which covers discourses, institutions, architectural institutions, reglemented decisions, laws, administrative measures, scientific statements, philosophical, moral or philanthropic teachings, in brief, what is said and what is not said. So much for the elements

of the dispositive. The dispositive itself is the net which can be woven between these elements. (Foucault, 1978: 119f.)

Foucault goes on to differentiate: 'Between these elements there is, whether discursive or not, a play of changing positions and functions which in turn can be very varied' (Foucault, 1978: 120). He understands 'by dispositive a kind of – say – formation whose major function at a given historical point in time was to respond to an urgency (original French, "urgence"; I.B./R.T.). The dispositive, therefore, has a mainly strategic function' (Foucault, 1978: 120). Having differentiated between discursive and non-discursive in the above cited initial definition, a few pages further on he goes on to say: 'In view of what I want with the dispositive it is of hardly any importance to say: this is discursive and that is not' (Foucault, 1978: 125).

Foucault is in an embarrassing situation here. The three psycho-analysts with whom he is debating have pushed him into a tight corner. It is noticeable that his interview partners are getting on his nerves. He is becoming impatient, even cross.

This can be felt even more clearly, when he proceeds:

Compare, for example, the architectural plan of the École Militaire by Gabriel with the actual École Militaire building: what is discursive, what is institutional? All that interests me is whether the building corresponds to the plan. However, I do not believe that it would be of great importance to undertake this division because my problem is not a linguistic one. (Foucault, 1978: 125)

Foucault liberates himself – and us – from linguistics that is not based on thought and consciousness; he subordinates language, and therefore also linguistics, to thought and basically makes them into a department of the cultural sciences whose objects are the conditions and results of sensory human activity – sensory because thought and consciousness are the preconditions of human activity.

After his archaeological endeavours to reconstruct the development of knowledge entirely materialistically, Foucault arrived at the conviction that it is not speech/the text/the discourse alone which moves the world, and he found, or rather set up, the dispositive in order to interpret his historical and current reality more appropriately. With this determination of dispositive, the question has to be examined intensively as to the connection between discourse and dispositive and/or discourse and reality.

Foucault clearly sees a co-existence of discourse and reality and/or objects; they are the elements of the dispositive which is the net hung between these elements and/or links them. Foucault is, however, not able to say in what quite concrete relationship and/or, to put it more pointedly, in what empirical relationship discourses and things and/or events/reality are linked to one another. He was indeed interested in the '"nature of the connection", which can be produced between these heterogeneous elements'. He sees between these elements 'whether discursive or not, a play of changing positions and functions, which' – as he says – 'in themselves can in turn be very varied' (1978: 120). Furthermore, he sees the dispositive as a kind of 'formation whose major function it has been at a given historical point in time to respond to an urgency (original French, "urgence"; I.B./R.T.)'. He also recognizes that therefore the dispositive has 'a primarily strategic function' (Foucault, 1978: 120). Such an urgency could, for instance, exist in the re-absorbing of a liberated social mass which inevitably had to be a problem for a capitalist society, and so on.

Foucault wishes to show 'that what I call dispositive is a far more general case of episteme. Or rather, that the episteme in contrast to the dispositive in general, which itself is discursive and non-discursive and whose elements are a lot more heterogeneous, is a specifically discursive dispositive' (Foucault, 1978: 123). In this respect we are not only dealing with spoken and written knowledge (episteme) but also with the entire knowledge apparatus with which a goal is achieved. Accordingly epistemes are not only the discursive part in the knowledge apparatus, but knowledge also 'lives' and 'acts' in the actions of people and in the objects they produce based on knowledge. What is meant here exactly is well illustrated in 'surveiller et punir' ('discipline and punish'), which I merely mention here (Foucault, 1989).

Yet, here the following becomes evident: Foucault assumes a dualism of discourse and reality. He did not see that the discourses and the world of objectivities and/or realities are substantially interrelated and do not exist independently. In the dispositive various elements are assembled which are linked to one another, as he says, and this connection constitutes the dispositive (see also Deleuze, 1992 and Balke, 1998).

Evidently Foucault sees the emergence of dispositives as follows: an urgency emerges and an existing dispositive becomes precarious; for this reason a need to act results and the social and hegemonial forces which are confronted with it assemble the elements which they can obtain in order to encounter this urgency, that is speech, people, knives, cannons, institutions, and so on in order to mend the 'leaks' – the urgency – which has arisen, as Deleuze says (Deleuze, 1992 and Balke, 1998).

What connects these elements is quite simply that they serve a common end, which is to fend off the momentary or permanent urgency. An 'inner bond' – of whatever kind – which would tie them together does not, however, become evident in Foucault's understanding of dispositive.

Yet this bond exists in the form of sensory human activity which mediates between subject and object, the social worlds and realities of objects, in other words, through non-discursive practices, which at least in Foucault's definition of dispositive do not explicitly come about. By relating back to sensory activity I am introducing the theoretical base of my second line of argument, that is the activity theory based on Marx and developed by Vygotsky and especially A.N. Leontjev, the nucleus of which, because of its importance in this context, I would like to illustrate.[9] However, it is also necessary to place this approach, which is in essence an ideology-critical one, on a discourse-theoretical foundation.

As already said, we as people are evidently capable of allocating meanings to 'things', in other words of giving reality a meaning; moreover, only by giving things meanings do we make them into things. I can, for example, allocate the meaning table to a piece of wood that I find in the forest and then eat my bread from it and put my mug on it. A thing to which I allocate no meaning is not a thing to me; indeed it is completely nondescript to me, invisible or even non-existent; I do not even see it, because I overlook it. I do not see the bird that the forester sees (forester syndrome). Perhaps I see a red spot. And what do I say about it when I see it? – 'That is a red spot.' And, in fact, to me that is the meaning of the red spot to which I can allocate the meaning red spot. Whether it is a flower, a bird or the recently dyed hair of Lothar Matthäus who is going for a walk in the woods, because he was injured playing in the last football match and therefore cannot train today, is not visible to me, is not there, is beyond my range. Of course, a friend can say to me, 'look, that is Lothar Matthäus's hair, and he used to be captain of the German national team.' Then I can say, 'Yes, OK, I know him', or else, 'No, that was definitely a bird or a flower.'

What I want to say by this is that all meaningful reality is existent for us because we make it meaningful[10] or because it has been allocated some meaning by our ancestors or neighbours and is still important to us. It is like King Midas with his gold: everything he touched turned to gold. Thus, everything to which we allocate meaning is real to us in a certain way, because, when and how it is meaningful to us.

Ernesto Laclau expressed this context elegantly when he wrote,

> By 'the discursive' I understand nothing which in a narrow sense relates to texts but the ensemble of phenomena of the societal production of meaning on which a society as such is based. It is not a question of regarding the discursive as a plane or dimension of the social but as having the same meaning as the social as such . . . Subsequently, the non-discursive is not opposite to the discursive as if one were dealing with two different planes because there is nothing societal that is determined outside the discursive. History and society are therefore an unfinished text. (Laclau, 1981: 176)

One has to ask, however, why, when, under what conditions and how do I allocate which meaning to 'things', in other words, how is the 'gap' between discourse and reality closed? With Leontjev's activity theory this happens when I derive a motive from a particular need and subsequently endeavour to achieve a certain aim for which one uses actions, operations and raw material, in other words, by working. The products thus created can be utility commodities but also new thoughts and plans from which in turn new sensory activities can result in new products, and so on. The psychologist Foucault, strangely, did not know the activity theory based on the materialistic psychology of the early 1930s, or possibly he rejected it as appearing to him to be too subject-based. Yet this approach is interesting because the theory allows discussion of the mediation between subject and object, society and objective reality by sensory activity. He overlooked the fact that the consequences and/or the 'materializations through work' of past speech and/or preceding discourses also belong to reality, as they are materializations of thought complexes. These have been implemented by people acting in their non-discursive practices, by means of which they have erected and furnished houses and banks and made benches, which incidentally – as demonstrated – only exist for as long as they are and remain embedded in discourses. The institution, bank, for example, which belongs to the dispositive capital, stops having this function when it no longer has a discursive base to stand on: it becomes meaningless, reduced to nothing apart from purely 'natural' matter (the latter itself becoming meaningful of course, if we call it thus), or 'discursified anew' into another objectivity having been allocated a new meaning. Then the bank is, for instance, lived in by beggars who make it into their shelter.[11]

Foucault also sees this and writes:

> It is not objects which remain constant, not the area which they form, neither is it the point of their emergence or the way in which they are characterized, but it is the creation of the interrelations of the surfaces where they appear, distinguish themselves from each other, where they are analysed and can be specified. (1988: 71)

To put it in a nutshell: if the discourse changes, the object not only changes its meaning, but it becomes a different object; it loses its previous identity.

This can either take place as a fracture or as a long, extended process in which, mostly unnoticed, yet in effect completely, everything changes.

Foucault is extremely reluctant, as he says, 'to define objects without a relationship to the basis of the things' (Foucault, 1988: 72). A little further on he says, it is his concern that the discourses are 'to be treated as practices which systematically form the objects of which they speak' (Foucault, 1988: 74).

However, he does not manage to proceed beyond this point, because in my opinion he does not understand the mediation between subject and object, society and discourse as being brought about by work/activity and/or non-discursive practices. The discursive practices remain verbal for him, strictly separated from the non-discursive practices, and he adheres to the separation between intellectual activity and (nonintellectual) physical work. In this respect he is in fact a child of his times or his origin, in which the bourgeoisie regarded physical work as completely unintellectual. He knows that signs serve more than to signify things and he sees: 'this "more" makes them irreducible to speech and language' (Foucault, 1988: 74). He would also like to illustrate and describe this 'more' (1988), in which, in my opinion, he does not succeed. He cannot really grasp this 'more'. In my opinion, this surplus is the knowledge which serves the conversion of knowledge of any kind – and of knowledge which still has to be articulated – into objects: knowledge about statics, for example, or about the nature of material, tools, routine knowledge, which flows into any work as 'numb intellectual actions', but which is not or only seldom articulated and in many cases even impossible to articulate. Consider, for example, the knowledge of a steelworker at the blast furnace who sees when the steel is ready or what ingredients are still missing, but cannot say why this is the case. In a certain way, what we have here is knowledge that has become independent, a routine.

Thus, one could say: reality is meaningful and exists in the form in which it exists only as long as the people, all of whom are bound up or 'knitted into' the (socio-historic) discourses and who are constituted by them, have allocated and will continue to allocate meaning to it. Should the latter no longer be the case, the objects change, or lose their meaning. At best the original meaning can be reconstructed as the former meaning, which has become entangled with other meanings or which has ceased to exist. Even when one observes the night sky and sees in the constellation of stars certain signs of the zodiac, this is the result of a discourse. One only sees signs of the zodiac, because one has learnt to see them and possibly to guess that somewhere there is a god or there is not.

The allocation of meaning is, however, not an unbinding symbolic action, but means the revival of what one comes across, re-shaped and changed. If, under these conditions we consider the collective symbolism that is popularly used when talking of immigrants, we will realize that many people who have learnt to carry out corresponding allocations of meaning, really feel that foreigners are floods, which have to be held back or against which dams have to be erected, or they are even felt to be lice and pigs, which one can crush or slaughter.

Bernhard Waldenfels (1991) confirms at several points the criticism of Foucault, outlined above, by whom he himself was inspired, when he writes:

> [it] is unclear how the border between discursive and non-discursive practices is drawn and how it is bridged [by Foucault, S.J.], it remains unclear whether it has to be drawn at all. I believe that in a certain way Foucault had manoeuvred himself into a blind alley by conceiving the formation of the order of history in his theory first as the orders of knowledge (epistemes), then as orders of speech (discourse) instead of starting with an order which is divided up into

the different behavioural registers of people, e.g. their speech and action (!),
but also their views, their physical customs, their erotic relationships, their
techniques, their economic and political decisions, their artistic and religious
forms of expression and a good deal more. One cannot see why any one such
area should be spared the functionality which Foucault developed one-sidedly
on the base of speech. (Waldenfels, 1991: 291)

In addition Waldenfels remarks that Foucault even exceeded these limits
at several points and continues:

in *L'archéologie du savoir* (archaeology of knowledge) the discourse is mentioned that deals with forms and expressions of politics, such as the function of
the revolutionary instance which can neither be traced back to a revolutionary
situation nor to a revolutionary consciousness. . . . Here, too, Foucault preferred to experiment. (Waldenfels, 1991: 291f.)

This ought to encourage us to experiment further and, equipped with
Foucault's 'box of tools', in which theoretical and practical instruments
are to be found, to develop some of his ideas further or to bring them to
a conclusion. This I have endeavoured to do in this text. Firstly, by
repositioning Foucault's definition of discourse, which is too strongly
caught up in the verbal, and which, moreover, is not replaced by that of
the dispositive but is incorporated into it, and I have taken it back a step
to the place where human thought and knowledge are situated, i.e. the
consciousness. This is where the contents of thought (including affects,
ways of seeing, and so on) are situated which provide the base for
the shaping of reality by work. In so doing I have, secondly, made the
activity theory fertile for discursive theory, the former theory being the
one which indicates how the subjects and objects of reality are mediated
by each other. Foucault saw discourse primarily as being somehow
mediated by reality, and thus occasionally approaches the ideas of constructivism. By discussing Leontjev I have been able to determine the
subject as the link which connects discourses with reality. Subjects do
this in the sum of their activities which, in the way they actually take
effect, are neither planned by a single individual nor a group. It is,
however, human consciousness and physical being (physical strength)
which in this respect takes effect and shapes reality. Everything that is
human consciousness is constituted discursively, that is through knowledge. It is also the subjects, incidentally, which bring the knowledge into
play that has become independent, a routine. This knowledge, too, is
handed down in the discursive and non-discursive practices and manifestations and is in principle reconstructable, re-accessible.

The problem I have touched upon in this discussion I will now
endeavour to summarize and bring to a conclusion: I have the impression
that the difficulties in the determination of the dispositive are related to a
failure to determine the mediation between discourse (what is said/what

has been said), non-discursive practices (activities) and manifestations (products/objects). If I, like Leontjev and others, regard these manifestations as materializations/activities of knowledge (discourse) and non-discursive practices as the active implementation of knowledge, a context can be produced that will probably solve many of the problems.

The sociologist Hannelore Bublitz provides a detailed discussion of this problem in her recent book, *Foucaults Archäologie des Unbewussten* (Foucault's archaeology of the unconscious) (Bublitz, 1999: 82–115), in which in particular she also underlines the function of the dispositive nets for the modern subject formation. She claims: 'although, therefore, Foucault on the one hand sees the non-discursive and the discursive as opposites he advocates the thesis that, "what is done and what is said are not opposite"'. Rather he assumes 'that the entire "civilized" occidental society appears as the "complex net of various elements – walls, space, institutions, regulations, discourses", as a "factory for the production of suppressed subjects"' (Bublitz, 1999: 90).

To conclude, the question that still has to be answered is whether and how discourses and dispositives can be analysed at all.

The method of discourse and dispositive analysis

The theoretical discussion of discourse and dispositive theory outlined above also forms the general theoretical foundation of the analytical method proposed in the following. This also draws on linguistic instruments (figurativeness, vocabulary, pronominal structure, argumentation types, and so on) with whose aid we can investigate the more discrete means that take effect in texts as elements of discourses. However, I will dispense with a detailed presentation of the (strictly) linguistic toolbox since one can derive it cautiously and selectively from good works on style and grammar.[12]

At the same time the linguistic toolbox represents merely one drawer in the discourse-analytical 'toolbox' which can be filled with very various instruments according to the texture of the object to be investigated. Yet there is a standard repertoire which I will describe later this chapter. Moreover, in what follows, emphasis will be placed on activity and discourse-theoretical principles.

The structure of discourse

Discourses and/or 'societal flows of knowledge through time' represent in their entirety a gigantic and complex 'milling mass'.

In the first place, therefore, the question arises how discourses can be analysed at all in spite of their constant rampant growth and interwoven nature. In order to do this, I will first make some terminologically pragmatic suggestions that are capable of rendering the principal structure of discourses transparent and only as a result of which they can actually be analysed.

Special discourses and interdiscourses   Fundamentally, special discourses (of (the) science(s)) are to be distinguished from inter-discourse, whereby all non-scientific discourses are to be regarded as components of the inter-discourse. At the same time, elements of the scientific discourses (special discourses) constantly flow into the interdiscourses.

   To identify the structure of discourses I suggest the following operationalization aids.

Discourse strands   In general societal discourse a great variety of themes arise. 'Thematically uniform discourse processes' I call 'discourse strands'. Each discourse strand has a synchronic and diachronic dimension. A synchronic cut through a discourse strand has a certain qualitative (finite) range.[13] Such a cut is made in order to identify what has been 'said' and/or what is, was and will be 'sayable' at a particular past, present or future point in time, in other words, in a respective 'present time' in its entire range.

Discourse fragments   Each discourse strand comprises a multitude of elements which are traditionally called texts. I prefer the term discourse fragment to 'text' since texts (can) address several themes and thus contain several discourse fragments. What I call a discourse fragment is therefore a text or part of a text which deals with a certain theme, for example, foreigners/foreigners' affairs (in the broadest sense). Conversely, this means that discourse fragments combine to constitute discourse strands.

Entanglements of discourse strands   It has to be considered, then, that a text can make references to various discourse strands and in fact usually does, in other words: in a text various discourse fragments can be contained; these emerge in general in an entangled form. Such a discursive entanglement (of strands) exists when a text clearly addresses various themes, but also when a main theme is addressed in which, however, references to other themes are made. Such is the case with a commentary which deals with two themes that have, or appear to have, nothing to do with one another. In this case there are two different discourse fragments which are, however, entangled with one another. On the other hand, though, a thematically uniform text (= discourse fragment) can make more or less loose references to other themes and tie the treated theme to one or several others at the same time. This is, for instance, the case when in a text on the theme of immigration reference is made to the economic discourse strand or a discourse on women, and so on. Thus a

corresponding commentary could, for example, conclude: 'and integration costs money, by the way' or, 'one also has to consider that with
people from that country, patriarchy plays a completely different role
than with us'. In these instances one can speak of discursive knots, the
discourse strands forming loose knots. Such 'occasional knots' as
opposed to constantly entangled strands can therefore be seen as a lesser
form of entanglement.

Discursive events and discursive context   All events have discursive roots; in
other words, they can be traced back to discursive constellations whose
materializations they represent. However, only those events can be seen
as discursive events which are especially emphasized politically, that is
as a general rule by the media, and as such events they influence the
direction and quality of the discourse strand to which they belong to a
greater or lesser extent. To give an example, the grave consequences of
the nuclear MCA (maximum credible accident) in Harrisburg can be
compared with those in Chernobyl. Whereas, however, the former was
kept secret by the media for years, the latter was made into a media-
discursive mega event which had an impact on politics in the entire
world. Whether an event, for instance an anticipated serious accident in
the chemical industry, becomes a discursive event or not, depends on the
respective political power constellation and developments. Discourse
analysis can establish whether such anticipated events will become discursive events or not. If they do, they influence the further discourse
considerably: Chernobyl contributed to a changing nuclear policy in
Germany, which – albeit hesitantly – might lead to its refusal to use
nuclear power. An opposing environmental ('green') discourse which
had been developing for some time, would hardly have been capable of
achieving this goal. It can at the same time be observed that a discursive
event, such as the one just described, can have an impact on the entire
discourse on new technologies by re-directing attention, for instance, to
the necessity of developing new energy sources.

   To quote another example, the electoral success of the FPÖ (Freedom
Party of Austria) in 1999 met with considerable media coverage. As a
result, and with the FPÖ (and indirectly Jörg Haider) becoming part
of the government, the situation triggered a far greater worldwide
response, thus becoming a discursive mega event, which for months kept
the European and US press in suspense. Here again an impact on other
discourses could be observed: on discourses of the extreme right wing in
other European and non-European countries.

   The identification of discursive events can also be important for the
analysis of discourse strands, because sketching them marks out the
contours of the discursive context to which a current discourse strand
relates. In this way the analysis of a synchronic cut through a discourse
strand can, for example, find its historic roots by referring this synchronic
cut back to a chronology of the discursive events that thematically belong

to the discourse strand at stake. Such historic references are particularly helpful to the analysis and interpretation of current cuts through discourse strands.[14]

Discourse planes The respective discourse strands operate on various discursive planes (science(s), politics, media, education, everyday life, business life, administration, and so on). Such discourse planes could also be called the societal locations from which 'speaking' happens. It can also be observed that these discursive planes impact on one another, relate to one another, use each other and so on. In this way, for example, discourse fragments from the special discourse of science or from political discourse can be included on the media plane. Furthermore, we can also observe that the media can include everyday discourse, package it, focus it, and also, particularly, in the mass-circulation yellow press à la Bild (Germany) or Kronenzeitung (Austria) sensationalize and 'doll it up' in a populist form. In this way, incidentally, the media regulate everyday thinking and exercise considerable influence on what is conductible and conducted politics. Consider, for example, the image of Jörg Haider, which, without the kind of media reporting that normalizes right-wing populism, would hardly have come about.

We also have to pay attention to the fact that the individual discourse planes are so tightly interwoven that, for example, even media that are renowned for having a leading role take over information and contents of any kind that have already been carried in other media. This adds to the justification of referring to the media discourse, which as a whole, but specifically concerning the dominant media in society, can essentially be regarded as uniform. It does not, however, rule out the possibility that various discourse positions can achieve different degrees of impact, from strong to weak.

Discourse position The category of discourse position, referring to a specific ideological location of a person or a medium, proves to be very helpful. Margret Jäger defines the category of discourse position as follows:

> With discourse position I understand the [ideological, S.J.] location from which the participation in the discourse and assessment of it for individuals and/or groups and institutions result. It produces and reproduces the special discursive entanglements, which feed on the hitherto experienced and current life situation of those involved in the discourse. Thus, the discourse position is the result of the involvement in, of being 'knitted into', various discourses to which the individual has been subjected and which it has processed into a certain ideological position during the course of its life. (M. Jäger, 1996: 47)

What applies to the subject correspondingly applies to the media and indeed to entire discourse strands. They, too, form certain discourse

positions, which shape overall reporting with varying degrees of strin-
gency. Attention has to be paid to the fact that:

> groups and individuals can assess this discourse system in a variety of ways.
> For instance, the hegemonial discourse can occupy the symbol of an aeroplane
> in a positive way, whereas the anti-hegemonial discourse rejects aeroplanes
> and idealizes trees, bicycles, etc. What is important in this respect is, however,
> that deviating discourse positions relate to the same discursive basic structure
> (Link, 1986). (Jäger, 1996: 47)

Such discourse positions can basically only be revealed as the result of
discourse analyses. It can be observed, however, that they belong to the
general knowledge of a population in a rough form. The self-descriptions
of newspapers, for example, as 'independent' or 'non-partisan' should
always be regarded with distrust. At the same time, it should be indicated that discourse positions within a dominant or hegemonial discourse are rather homogeneous, which can in turn be regarded as the
effect of the respective hegemonial discourse. Within the paramount
discourse there can of course be various positions which, however, can
agree in principle about not putting in doubt the ruling economic system.
Discourse positions which deviate can frequently be allocated to more or
less stringent opposing discourses. This does not rule out the fact that
opposing discursive and fundamentally oppositional discourse elements
can be subversively introduced into the hegemonial discourse. An
example of this would be the popular figure of speech 'time is money',
which might well be understood by some people as a criticism of
capitalism.

The overall societal discourse in its entanglement and complexity In a given
society discourse strands form the overall societal discourse in a state of
complex entanglement. In this respect it has to be considered that 'given
societies' are never (entirely) homogeneous; therefore under certain
circumstances one has to operate with social sub-groups of a society. In
the Federal Republic of Germany, however, there has evidently been a
strong ideological homogenization of the overall societal discourse,
subsequent to the political turnabout in 1989, which will not be easy to
break down (see Teubert, 1997, 1999). Attention should also be paid to
the fact that the overall discourse of a society is a partial discourse of a
(naturally heterogeneous) global discourse or, in other words, of the
worldwide discourse which – very cautiously put – has at the same time
been homogenized (in the Western world) since 1989 and is tending to be
re-polarized (from 'the West versus the East' to 'the West versus the
Orient, Islam').

No doubt, the overall societal discourse presents a particularly
entwined and interdependently deeply rooted net. Discourse analysis
has the aim of untangling this net and proceeds as a rule by first working

out the individual discourse on individual discourse planes. An example of this would be: the media–immigration discourse (strand). Such an analysis would be joined by others, such as the analysis of the political discourse strand on immigration, of the everyday discourse on immigration, and so on.

Subsequent to such analyses, as a general rule the question can be asked how the discursive planes of the entire discourse strand concerned relate to one another. In this context the question would have to be answered, if and how the political discourse strand dovetails with that of the media and the everyday discourse strand, how and whether that of the media 'influences' that of the everyday discourse strand and thus 'eats into it' as it were, and so on.

History, present and future of discourse strands In addition, discourse/ discourse strands have a history, a present and a future. Thus, it would be necessary to analyse longer timeframes of discursive processes in order to reveal their strength, the density of the entanglement of the respective discourse strands with others, changes, fracture, drying-up and re-emergence. In other words, it would be (in accordance with Foucault) necessary to carry out an 'archaeology of knowledge' or as he later said 'a genealogy'. This would be the basis for a discursive prognostic concept, possibly taking the form of unfolding scenarios, which would, however, also have to take into account the various discursive events (events given great media coverage) that can be anticipated in future.

Such a project would of course be enormous and could only be approached in the form of a large number of single projects. Yet such single projects are very useful because they allow very reliable statements to be made on certain discursive areas. Such statements can, for instance, be the basis from which to change the 'knowledge' of and the attitude towards foreigners and thus in turn have an impact on the further course that the discourse strand takes.

On the question of the completeness of discourse analyses

With the question of how complete discourse analyses are, we are asking how representative, reliable and generally valid they are. The analysis is complete when it reveals no further contents and formally new findings. On the whole, this completeness is achieved – much to the irritation of primarily quantitative empirical social scientists who as a rule work with massive amounts of material – surprisingly quickly, because discourse analysis deals with the respective fields of what can be said. The arguments and contents which can be read or heard on the theme of immigration at a certain societal location at a certain time are astonishingly limited (and, in fact, mostly in the ambiguous sense of this word). Quantitative aspects do, however, also play a certain role: the frequency with which particular arguments emerge can be recorded. In this way the statements on a certain theme can be registered, which, for example, have a slogan character whose dissemination always goes hand in hand with the fact that it addresses whole lists of judgements and prejudices. The quantitative aspect of discourse analysis is accordingly always of less relevance to the significance of discourse analysis than the qualitative. These statements apply especially to making a synchronic cut through the discourse strand. Historically oriented analyses can proceed by conducting several synchronic cuts through a discourse strand – based on discursive events, for example – and subsequently comparing them with each other. Such analyses provide information on changes to, and continuities of, discourse processes through time.

Little toolbox for conducting discourse analyses

In a brief summary I would now like to introduce our 'toolbox' to be used when conducting discourse analyses, though these cannot be explained in detail here (see S. Jäger, 1999).[15]

In the following the practical approach to the discourse-analytical discussion of empirical (text) material will be addressed. In order to conduct a complete investigation additional steps have to be taken. These entail first and foremost a justification of the project and what is to be investigated, accompanied by an explanation of the theoretical approach and method ('theoretical part'), which is necessary and useful to understand and follow the analysis.

Selection of the 'object' to be investigated, justification of the method and research-pragmatic suggestions to avoid short cuts and simplifications

The first thing the researcher must do is to locate precisely his/her investigation (the object to be investigated). There are several possible traps one can run into here. For example, if the issue at stake is how racism is disseminated in the media or in everyday life, one should not take the term racism as a kind of magnifying glass and with it launch a search for the expression of this ideology. Instead, one should endeavour to determine the location at which such ideologies are expressed. Such a location is the discourse on immigrants, refugees, asylum, and so on. This discourse (strand) provides the material which has to be investigated.

Mostly one has to concentrate (initially) on one discourse plane, for instance, the media. In some cases, however, several planes can also be investigated at the same time or, in addition, several sectors of the plane, for example, women's magazines, news programmes on television. Frequently one will only be able to investigate a partial sector of the discourse plane, for example, printed media, popular media (pop songs). Why the investigation is dedicated to this sector has to be explained precisely: for example, because it promises to demonstrate in a special way, how a theme is disseminated to the masses, or because this sector has not previously been investigated (in which case, of course, other sectors which have already been investigated should also be dealt with).

A 'synchronic' cut through the discourse strand which, insofar as it has become 'what it is', is at the same time diachronic-historic, can look different according to the theme and the discourse plane. In the case of printed media and the way they deal with the theme biopolitics consistently a whole year could be examined but seldom in very great detail. This is because even by thorough reading of the newspapers concerned, the range of the discourse strand at issue might only be qualitatively completely covered over a longer period of time. In contrast to this the presentation of women in pop songs can (probably) be achieved using a few examples, because we can expect to find extremely exemplary densities. (But this must be proved!)

It is important to identify the sub-themes of the discourse strand in the respective sector of the discourse plane and to allocate them (approximately) to the superior themes, which in their entirety constitute the discourse strand of the newspaper and/or of the sector concerned on the discourse planes.

The interplay of several discursive planes in regulating (mass) consciousness is particularly exciting but extremely labour intensive. Here one has to search for well-justified examples from the various discourse planes and exemplify their interplay. The problem is compounded when the interplay (the entanglements of various discourse strands) also has to be investigated.

Method

A possible method for a (simple) discourse analysis (following the introduction and justification of the theme (discourse strand)) is as follows:

1   brief characterization (of the sector), of the discourse plane, for example printed media, women's magazines, pop songs, videos;
2   establishing and processing the material base or archive (see analysis guideline for processing material below);
3   structure analysis: evaluating the material processed with regard to the discourse strand to be analysed;
4   fine analysis of one or several articles (discourse fragments) which are as typical as possible of the sector, for instance, and also of the discourse position of the newspaper; this article (discourse fragment) has of course to be allocated to a superior theme;
5   this is followed by an overall analysis in the sector concerned, for example, in the newspaper concerned; this means that all the essential results that have hitherto been gained are reflected upon

and added to an overall statement on the discourse strand in the newspaper or sector concerned; the question hovering over this concluding part could for instance be, 'what contribution is made by the newspaper concerned towards (the acceptance of) biopolitics in the Federal Republic of Germany at the present time and what future development can be expected?'

This is not necessarily a table of contents which has to be adhered to slavishly. Variations are in fact possible. One should, however, pay attention to the fact, that we are dealing with the discourse analysis of the discourse strand at issue, of the sector concerned, on a discourse plane, for example of the newspaper in question.

Processing the material

Preliminary remarks   The following provides a kind of analytical guideline for processing the material. It is geared to the special problems involved in media analysis. Processing the material is both at the base and at the heart of the subsequent discourse analysis. It should be conducted with extreme care and (in the case of larger projects and several collaborators) it has to be conducted in the same sequence by all those involved without proceeding schematically. This is because the synoptic analysis (comparative concluding analysis) that follows the individual investigations of a respective newspaper or magazine in a certain year, relies on the capacity to line up the results systematically alongside each other. While processing the material, ideas and interpretation approaches can or should be incorporated whenever one has such ideas. Such interpretative passages should, however, be especially marked, for instance by underlining or the use of italic script.

The following list provides an overview of the analytical steps to be undertaken and the instrumentarium (toolbox) to be used.

Analytical guidelines for processing material   The following list incorporates a suggestion for the analytical procedure:

1 Processing material for the structure analysis, e.g. of the entire selected discourse strand of a newspaper/magazine
  1.1 *General characterization of the newspaper: political localization, readership, circulation, etc.*
  1.2 *Overview of (e.g.) the medium in question reviewing an entire year of the selected theme*
    1.2.1 List of the articles covered which are relevant to the theme with corresponding particulars of the bibliographic data: abbreviated note form on the theme; particulars of the kind of journalistic text, possible peculiarities; particulars

of the section in which the article appears in the case of weekly newspapers/magazines, etc.

1.2.2 Summary of the theme addressed/covered by the newspaper/magazine; qualitative evaluation; striking absence of certain themes which had been addressed in other years of publication investigated; presentation, timing and frequency of certain themes with a view to possible discursive events

1.2.3 Allocation of single themes to thematic areas (concerning the biopolitical discourse strand, for instance, to the following sub-themes: 'illness/health', 'birth/life', 'death/dying', 'diet', 'economy', 'bio-ethics/concept of what is human' and to possible discourse strand entanglements (for instance: 'economy', 'fascism', 'ethics/morals', etc.)

1.3 *Summary of 1.1 and 1.2: determination of the discourse position of the newspaper/magazine with regard to the theme in question*

2 Processing the material for the sample fine analysis of discourse fragments of an article or a series of articles and so on, which is/are as typical as possible of the discourse position of the newspaper

2.1 *Institutional framework: 'context'*

2.1.1 Justification of the selection of the (typical) article(s)

2.1.2 Author (function and significance for the newspaper, special areas of coverage, etc.)

2.1.3 Cause of the article

2.1.4 In which section of the newspaper/magazine does the article appear?

2.2 *Text 'surface'*

2.2.1 Graphic layout, including pictures and graphs

2.2.2 Headlines, headings, subheadings

2.2.3 Structure of the article in units of meaning

2.2.4 Themes addressed by the article (discourse fragments) (other themes touched upon, overlapping)

2.3 *Rhetorical means*

2.3.1 Kind and form of argumentation, argumentation strategies

2.3.2 Logic and composition

2.3.3 Implications and insinuations

2.3.4 Collective symbolism or 'figurativeness', symbolism, metaphorism, etc., in language and graphic contexts (statistics, photographs, pictures, caricatures, etc.)

2.3.5 Idioms, sayings, clichés

2.3.6 Vocabulary and style

2.3.7 Players (persons, pronominal structure)

2.3.8 References: to (the) science(s), particulars of the sources of knowledge and so on

2.4   *Ideological statements based on contents*
   2.4.1   What notion of, for instance, the human being, underlies the article/does the article convey?
   2.4.2   What kind of understanding of, for instance, society, underlies the article/does the article convey?
   2.4.3   What kind of understanding of, for instance, technology underlies the article/does the article convey?
   2.4.4   What is the future perspective which the article sets out?
2.5   *Other striking issues*
2.6   *Summary: localization of the article in the discourse strand (see 1.3 above); the 'argument', the major statement of the entire article; its general 'message'*
2.7   *Concluding interpretation of the entire discourse strand investigated with reference to the processed material used (structure and fine analysis/analyses)*

After repeated treatment of the processed material, justification of connections between the various planes on which material has been processed, additions to interpretative approaches, rejection of too weakly justified interpretative approaches, and so on, a complete package of processed material with as few gaps as possible is now provided. With this the foundation has been laid for conducting an overall analysis of the discourse strand in question. As far as the aesthetic aspect of the analysis is concerned, rules cannot and should not be prescribed. What the final result looks like depends on the quality of the 'writing style', the target group, the place of publication, and so on. The most important thing is that the presented argumentation is stringent, rich in material and convincing.

When dealing with several text corpora (for example, several newspapers, films, and so on), an additional comparative (synoptic) analysis follows, especially when striving for statements about complete discursive planes.

Initial considerations on the analysis of dispositives

Discourses are not phenomena which exist independently; they form the elements – and are the prerequisite – of the existence of so-called dispositives. A dispositive is the constantly evolving context of items of knowledge which are contained in speaking/thinking – acting – materialization. To visualize the concept of the dispositive in the form of a figure, imagine a triangle, or rather a circle rotating in history with three central 'transit points or transit stations'. These are:

1   discursive practices in which primarily knowledge is transported;
2   actions as non-discursive practices, in which, however, knowledge is transported, which are preceded by knowledge and/or constantly accompanied by knowledge;

3 manifestations/materializations which represent materializations of discursive practices through non-discursive practices, whereby the existence of manifestations ('objects') only survives through discursive and non-discursive practices.

The dispositive has a certain consistency. But it is also always subject to historical change. In addition, the constant impact of other dispositives has to be heeded.

In order to establish the (respective) current state of such a dispositive one can analyse this 'triangle', or this circle rotating in history comprising three 'transit stations' (discourse, action, manifestations/materializations), using a synchronic cut.

The dispositives circulate with one another and penetrate each other. A certain concrete discursive practice is, as a rule, of significance to several dispositives. An example would be discourse on traffic. This entangles itself with the economy, with illness, health, and so on. Perhaps it is precisely such entanglements which glue society together and convey its context. The 'triangle' – or the circle rotating in history – represents a rough analytical simplification of the term dispositive and is therefore only appropriate as a basic thought pattern, as a strongly simplified model, which one can conceive of as shown in Figure 3.1:

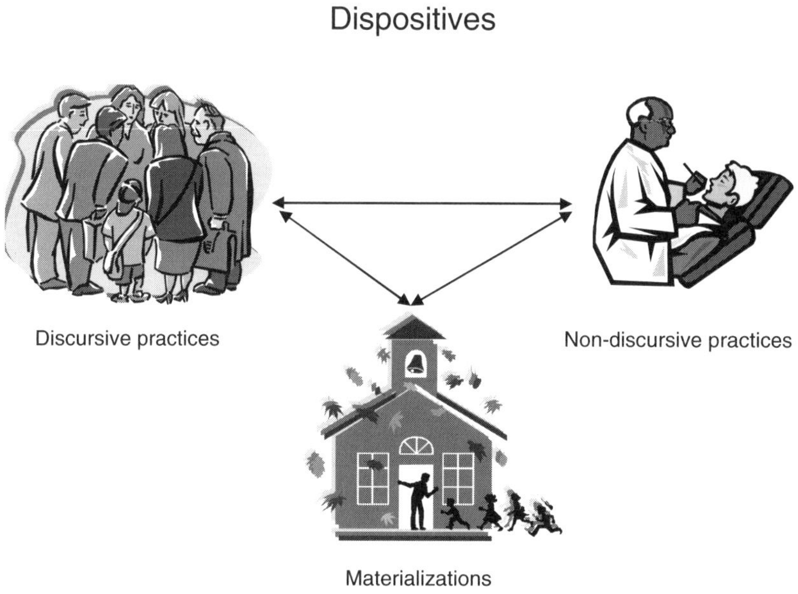

Dispositives

Discursive practices   Non-discursive practices

Materializations

FIGURE 3.1   *Dispositives*

Dispositive analysis whose object of investigation is the evolving context of knowledge, action and manifestations, therefore has to cover the following steps:

1 reconstruction of knowledge in the discursive practices (as illustrated above, whereby such an analysis forms the foundation for the further analytical steps of a dispositive analysis by directing attention to the following aspects of the dispositive to be investigated, for example, to 'blank areas' in the discourse, important manifestations which belong to it, and so on);
2 reconstruction of knowledge which underlies the non-discursive practices;
3 reconstruction of the non-discursive practices which have led to the manifestations/materializations and the knowledge contained therein.

The reconstruction of knowledge, which in fact always results in texts, also always covers the form in which knowledge emerges, that is how it presents itself, whether this knowledge comes to light openly, whether it disguises itself – in the shape of implications – how it is packaged argumentatively, and so on. At this point one should recall yet again that the term knowledge is used here in a very broad sense and must therefore in no way be regarded as being equal to 'recognition', and that it also covers feelings, affects and so on; in other words, all aspects of the human consciousness.

While the analysis of the discursive components of the dispositive has already been discussed at length, several questions still have to be asked:

1 How can the knowledge that underlies and accompanies the actions and/or non-discursive practices be reconstructed?
2 How can we get at the manifestations/materializations for the analysis of dispositives and how can we process them, so that we can establish the knowledge that underlies them?

Knowledge in actions

Actions can be observed and described. The point is how to reconstruct the knowledge that conditions and accompanies them. To take a simple example, a person is being observed walking along the street and looking for a baker's shop in which he/she buys a loaf of bread. I now have to find out what this person knows and wants. He/she knows that he/she has to go to a certain place to be able to buy bread. He/she knows that he/she has to dress in a certain way (put on shoes, and so on). He/she knows that he/she has to cross a street, and that in so doing he/she has to take care with the traffic and respect the highway code.

Furthermore, he/she knows that a baker's shop is situated at a certain place in a street, which he/she has to keep a look out for. He/she knows that he/she can get bread there and that he/she has to have money ready to pay for it. In fact, there is a large quantity of knowledge that underlies such a simple action as buying bread, the complexity of which I would merely like to hint at here.

This was a very simple example. A more complex one would be: I observe a person who has dug a hole at the edge of a street and is working away at a large pipe in this hole. That is all I observe! A precondition of the fact that the knowledge connected with this action can be reconstructed is that I – in a similar way to the buying bread example, but at a much more sophisticated level – have knowledge at my disposal that assists me to understand what this person is doing on the basis of his/her knowledge. I am lacking – at least in part – this knowledge, so that if I want to understand what this person is doing, I can address him/her and ask him/her, what and why he/she is doing what he/she is doing. He/she might well reply: 'I am mending a burst pipe.' Equipped with this knowledge, I understand a lot better what the person is doing. I could be content with this, but decide to ask further, 'But why are you doing it?' He/she might answer, 'To mend the burst pipe.' He/she might add, 'It is my job!' and even add, 'I have to earn money somehow!' and so on. The knowledge hidden in this activity is in fact quite complex; basically it can be traced back and extended to include the question as to the necessity or economic practice of dependent wage labour.

A far more complex action, where underlying knowledge is a lot harder to reconstruct, would be, for instance, observing a person who goes to a bank to sign a cheque. What is visible to me is exceptionally little; a precondition of interpreting it is a huge amount of knowledge with the help of which I can understand what this person is doing and/or can reconstruct the 'hidden' knowledge in his/her action.

Knowledge in manifestations/materializations

I observe an object, a house, a church, a bicycle. In contrast to the preceding examples, I cannot ask any of these objects for their knowledge. They do not have a meaning to themselves and are also incapable of giving me any information. Therefore I must, to begin with, rely on my own knowledge in order to be able to reconstruct the knowledge and action that were the preconditions for the production of these objects. Not only that, but it has to be determined whether the object is a church, a stable, a museum or a public convenience is hardly, if at all, the kind of information which it actively provides me with. I have to extend my knowledge, analyse, ask experts and users, consult statistics, maps, books, and so on. Only then can I establish the knowledge that has flowed into the object in question.

One has to ask, of course, how to proceed with very complex dispositives (as dispositive packages), for example, the war in Kosovo,
especially since access to it was very difficult. To what extent can one
rely on existing discursivization, that is statistics, photographs, reports,
media commentaries, and the like? How can the discourse positions
which flow into them be recognized – by comparison with others? Here
we have an additional problem, that of mental or objective discursivization, which still does not exist if one personally questions the manifestations as to the knowledge which has flowed into them.

Here, again, we are not dealing with the establishment of 'truths' but
with allocations that have a certain validity, yet which are always
interwoven with interests. Thus, our view must always be directed
towards these interests as well, including our own.

Special problems emerge here, such as the fact that one does not only
establish neutral knowledge, but that interpretations already flow into it
and, moreover, knowledge is forgotten and re-interpretations and the
veiling of knowledge take place.

A general rule applies here: in no way can I rely on my own
knowledge to reconstruct the knowledge that preconditions an object.

In addition, the knowledge which originally 'flowed into' an object
through an allocated meaning is not, or at least no longer completely,
identical with the object in the present time. The object may, in the course
of its history, have been allocated another meaning which is different
from the meaning that was originally allocated to it. 'Legends' might
have been formed and re-adjustments may have emerged. Consider, for
instance, the current use of a church as a museum or a stable for horses
or the contradictory testimonies of a witness to a traffic accident.

There is a further problem: where there is knowledge, there is power.
Where materializations exist, power and knowledge have been at work
and continue to be so, since otherwise the materializations lose their
meaning and rot. Power as such is not visible. Can it be made visible –
perhaps in an indirect way or in the form of effects? All knowledge is, of
course, linked to power. In all knowledge which prevails, power prevails. It is generated by power and exercises power. Thus, where there is
knowledge, there is power. Where knowledge is weakened, power can
be weakened.

If we consider the dispositive as the concrete context in which the
three knowledge aspects work in connection with one another, a form of
analysis is possible, which is, however, very complex. Michel Foucault's
book *Surveiller et punir* (supervise and punish) (Foucault, 1989) represents such a dispositive analysis. And also Victor Klemperer's diaries
can be read as a dispositive analysis (Klemperer, 1995). Neither of them
have provided an explicit method, but have applied it implicitly –
Foucault says 'experimentally' – by analysing the discourses, assembling
knowledge, consulting statistics, critically deconstructing them, drawing
conclusions from them, adding opinions to them and so on. Thus, the

considerations presented here cannot present us with a recipe, let alone ɑ method, which can be schematically applied. They do, however, trigger ideas as to how we can approach analytically the complex context of discourse, action and the resulting – developing or established – materializations and/or manifestations. At the heart of these endeavours is the discourse analysis that can also be related to texts and can be gained through the reconstruction of knowledge in non-discursive practices and materializations. An explicit method for this has yet to be – and will only be – developed in connection with concrete research projects. This would also contribute to bridging the existing gap between discourse analysis and empirical social research.

Notes

1 Sources are given in the language the author consulted, both in the text and the bibliography. Titles of the sources provided in the text and footnotes of the author's original manuscript have been translated into English – using the titles of corresponding English-language publications if available – and have been added in parentheses.

2 For the difference between this and other discourse-theoretical approaches, see S. Jäger, 1996b.

3 A detailed presentation (with examples of applications) is contained in my *Critical Discourse Analysis* (CDA), which appeared in 1999 in a revised and extended edition (S. Jäger, 1999). The CDA provides the foundation for numerous projects, which have been conducted at the Duisburg Institute for Linguistics and Social Research (Duisburger Institut für Sprach- und Sozialforschung (DISS)); see, for example, M. Jäger, 1996; Cleve, 1997; M. Jäger et al., 1997; Jäger et al., 1998; M. Jäger et al., 1998, etc.

4 For an introduction see Link, 1982.

5 'The term "power" is used which covers many individual, definable and defined mechanisms which appear capable of inducing behaviour or discourses' (Foucault, 1992: 32).

6 Especially Link, 1982; Drews et al., 1985; Link and Link-Heer, 1990; Becker et al., 1997.

7 See also Link, 1995, who underlines the formative constitutive force of discourses and understands discourse (as Foucault) as 'a material production instrument with which in a regulated way (social) objects (as for example "madness", "sex", "normality" etc.) and also the subjectivities corresponding to them are produced' (ibid.: 744).

8 See below for more on the problem of how complete and generalizable the statements of discourse analyses are.

9 Leontjev's reference to Marx soon becomes clear if we recall Marx's first thesis on Feuerbach, in which he demands: 'that the object, the reality, the sensory nature is (not only) to be dealt with in the frame of the *object or the ideology*; but *as human sensory activity, practice*, subjectively' (Marx and Engels, 1969 MEW 3: 5).

10 Jurt refers to Castoriadis for whom 'the societal things . . . are only what they are due to meanings' (Jurt, 1999: 11).

11 Foucault speaks in the *L'archéologie du savoir* (archaeology of knowledge) of relations which are not present in the object. In my opinion these are the discourses which at the same time keep the object alive from outside through the meaningful reference of people to them (Foucault, 1988: 68).

12 A strictly linguistic toolbox or instrumentarium means in this context grammatical and stylistic details that can be important to the analysis but are not absolutely necessary.

13 The problem of the complete treatment of a discourse strand hinted at here I will discuss below. This is of particular importance because the expressiveness and general validity of a discourse analysis is at stake.

14 Such an experiment is provided by Caborn, 1999.

15 We use such short texts when conducting projects as a kind of assistance or guide for first treatments of the given material. They serve as memory aids (or checklists).

4

The discourse-historical approach

Ruth Wodak

CONTENTS

Defining the approach

Theoretical background[1]

Struggles and contradictions characterize our modern world and Western societies. Nowhere is homogeneity to be found. On the contrary, ideological dilemmas (Billig, 1991), fragmentation (Hall, 1996) and multiple identities seem to be the answers to the challenges of globalization and neo-liberalist economies and ideologies (Muntigl et al., 2000). These tendencies are accompanied by a rise in nationalism and xenophobia, particularly from right-wing populist movements. Complex phenomena are seen as needing easy answers.

The complexities of modern societies in our fast changing world, where space and time seem to collapse (Harvey, 1996), can only be grasped by a model of multicausal, mutual influences between different groups of persons within a specific society and relationships between different societies. The great challenge, nowadays, is to explain the contradictions and tensions which occur between nation states and supranational entities on many levels (economies, science, technologies, communication, and so on). Causal models do not fit this complexity. I prefer to speak about a 'symptomatology', about relating and explaining the relationships between various 'symptoms' which we can study, in a more hermeneutic and interpretative way (see Wodak, 2000a). Moreover, I endorse a more pragmatically oriented theoretical approach, like the one developed by Nikos Mouzelis (1995). In his recent book *Sociological Theory: What Went Wrong?* (1995), Mouzelis introduces the idea of 'conceptual pragmatism' as a possible way out of the theory crisis in the social sciences. According to Mouzelis, social theory 'has as its major task to clarify conceptual tools and to construct new ones by following criteria of utility rather than truth' (1995: 9). Such a pragmatic approach to theory would not seek to provide a catalogue of context-less propositions and generalizations, but rather to relate questions of theory formation and conceptualization closely to the specific problems that are to be investigated. In this sense, the first question we have to address as researchers is not, 'Do we need a grand theory?' but rather, 'What conceptual tools are relevant for this or that problem and for this and that context?' Although the former question might invite exciting speculations, it moves away from problem oriented science.

Let us turn to the field of politics (in the narrow sense). If we take politicians, for example, as specific and not at all homogeneous groups of elites, then they are best seen both as shapers of specific public opinions and interests and as seismographs, that reflect and react to the atmospheric anticipation of changes in public opinion and to the articulation of changing interests of specific social groups and affected parties.[2] The relationships between media, politics (all genres) and 'people' are very complex. Up to now, we have not been able to provide clear answers about who influences who and how these influences are directed. Only interdisciplinary research will be able to make such complex relationships more transparent. Simple conspiracy theories do not seem valid in our global societies. In research of this kind, discourse analysis, and specifically critical discourse analysis (CDA), is only one component of the multiple approaches needed. Not only discursive practices are to be focused on, but also a wide range of material and semiotic practices. Thus, research in CDA must be multitheoretical and multimethodical, critical and self-reflective.

The discourse–historical approach, committed to CDA, adheres to the socio-philosophical orientation of critical theory.[3] As such, it follows a complex concept of social critique which embraces at least three interconnected aspects, two of which are primarily related to the dimension of cognition and one to the dimension of action (see Reisigl and Wodak, 2001 for an extended discussion):

1 'Text or discourse immanent critique' aims at discovering inconsistencies, (self-)contradictions, paradoxes and dilemmas in the text-internal or discourse-internal structures.
2 In contrast to the 'immanent critique', the 'socio-diagnostic critique' is concerned with the demystifying exposure of the – manifest or latent – possibly persuasive or 'manipulative' character of discursive practices. With socio-diagnostic critique, the analyst exceeds the purely textual or discourse internal sphere. She or he makes use of her or his background and contextual knowledge and embeds the communicative or interactional structures of a discursive event in a wider frame of social and political relations, processes and circumstances. At this point, we are obliged to apply social theories to interpret the discursive events (see below, theory of context).
3 Prognostic critique contributes to the transformation and improvement of communication (for example, within public institutions by elaborating proposals and guidelines for reducing language barriers in hospitals, schools, courtrooms, public offices, and media reporting institutions (see Wodak, 1996a) as well as guidelines for avoiding sexist language use (Kargl et al., 1997)).

To summarize, and in contrast to some views on CDA, CDA is not concerned with evaluating what is 'right' or 'wrong'. CDA – in my view – should try to make choices at each point in the research itself, and should make these choices transparent. It should also justify theoretically why certain interpretations of discursive events seem more valid than others.

One methodical way for critical discourse analysts to minimize the risk of being biased is to follow the principle of triangulation. Thus, one of the most salient distinguishing features of the discourse–historical approach is its endeavour to work with different approaches, multimethodically and on the basis of a variety of empirical data as well as background information (see for example Wodak et al., 1998 and Wodak et al., 1999).

In investigating historical, organizational and political topics and texts, the discourse–historical approach attempts to integrate a large quantity of available knowledge about the historical sources and the background of the social and political fields in which discursive 'events' are embedded. Further, it analyses the historical dimension of discursive actions by exploring the ways in which particular genres of discourse are subject to diachronic change (Wodak et al., 1990; Wodak et al., 1994). Lastly, and most importantly, this is not only viewed as 'information': at this point we integrate social theories to be able to explain the so-called context.

The notion of 'discourse'

In accordance with other approaches devoted to CDA, as has already been implied, the discourse–historical approach perceives both written and spoken language as a form of social practice (Fairclough and Wodak, 1997). A discourse is a way of signifying a particular domain of social practice from a particular perspective (Fairclough, 1995: 14). We assume a dialectical relationship between particular discursive practices and the specific fields of action (including situations, institutional frames and social structures), in which they are embedded. On the one hand, the situational, institutional and social settings shape and affect discourses, and on the other, discourses influence discursive as well as non-discursive social and political processes and actions. In other words, discourses as linguistic social practices can be seen as constituting non-discursive and discursive social practices and, at the same time, as being constituted by them.

In the following, I would like to make a distinction between 'discourse' and 'text', also following Lemke's interesting approach (Lemke, 1995).

'Discourse' can thus be understood as a complex bundle of simultaneous and sequential interrelated linguistic acts, which manifest themselves within and across the social fields of action as thematically interrelated semiotic, oral or written tokens, very often as 'texts', that belong to specific semiotic types, that is genres (see Girnth, 1996). The most salient feature of the definition of a 'discourse' is the macro-topic, like 'unemployment'. Interdiscursivity can be seen when, for example, a racist argument (taken from the discourse on immigration restrictions) is used while arguing for other policies to combat unemployment. Each macro-topic allows for many sub-topics: 'unemployment' thus covers sub-topics like 'market', 'trade unions', 'social welfare', 'global market', 'hire and fire policies' and many more. Discourses are open and hybrid and not closed systems at all; new sub-topics can be created, and intertextuality and interdiscursivity allow for new fields of action. Discourses are realized in both genres and texts.

'Texts' can be conceived as materially durable products of linguistic actions (see Ehlich, 1983; Graefen, 1997: 26; Reisigl, 2000). A 'genre' may be characterized, following Norman Fairclough, as the conventionalized, more or less schematically fixed use of language associated with a particular activity, as 'a socially ratified way of using language in connection with a particular type of social activity' (Fairclough, 1995: 14). Thus, a proposal on combating unemployment manifests certain rules and expectations according to social conventions. The proposal itself follows certain textual devices; the contents follow certain ideological concepts put forward by a specific political group (like the trade unions).

'Fields of action' (Girnth, 1996) may be understood as segments of the respective societal 'reality', which contribute to constituting and shaping the 'frame' of discourse. The spatio-metaphorical distinction among different fields of action can be understood as a distinction among different functions or socially institutionalized aims of discursive practices. Thus, for example, in the area of political action we distinguish between the functions of legislation, self-presentation, the manufacturing of public opinion, developing party-internal consent, advertising and vote-getting, governing as well as executing, and controlling as well as expressing (oppositional) dissent (see Figure 4.1 below). A 'discourse' about a specific topic can find its starting point within one field of action and proceed through another one. Discourses and discourse topics 'spread' to different fields and discourses. They cross between fields, overlap, refer to each other or are in some other way socio-functionally linked with each other.

We can represent the relationship between fields of action, genres and discourse topics with the example of the area of political action in Figure 4.1 below.

Figure 4.2 further illustrates the interdiscursive and intertextual relationships between discourses, discourse topics, genres (as types) and texts (as tokens).

In this diagram, interdiscursivity (for example, the intersection of discourse A and discourse B) is indicated by the two big overlapping ellipses. Intertextual relationships in general are represented by dotted double arrows. The assignment of texts to genres is signalled by simple arrows. The topics to which a text refers are indicated by small ellipses to which simple dotted arrows point, the topical intersection of different texts is signalled by the overlapping small ellipses. Finally, the specific intertextual relationship of thematic reference of one text to another is indicated by simple broken arrows (see application in the methodology below).

Our triangulatory approach is based on a concept of 'context' which takes into account four levels. The first one is descriptive, while the other three levels are part of our theories on context (see Figure 4.3):

1 the immediate, language or text internal co-text;
2 the intertextual and interdiscursive relationship between utterances, texts, genres and discourses;
3 the extralinguistic social/sociological variables and institutional frames of a specific 'context of situation' (middle range theories);
4 the broader sociopolitical and historical contexts, which the discursive practices are embedded in and related to ('grand' theories).

In our example (see the case-study in this chapter), I will illustrate each level of context and make the sequential analysis transparent, following the categories of analysis which will be defined below.

The history of the discourse–historical approach

The research programme

In this chapter, I would like to focus on the study of discourses of discrimination. However, I would first like to stress the most important characteristics of our discourse–historical CDA approach:

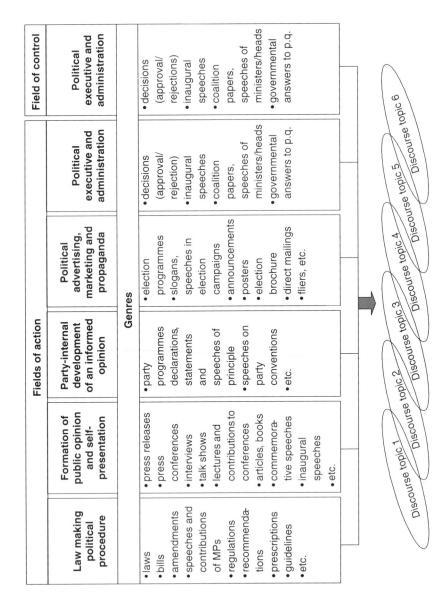

FIGURE 4.1   Selected dimensions of discourse as social practice

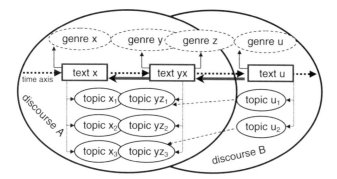

FIGURE 4.2 *Interdiscursive and intertextual relationships between discourses, discourse topics, genres and texts*

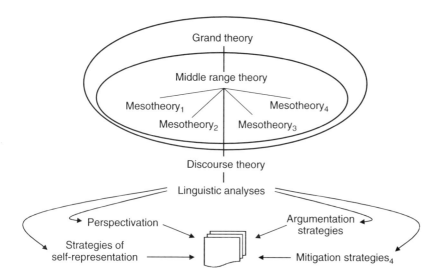

FIGURE 4.3 *Levels of theories and linguistic analysis*

1 The approach is interdisciplinary.
2 Interdisciplinarity is located on several levels: in theory, in the work itself, in teams, and in practice.
3 The approach is problem oriented, not focused on specific linguistic items.
4 The theory as well as the methodology is eclectic; that is theories and methods are integrated which are helpful in understanding and explaining the object under investigation.
5 The study always incorporates fieldwork and ethnography to explore the object under investigation (study from the inside) as a precondition for any further analysis and theorizing.

6　The approach is abductive: a constant movement back and forth between theory and empirical data is necessary.

7　Multiple genres and multiple public spaces are studied, and intertextual and interdiscursive relationships are investigated. Recontextualization is the most important process in connecting these genres as well as topics and arguments (topoi).

8　The historical context is always analysed and integrated into the interpretation of discourses and texts.

9　The categories and tools for the analysis are defined according to all these steps and procedures as well as to the specific problem under investigation.

10　Grand theories serve as a foundation (see above). In the specific analysis, middle range theories serve the analytical aims better.

11　Practice is the target. The results should be made available to experts in different fields and, as a second step, be applied with the goal of changing certain discursive and social practices.

Political and discriminatory discourses

The study for which the discourse–historical approach was actually developed, sought initially to trace in detail the constitution of an anti-Semitic stereotyped image, or 'Feindbild', as it emerged in public discourse in the 1986 Austrian presidential campaign of Kurt Waldheim (Wodak et al., 1990; Mitten, 1992; Gruber, 1991). Briefly summarized, we analysed, on the one hand, the linguistic manifestations of prejudice in discourse, embedded in the linguistic and social context (for example, newspaper reports or news bulletins in Austria). On the other hand, we confronted the latter texts with other facts and context phenomena (the reporting in the United States, which of course was also biased in certain aspects). Thus, we contrasted one report with the comments on the report, with the historical knowledge. In other words, we did not rely on the 'meta-data' alone. We compared Waldheim's story with the historical facts about Wehrmacht atrocities in the Balkans and the deportation of Jews from Greece. In this way we were able to detect and depict the disfiguring of facts and realities. Our comparison of the *New York Times* with the reports in the Austrian press and statements of politicians proved that this distortion was complete and systematic.

　Our data comprised both oral and written texts. Three newspapers were read systematically, every day, during the four months of the presidential election campaign (March to June 1986), and then at regular intervals after June 1986 (*Presse, Neue Kronen Zeitung*, the *New York Times*). Daily radio and television news, interviews, television discussions, hearings, larger news documentary series (about 50 hours of video), discussions in diverse institutional settings and the vigil commemorating Austrian resistance in June 1987 on Stephansplatz in Vienna ('Mahnwache') were integrated into the analysis. Thus, very different degrees of formality and very different settings were taken into account. We prepared an exhibition with some of our material (see Wodak and de Cillia, 1988) which we presented in March 1988, and even filmed discussions which occurred when people visited the exhibition.

The following two-year research project was carried out on the occasion of the Austrian 'Gedenkjahr 1988', the year in which the 50th anniversary of Austria's occupation by Hitler was commemorated. In the study, entitled 'Languages of the past' (see Wodak et al., 1994), the main interests of investigation were firstly the publication and the media treatment of the report by a commission of seven international historians on former president Waldheim's Nazi past in February 1988; secondly the official political commemoration of the Austrian 'Anschluss' in March 1938; thirdly the unveiling of a 'memorial against war and fascism' by the sculptor Alfred Hrdlicka in November, as well as the controversial discussions that preceded it for several months; fourthly the premiere of the play *Heldenplatz* by Thomas Bernhard in November, which deals with Austrian anti-Semitism then and now and its psycho-terrorizing long-term impact on surviving Jewish victims; and finally the commemoration of the fiftieth anniversary of the November pogrom. The data of this interdisciplinary discourse–historical study specifically included a great variety of media genres (all kinds of printed media, radio reports, television news broadcasts, television and newspaper series) as well as statements and addresses of Austrian politicians. The rich data allowed for a differentiated examination of the official political and media recollection, and a critical reconsideration of the Austrian National Socialist past, of the often conflicting narratives on Austrian history and of some related convenient myths, such as 'Austria as the first victim of the Nazi politics of dictatorship and territorial expansionism'.

The discourse–historical approach has been further elaborated in a number of more recent studies, for example, in a study on racist discrimination against immigrants from Romania, and in a study on the discourse about nation and national identity in Austria (Matouschek et al., 1995; Wodak et al., 1998, 1999). The latter study was concerned with the analysis of the relationships between the discursive construction of national sameness and the discursive construction of difference leading to political and social exclusion of specific out-groups. These questions were investigated in a series of case studies on the Austrian identity and nation. Taking several current social scientific approaches as a point of departure, we developed a method of description and analysis that has applications beyond the discursive production of national identity in the specific Austrian examples studied. Our findings suggested that discourses about nations and national identities rely on at least four types of discursive macro-strategies: constructive strategies (aiming at the construction of national identities), preservative or justificatory strategies (aiming at the conservation and reproduction of national identities or narratives of identity), transformative strategies (aiming at the change of national identities), and destructive strategies (aiming at the dismantling of national identities). Depending on the context – that is to say, on the social field or domain in which the 'discursive events' related to the topic under investigation take place – one or other of the aspects connected with these strategies is brought into prominence.

In all of the four studies taken from the Austrian context, discriminatory, racist and anti-Semitic as well as chauvinist utterances sometimes occurred simultaneously, especially in everyday conversations (which for the first study were tape recorded in the streets). In more official settings, nationalist, racist and anti-Semitic stereotypes occurred in a more vague form, mostly as allusions and implicit evocations triggered by the use of vocabulary which was characteristic of the historical period of National Socialism. Thus, in all these studies, it was possible to follow the genesis and transformation of arguments, the recontextualization throughout different and important public spaces resulting from the social interests of the participants and their power relations (see Muntigl et al., 2000; Reisigl and Wodak, 2001). All these studies now make it possible to attempt to construct broader explanations for the specific application of discourses of sameness and difference.

The analysis of discriminatory discourse: the case-study of the FPÖ petition 'Austria first' 1992–3

Categories of analysis

The specific discourse-analytical approach applied in the four studies referred to was three-dimensional: after firstly having established the specific contents or topics of a particular discourse with racist, anti-Semitic, nationalist or ethnicist ingredients, secondly the discursive strategies (including argumentation strategies) were investigated. Then thirdly, the linguistic means (as types) and the specific, context-dependent linguistic realizations (as tokens) of the discriminatory stereotypes were examined.

In the following section, we shall describe from an abstract viewpoint some of the discourse-analytical tools useful in the analysis of discourses about racial, national and ethnic issues. There are several discursive elements and strategies which, in our discourse-analytical view, deserve to receive special attention. Selecting five of the many different linguistic or rhetorical means by which persons are discriminated against in an ethnicist or racist manner, we orientate ourselves to five simple, but not at all randomly selected questions:

1 How are persons named and referred to linguistically?
2 What traits, characteristics, qualities and features are attributed to them?

TABLE 4.1   *Discursive strategies*

Strategy	Objectives	Devices
Referential/nomination	Construction of in-groups and out-groups	• membership categorization • biological, naturalizing and depersonalizing metaphors and metonymies • synecdoches (pars pro toto, totum pro pars)
Predication	Labelling social actors more or less positively or negatively, deprecatorily or appreciatively	• stereotypical, evaluative attributions of negative or positive traits • implicit and explicit predicates
Argumentation	Justification of positive or negative attributions	• topoi used to justify political inclusion or exclusion, discrimination or preferential treatment
Perspectivation, framing or discourse representation	Expressing involvement Positioning speaker's point of view	• reporting, description, narration or quotation of (discriminatory) events and utterances
Intensification, mitigation	Modifying the epistemic status of a proposition	• intensifying or mitigating the illocutionary force of (discriminatory) utterances

3 By means of what arguments and argumentation schemes do specific persons or social groups try to justify and legitimize the exclusion, discrimination, suppression and exploitation of others?

4 From what perspective or point of view are these labels, attributions and arguments expressed?

5 Are the respective utterances articulated overtly? Are they intensified or are they mitigated?

According to these questions, we are especially interested in five types of discursive strategies, which are all involved in the positive self- and negative other presentation. We view, and this needs to be emphasized, the discursive construction of 'us' and 'them' as the basic fundaments of discourses of identity and difference. And such discourses are salient for discourses of discrimination.

By 'strategy' we generally mean a more or less accurate and more or less intentional plan of practices (including discursive practices) adopted to achieve a particular social, political, psychological or linguistic aim. As far as the discursive strategies are concerned, that is to say, systematic ways of using language, we locate them at different levels of linguistic organization and complexity (see Table 4.1).[4]

Arguing for and against discrimination

The different forms of social exclusion and discrimination can be discussed inter alia by means of topoi, both arguing for and against racism, ethnicism and nationalism.

TABLE 4.2   *List of topoi*

1	Usefulness, advantage	9	Finances
2	Uselessness, disadvantage	10	Reality
3	Definition, name-interpretation	11	Numbers
4	Danger and threat	12	Law and right
5	Humanitarianism	13	History
6	Justice	14	Culture
7	Responsibility	15	Abuse
8	Burdening, weighting		

Within argumentation theory, 'topoi' or 'loci' can be described as parts of argumentation which belong to the obligatory, either explicit or inferable premises. They are the content-related warrants or 'conclusion rules' which connect the argument or arguments with the conclusion, the claim. As such, they justify the transition from the argument or arguments to the conclusion (Kienpointner, 1992: 194).

The analysis of typical content-related argument schemes can be carried out against the background of the list of topoi, though incomplete and not always disjunctive, given in Table 4.2 (see for example Kindt, 1992; Kienpointner, 1992, 1996; Kienpointner and Kindt, 1997; Kopperschmidt, 1989; Wengeler, 1997; Reeves, 1989).

The topos of advantage or usefulness can be paraphrased by means of the following conditional: if an action under a specific relevant point of view will be useful, then one should perform it (for example, the usefulness of 'guest workers' for a national economy). To this topos belong different subtypes, for example the topos of 'pro bono publico', ('to the advantage of all'), the topos of 'pro bono nobis' ('to the advantage of us'), and the topos of 'pro bono eorum' ('to the advantage of them'). In a decision of the Viennese municipal authorities (Amtsbescheid der Magistratsabteilung 42), the refusal of a residence permit is set out as follows:

> Because of the private and family situation of the claimant, the refusal of the application at issue represents quite an intrusion into her private and family life. The public interest, which is against the residence permit, is to be valued more strongly than the contrasting private and family interests of the claimant. Thus, it had to be decided according to the judgement.

Like the topos of advantage or usefulness, the topos of uselessness/disadvantage is also a specific causal argumentation scheme, but in contrast to the former, the latter relies on the conditional. If one can anticipate that the prognosticated consequences of a decision will not occur, or if other political actions are more likely to lead to the declared aim, the decision has to be rejected. If existing rulings do not help to reach the declared aims, they have to be changed. This topos was employed in Austria in 1992, when the *'Verbotsgesetz'* – the law against revitalizing the National Socialist ideology and practices (*'Wiederbetätigung'*) and against the dissemination of the so-called *'Auschwitzlüge'* – was amended.

The topos of definition or topos of name-interpretation or locus a nominis interpretatione can be traced back to the following conclusion rule: if an action, a thing or a person (group of persons) is named/ designated (as) X, the action, thing or person (group of persons) carries or should carry the qualities/traits/attributes contained in the (literal) meaning of X. This topos is employed if immigrant workers in Austria or Germany are euphemistically called *'Gastarbeiter'* ('guest workers'). The term implies that, because they are 'only guests', they will or they must return to the countries they came from.

The topos of danger or topos of threat is based on the following conditionals: if a political action or decision bears specific dangerous, threatening consequences, one should not perform or do it. Or, formulated differently: if there are specific dangers and threats, one should do something against them. There are many subtypes of this scheme of argument. Here we mention only one of them, namely the topos of threat of racism, which goes as follows: if too many immigrants or refugees enter the country, the native population will not be able to cope with the situation and become hostile to foreigners. This argument scheme can lead to a victim–victimizer reversal. The victims thus are made responsible for the prejudices directed against them.

The topos of humanitarianism can be paraphrased by the following conditional: if a political action or decision does or does not conform with human rights or humanitarian convictions and values, one should or should not perform or take it. This topos can be employed in every situation where one argues against unequal treatment and discrimination and for the recognition of 'racialized', ethnic, religious, gender or other differences.

It is closely connected with the topos of justice that is based on the principle and claim of 'equal rights for all'. As a conditional phrase, it means that if persons/actions/situations are equal in specific respects, they should be treated/dealt with in the same way. For example: as far as social security is concerned, workers should be treated equally, that is to say, irrespective of their citizenship, as they make the same social security payment contributions.

A third argumentation scheme closely related to the two topoi just mentioned is the topos of responsibility. It can be summarized by the conditional formula: because a state or a group of persons is responsible for the emergence of specific problems, it or they should act in order to find solutions to these problems. Although this topos is very often employed to argue against discrimination or for 'compensation' or 'reparations' for a committed crime (for example, a Nazi crime), it can also serve the opposite aim, for example in cases where a government is held responsible for unemployment and required to reduce the quota of immigrants as they are falsely considered to be the cause of unemployment.

The topos of burdening or weighing down is to be regarded as a specific causal topos (a topos of consequence) and can be reduced to the following conditional: if a person, an institution or a country is burdened by specific problems, one should act in order to diminish these burdens. Within this context, one can find the metaphorical phrase '*das Boot ist voll*' ('the boat is full/overcrowded') when legitimating immigration restrictions.

The topos of finances can be characterized by the following conclusion rule: if a specific situation or action costs too much money or causes a loss of revenue, one should perform actions which diminish the costs or help to avoid the loss. This topos, which is a specific causal topos (topos of consequence), comes close to the topos of burdening. It is employed implicitly by the former Governor of Upper Austria when he argues against the accommodation of Romanian refugees in the community of Franking: 'Here, we are dealing with people whose origin one can explicitly identify by looking at them, and thus, one is afraid of losses within the framework of tourism'.[5] In this example, the topos of finances focuses on allegedly negative socio-economical consequences.

The topos of reality is rather a tautological argumentation scheme that can be paraphrased as follows: because reality is as it is, a specific action/decision should be performed/made. A general example would be: social, economic and political realities have changed and the Asylum Act no longer fits. Therefore, the law must also be changed.

The topos of numbers may be subsumed under the conclusion rule: if the numbers prove a specific topos, a specific action should be performed or not be carried out. This topos can become fallacious if it is related to incorrectly presumed majorities which are not verified empirically.

The topos of law or topos of right can be condensed in the conditional: if a law or an otherwise codified norm prescribes or forbids a specific politico-administrative action, the action has to be performed or omitted. The use of this topos is institutionalized in politico-administrative genres such as rejections of applications for residence permits (see van Leeuwen and Wodak, 1999).

The topos of history can be described as follows: because history teaches that specific actions have specific consequences, one should perform or omit a specific action in a specific situation (allegedly) comparable with the historical example referred to. A specific subtype of this argumentation scheme is the existing Ciceronian topos of *historia magistra vitae*, of 'history teaching lessons' (see Wodak et al., 1998: 205–7).

The topos of culture is based on the following argumentation scheme: because the culture of a specific group of people is as it is, specific problems arise in specific situations. This topos is employed by Jörg

Haider, the former leader of the Freedom Party, in combination with the topos of danger in his appeal that, 'The greatest damage that one can do to a people is to put the identity, cultural heritage, and the opportunities of its young people negligently at stake. That is why we have introduced the "Austria first" petition. In order to guarantee Austrians their right to a fatherland'.[6]

The last topos to mention in this section, the topos of abuse, extensively employed in the petition campaign, can be paraphrased by the following conclusion rule: if a right or an offer for help is abused, the right should be changed, or the help should be withdrawn, or measures against the abuse should be taken. Rightist politicians fall back upon this topos when they argue for restricting asylum policy by means of reference to an alleged abuse of the asylum law. The topos of abuse is also employed when a change to the social security law is demanded by politicians who are hostile to foreigners, and an attempt is made to account for this claim in the accusation that aliens exploit the welfare system or social security system of the state in which they are or have been working. Point 10 of the petition and several passages of its 'explanation', rely on this topos.

The 'Austria first' petition

The historical context – the need for ethnography   At this point, I will start by providing a few contextualizing remarks on the history of the FPÖ. After the Second World War, in 1949, liberals with a strong German National orientation and with no classical liberal tradition (see Bailer-Galanda and Neugebauer, 1993: 326) who felt unable to support the SPÖ or the ÖVP founded the VDU ('Verband der Unabhängigen'), which became an electoral home for many former Austrian Nazis. The FPÖ, founded in 1956, was the successor party to the VDU; it retained an explicit attachment to a 'German cultural community'. In its more than 40-year-old history, the FPÖ has, therefore, never been a liberal party in the European sense, although there were always tensions between more liberal and more conservative members of the party. In 1986, Haider was elected as leader of the party and unseated Norbert Steger, a liberal leader. Since 1986, the FPÖ has gained many votes and had by October 1999 risen to 26.91 per cent of all the votes cast in Austria (1,244,087 voters). The FPÖ's party policy and politics in 1993 was anti-foreigner, anti-European Union and widely populist, similar to Le Pen's party in France. Since the summer of 1995, the FPÖ has almost completely ceased to stress the closeness between the Austrian and the German cultural community because opinion polls demonstrated that the majority of Austrian citizens no longer accepted such a self-definition. In the autumn of 1997, the FPÖ presented a new party programme, which, in its calculated ambivalence, emphasizes Christian values. At present, the FPÖ is the largest right-wing party in Western Europe (for further information about the FPÖ see, among others, Scharsach, 1992; Scharsach and Kuch, 2000; DöW, 1993; Mitten, 1994; Bailer-Galanda and Neugebauer, 1997; Grünalternative Jugend, 1998). It is this party, which, more than any other Austrian party, persuasively sets the xenophobic anti-foreigner tone in Austrian domestic policies and, for a decade, has almost always made electoral advantage out of the populist business of sowing uncertainty and irrational xenophobic anxieties, which, for different reasons, were and are harboured or willingly adopted by a considerable proportion of voters. Since 4 February 2000, the FPÖ has been part of the Austrian government and has formed a coalition with the conservative ÖVP. This development caused a major upheaval internationally and nationally, and has led to sanctions by the 14 other member states of the European Union (see Wodak, 2000a, b for more details).

In applying our four-level theory model to the attempt to explain the FPÖ's success in the election of 3 October 1999, several middle range theories have to be drawn upon, to be able to interpret specific texts produced by the FPÖ and also the public debate about the slogans and programme of the FPÖ and the coalition programme of the new government (FPÖ and ÖVP from 4 February 2000). These include theories about populism, theories about coming to terms with the Austrian Nazi past, theories about the changes from social welfare states to neo-liberal economies, and finally theories about the rise of racism in times of globalization. Because of limitations of space and also because of the methodological focus of this chapter, I will only summarize the results of this kind of theoretical approach in the following diagram (see Figure 4.4), and refer readers to Wodak (2000b) which exemplifies our research programme in CDA with a focus on theory construction and interdisciplinarity according to the research questions posed there (based on ethnography, teamwork and extensive literature research as well as text analysis).

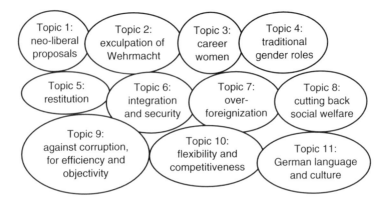

FIGURE 4.4   *Topics covered by the FPÖ*

The application of the discourse model   The second step, after having provided historical background information which is necessary to understand the object under investigation and is defined in its extent by the topics of the text itself as well as by the public debate about the petition and the allusions occurring there, is the attempt to apply the discourse model presented above to the specific Austrian populist discourse of 1993. In this model, the sub-topics which marked public discourses are collected by means of ethnographic explorations and the analyses of multiple genres (media, slogans, party programmes and so on, see Reisigl and Wodak, 2001: Chapter 4 for more details).

The strategic populist move to initiate the 'Austria first' petition was just one particularly drastic step in the FPÖ's policy of instigating hostile emotions against specific groups of foreigners. This step had an impact on all six of the main fields of political action we distinguished above: the areas of law making; of party internal opinion making; of the formation of public political opinion; of political advertising; of political administration; and of political control.

As a whole, the discourse about the 'Austria first' petition or 'anti-foreigner' petition mainly evolved in these fields of political activity around the following topics and in the following genres (see Figure 4.5).

We will now briefly illustrate the notion of interdiscursivity with a constructed, but plausible example that illustrates selected, potential interdiscursive and intertextual relationships between the Austrian discourse about the 'Austria first' petition and the Austrian discourse about 'national security' (see Figure 4.6, and see Reisigl and Wodak, 2001 for details).

The two discourses partly overlap, and this is symbolized in Figure 4.6 by the two large overlapping ellipses. The two specific texts selected from the whole discourse about the petition are the text of the petition itself and the text of a speech made by Jörg Haider during the campaign for the petition. The text of the 'Austria first' petition can be assigned to the political genre of 'petition for a referendum' and is primarily situated in the field of political control. The text of Haider's speech may be a hybrid mixture that contains elements of both an election speech and a pub conversation. This presupposed, it is primarily located in the field of political advertising or propaganda, but, in addition, also in the fields of political control and of formation of public opinion. This text may have been produced after the text of the petition itself and may explicitly refer to the petition text as a whole (as is indicated by the dotted double arrow), for example by a wording like 'as we demand in our petition', or simply share some topics with the petition text, without explicitly mentioning the petition (as indicated by the intersections of the small ellipses). Alternatively it may explicitly refer to specific topics of the petition text, by a wording like 'as we pick out as a central theme in point 2 of the petition' (as indicated by the simple, bending broken arrow). Let us further assume that this text speaks extensively about issues related to the

	Fields of action					Field of control
Genres	**Law making political procedure**	**Formation of public opinion and self-presentation**	**Party-internal development of an informed opinion**	**Political advertising, marketing and propaganda**	**Political executive and administration**	**Political executive and administration**
	• Alien Act • Asylum Act • Refugee Assistance Act • Residency Act • speeches and contributions of MPs • report and recommendation of parliamentary subcommitee • bills • amendments	• press releases • press conferences • interviews • demographic surveys and opinion polls • press articles (reports, comments, columns) • readers' letters • speeches/comments of MPs • speeches of ministers • books by politicians	• FPÖ party programme	• advertising for and against the petition • speeches/talks/slogans during campaign • announcements • posters • brochures • direct mail • advertising • flyers	• decisions (approval/rejection: asylum-stay-work) • report on the administration of the laws on aliens • governmental answers	• 'foreigner petition' for a referendum • grounds for the petition • parliamentary questions • speeches/contributions of MPs • press releases/conferences/declarations/statements of NGOs, human rights organizations, etc.

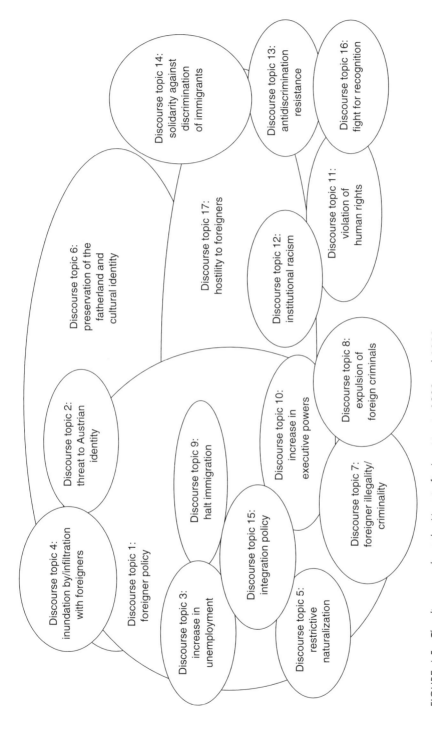

FIGURE 4.5   *The discourse about the 'Austria first' petition in 1992 and 1993*

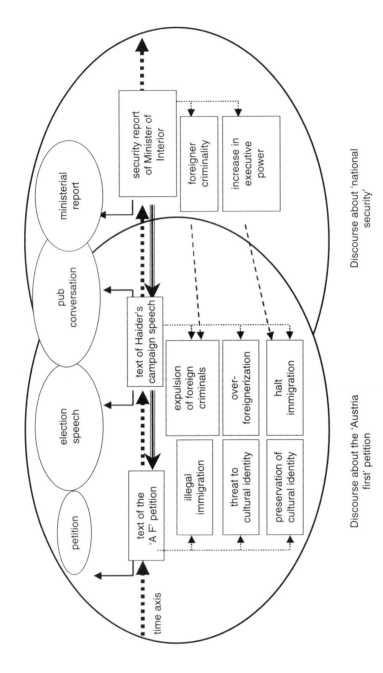

FIGURE 4.6 *Interdiscursive and intertextual relationships between the discourse about the 'Austria first' petition and the discourse about 'national security'*

topic of 'national security'. If this is the case, it also belongs to the political discourse about 'national security'. In this second discourse, many other texts participate, including the genre of ministerial reports, such as a specific security report of the Ministry of the Interior. As indicated by the dotted double arrow, this text may be intertextually related to the text of the petition. It may, for example, be related by explicit naming of the petition text in general, or by topical overlapping of the two texts without explicit reference. For reasons of clarity and comprehensibility, this intertextual relationship is not specifically indicated in Figure 4.6 above, as it would be if there were overlapping small ellipses. An example of this would be an ellipsis that represents the report's topic of internal national security and that overlaps with the ellipses standing for the topics of 'illegal immigration' and 'expulsion of illegal foreigners'. Intertextual relationship could also be established by the report's explicit thematic reference to topics of the petition. An example of this might be the report's reference to the demands in points 4 and 11 of the petition, in which the Austrian Freedom Party (FPÖ) requests an increase in executive powers (point 4), the creation of the legal basis for the possibility of immediate expulsion and an imposition of residence prohibitions for foreign criminals (see below). We can hypothesize that the ministerial report refers to these two topics and points out that these claims are already fulfilled by the official Austrian governmental policy. Finally, we may assume that there could exist an explicit intertextual or interdiscursive relationship between the report's topic of 'foreigner criminality' and the discourse about the Austria first petition (as indicated by the arrow pointing from the small ellipse symbolizing the topic of 'foreigner criminality' to the large ellipse indicating the whole discourse about the FPÖ petition). This would apply if, for example, the report were to tell us that in the public debate about the petition many of the prejudices about an allegedly high 'foreigner criminality' were reproduced, and that these prejudices are disproved by the criminal statistics contained in the report (see Reisigl and Wodak, 2000 for more details).

The petition   The next step in our methodology requires a description of the genre investigated as well as the necessary background information on this particular genre, a petition in the Second Austrian Republic.

According to Article 41 of the Austrian constitution, parliament is required to consider and vote on any petition that gathers at least 100,000 signatures. Unlike provisions for petitions elsewhere, Article 41 of the Austrian constitution requires only that parliament considers the petition, which must be in the form of a draft law.

In October 1992, after the Austrian government then consisting of a grand coalition between the ÖVP and SPÖ had rejected Haider's ultimatum to adopt the FPÖ's programme on immigration, his party launched the petition campaign to force the government's hand. Initially, Haider was convinced that they would get one million signatures for the petition (*Neue Kronen Zeitung*, 4 November 1992). This number then slowly dropped as the FPÖ became aware that large-scale opposition was forming against anti-foreigner sentiment: on 14 January 1993, 500,000 signatures were thought to be a total success (*Täglich Alles*). On 15 January 1993 Haider spoke of more than 500,000 signatures (*Standard*). On 26 January 1993, numbers increased to 750,000; on 30 January, Haider explicitly stated that anything under 500,000 would be a failure (*Täglich Alles*) and on 1 February, 1993 he said that 780,000 would be a total success. The massive propaganda campaign against the petition paid political dividends: although the 417,278 signatures collected, representing approximately 7 per cent of all eligible voters, amply exceeded the required minimum of 100,000, the number fell far short of the prophecies and speculations of the FPÖ and also of the votes the FPÖ had received in the most recent general election (782,648 or 16.6 per cent) or even the 700,000 that the FPÖ had (internally) projected (*Standard*, 2 February 1993).

We set out the petition in an English translation in the following box:

TITLE: PETITION 'AUSTRIA FIRST'

Subtitle: through the creation of legal measures which permanently secure the right to a fatherland for all Austrian citizens and, from this standpoint, ensure a restrained immigration policy in Austria

---

1   The adoption of a national law to anchor the national regulatory goal (*Staatszielbestimmung*) 'Austria is not an immigration country' into the federal constitutional law of 1920 (1929 version).

2   Legal standardization of a halt to immigration until the question of illegal immigration is satisfactorily resolved, until the housing shortage is eliminated, until unemployment is reduced to 5 per cent, as well as the creation of legal measures which ensure that subsidized housing is granted in future solely to Austrian citizens, to the extent that this is not prohibited by international agreements and norms.

3   The adoption of a federal law to institute a general registration requirement for foreign workers at their place of employment, whereby the work permit and application for health insurance are prerequisites for an identity card.

4   An increase in executive powers (in particular for foreign and criminal police), including their improved remuneration, and equipment for the detention of illegal immigrants and for greater effectiveness in the fight against crime, in particular organized crime.

5   The adoption of a federal law for the immediate creation of permanent border troops (customs, gendarmerie) instead of federal army troops.

6   The adoption of a federal law to change the law governing the organization of schools so that the proportion of pupils in compulsory and vocational school classes whose native language is not German is limited to 30 per cent; where the percentage of children whose native language is not German is higher than 30 per cent, regular classes for foreigners are to be established.

7   Easing the tension in the school situation by having children whose native language is not German participate in regular classes only if they possess sufficient knowledge of German (preparatory classes).

8   Creation of a regulation in party law that ensures that only Austrian citizens participate in party-internal primary proceedings, where lists are created for the general elections to general representational bodies.

9   The adoption of a federal law to restrict the practice of premature conferring of citizenship.

10   The adoption of a federal law to end illegal business activities (as, for example, in foreigner associations and clubs), as well as to establish rigorous measures against the abuse of social benefits.

11   Creation of the legal basis for the possibility of immediate deportation and imposition of residence prohibitions for foreign criminals.

12   The adoption of a federal law to establish an Eastern Europe foundation to prevent migrational movement.

The analysis   The analysis follows the categories defined above, in particular focusing on the use of topoi. Nevertheless, other categories are applied when they occur. The analysis is sequential, that is it proceeds clause by clause, detecting all salient features at once, and not – as would also be possible – applying one category after another throughout the whole text. This is justified by the coherence and cohesive structure of the text, which makes use of all linguistic strategies and mixes them with each other. The interpretation also has to make use of the theories mentioned above. Because of our definition of textual meaning as acquired in use, it would not make sense to count the appearance of certain categories, since the meaning and structure of the whole text would not be accounted for in such a manner (although specific frequencies would certainly be of relevance). In the following, I will deconstruct the first sentence in detail; the rest of the text analysis will consist of the flow of the whole argument and interpretation.

Already the title of the petition 'Austria first' presupposes that there might be alternative views which posit Austria 'next' or 'last' as attributes or predications. The elliptical and pithy demand implies that Austria – metonymically standing for 'the Austrians' – is to be given priority over other 'countries' (metonymically implying 'non-Austrians') and that the governing politicians are neglecting the interests of the country and its people. This slogan, which was also used by the FPÖ in 1994 in their campaign against Austria joining the European Union, and, even more recently, in a political campaign against the change of currency to the Euro, constructs the view – from the very beginning of the text – that the FPÖ is the party that is concerned with the interests of the country and strategically aims at dividing the electorate into 'good' patriotic Austrians who love the country, and 'bad' unpatriotic Austrians who do not give Austria and the Austrians preferential treatment. (This already implies an actor's analysis in that certain referential strategies apply; moreover, theories on populist propaganda are consistent with such an interpretation.) The genesis of this title and the diachronic development illustrate the historical dimension of our research programme. Also, the beginning of this petition with the construction of the two important groups of 'us' and 'them' makes our general framework of sameness and difference salient and is typical of political discourse and discourses of discrimination in particular.

The subtitle justifies and elaborates the aims of the petition: legal measures are needed, which secure the 'right to a fatherland or home' for all Austrian citizens and which also ensure a reluctant Austrian immigration policy. The evaluative, polysemous and, very often, geographically localized notion of 'fatherland/home' (*Heimat*) woos much more emotional connotations – not least from before and during the Nazi era – and for specific conservative addressees it is much more evocative and solidarity promoting than the terms 'nation' or 'state'. Thus, again we focus referential and predicational strategies at this point of the analysis. This term is used mainly by German nationalists or/and very traditional people who are 'rooted in the soil' and endorse a culturally and ethnically defined notion of nation, which in the case of the pan-German nationalists coincides with a sort of 'greater German' nation. Since around 1995, the Austrian People's Party and its former Vice-chancellor, Erhard Busek, have also frequently adopted and emphasized the high-value term '*Heimat*'. The President of the Republic, Thomas Klestil, uses this term quite often in his speeches to court Austrian national identification.

The subtitle mentions the first group of social actors who are not referred to in terms of metonymic reference. But who are these 'Austrian citizens', the first group of social actors linguistically constructed as beneficiaries? Is it everybody who possesses Austrian citizenship, which also means ethnic minorities and naturalized 'guest workers' who have lived in Austria for more than ten years, or only German-speaking Austrians? Although it is nowhere explicitly restricted to the German language community, and although this politonym seems merely to refer to a group of persons in terms of the possession of citizenship and of the assignment of the related political rights and duties, this last assumption could be derived from the rest of the petition (points 6, 7) where knowledge of the German language as a mother tongue is emphasized as a distinctive feature for school-age children of 'the Austrians'. These are presupposed to be against the children of 'foreigners' who allegedly do not speak German as a native language – although this is clearly untrue in the case of those schoolchildren who belong to the second or third generation of immigrants. At this point, the importance of intertextuality, the relationship with other texts, becomes clear. It also becomes clear that the whole text has to be considered to be able to interpret singular occurrences. And what does 'restrained' mean? This is – considering the 12 points of the petition – obviously a euphemism for 'most restrictive', for the FPÖ calls for an at least a temporary 'halt to immigration'. This mitigating language use is part of the FPÖ's positive self-presentation and may aim at inviting even voters from the political centre to sign the petition. This interpretation uses other genres and texts and also refers to other discourses in the Austrian public debate.

Summarizing the analysis of these first clauses, the simultaneity of theory, categories, intertextuality and interdiscursivity becomes apparent. In these first clauses, we find mainly referential and predicational strategies, although actors' analysis is also relevant as well as some features of the Hallidayan transitivity analysis. It would be impossible to grasp the meaning of these units without the contextual information, the knowledge of the history of the FPÖ, the ethnography and investigation of other genres, and theories about right-wing populist propaganda in the specific Austrian context.

Let us now conduct the remainder of the analysis more briefly. The underlying assumptions become very clear as soon as one reads the first proposal: 'Austria is not a land of immigration' should be stated in the constitution itself. As Mitten (1994: 29–30) states, 'its initial provision [. . .] was not only demagogic, but also unmitigated nonsense. As the studies of the Austrian demographers Heinz Fassmann and Rainer Münz have shown, Austria has always been a country of immigration and emigration', and the population and economy would stagnate and decline without immigration (Fassmann and Münz, 1992, 1996; Fussmann et al., 1997). At this point in the analysis, it becomes very clear again that background information has to be included.

Except for the more polemic rhetoric, points 2, 3, 4, 8 and 12 of the petition do not diverge significantly from governmental policies in Austria. That is to say, certain demands in the petition – such as obliging foreign workers to show identification papers at their place of employment (point 3), increasing the numbers and salaries of the police (point 4), denying voting rights to legal foreign residents (point 8) or establishing a foundation to provide economic aid to Eastern Europe, thus discouraging migration (point 12) – largely reproduced projected government policies, or proposals already under consideration by the government. In general terms, it is primarily the diction of the government that diverges from the discursive practices and instigating populism of the FPÖ opposition. Only such an extreme demand as that for the 'legal standardization of a halt to immigration until the question of the illegal foreigner question [sic] is satisfactorily resolved' seems unlikely to be formulated by government politicians. As far as this formulation is concerned, at least two remarks must be made. Firstly, the formulation 'illegal foreigner question' sounds ambiguous, if not ungrammatical. Taken literally, it allows an interpretation which means nearly the converse of what the petition's authors intended to express. Then, the passage can no longer be paraphrased by 'the question of illegal foreigners', in which case it still remains unclear what 'illegal' should mean, although points 3, 4, 10 and 11 indicate several possible interpretations. Moreover, the formulation points back to and questions the way the FPÖ 'asks the foreigner question', meaning that the FPÖ, in making a 'foreigner issue', or 'foreigner problem', places itself outside the frame of legality. Secondly, the term 'satisfactory' is wide open to different interpretations, and the question arises of who will determine when the solutions are satisfactory. The respective actors are not mentioned, but clearly implied are the FPÖ and their followers.

Next, we turn to the actors' analysis. In general, the actors who are constructed implicitly or explicitly throughout the whole text by reference and predication fall into two groups. On the one hand, there are immigrants (a spatializing actionym), illegal foreigners or aliens (two criminonyms which presuppose the prejudice that 'foreigners are criminal'), foreign employees (an econonym related to the prejudiced suspicion that foreigners would do illicit work), foreigners or aliens carrying on organized crime (again, a prejudiced criminalization), foreigners' children who speak a non-German native language (a referential and predicational identification in terms of negative linguification), clubs of foreigners (a collectivizing 'organizationalization'), aliens doing illicit work (an economizing criminalization), aliens abusing the social welfare system (a criminalization that reproduces the prejudice that 'foreigners are socio-parasites'), non-nationals being naturalized prematurely (a politicizing questioning of political rights) as well as foreign criminals and perpetrators (again, two criminonyms). In the whole text, thus, the other is negatively connotated already through lexical choice. In passing, I would like to emphasize that 'foreigners' and 'aliens' mean primarily 'third-country nationals'. On the other hand, there are the Austrian citizens (the above mentioned politonym), Austrian voters (an actionalizing politonym), Austrian security forces, strictly speaking, police and customs authorities ('executionalizing' politonyms) and the Austrian army (a militarionym). This dichotomous black-and-white portrayal implicitly and explicitly constructs a two-part world and insinuates a rather clear frontier between an Austrian world of 'law and order' and a non-Austrian world of 'crime and disorder'. Foreigners are depicted as aliens who are illegal and criminal and who do not speak or understand German. The referential exterritorialization by naming them 'Ausländerinnen' is expanded here by prejudiced predication and discriminatory argumentation – up to the point where it may be concluded that 'foreigners', that is primarily 'third-country nationals', are people the FPÖ does not want to have living in Austria.

There are passages in the petition and its rationale which are not only polemical rhetorically, but also explicitly racist or which at least ascribe ethnic significance to social problems that have social and political causes beyond the 'foreigners'' influence. At this point, we can refer to argumentation analysis and apply the categories of topoi defined above. Point 6 – relying on a combination of the topos of burden with the topos of threat and the topos of culture – requests the segregation of schoolchildren according to their knowledge of German. This would not only contradict international agreements; it would introduce a discriminatory ethnic criterion into the school system. This means, it should be noted, that children are not directly characterized by their proficiency in German, but only by their mother tongue.

Other discriminatory stipulations, like relating unemployment and housing shortages to the 'foreigner problem', clearly offer explanations for problems which are causally unrelated to the presence of foreigners in Austria. Similar fallacious topoi of consequence and argumenta ad consequentiam are employed in discriminatory discourses against 'foreigners' – whoever they may be – in many Western European countries.

Point 9, the curbing of 'premature conferring of citizenship', is again open to many readings. When is naturalization 'premature' and when is this conferring legally acceptable? In view of the fact that Austria, at the time during which the petition campaign was promoted, already had one of the most restrictive citizenship laws in Europe, such a claim shows the rightist orientation of the FPÖ in an even more alarming light.

Point 10 openly manifests prejudiced hostility to foreigners by a topos of threat and a topos of abuse. On the one hand, 'clubs of foreigners' are viewed to be illegal and threatening to the 'Austrian' economy. On the other hand, 'foreigners' are presented as abusers of the Austrian welfare system. There are good reasons for assuming that one of the basic motivations for this demand – which borders on the violation of the basic right of freedom of assembly – is the FPÖ's fear of a multicultural society.

Point 11 asks for the establishment of legal instruments that allow for the immediate deportation of foreign criminals. The presupposed equation of 'illegality' and 'criminality' clearly ignores the fact that, from a viewpoint that puts human rights above the rights of a nation state, to implement a very restrictive, inhuman law to the letter can mean committing a grave wrong that is not legitimized.

Point 12 demands the investment of funds for Eastern Europe to prevent immigration as such. This demand seems to be the thin veneer of democracy in the 'anti-foreigner petition'. It cannot, however, mask the central discriminatory claims of the petition.

The FPÖ circulated a brochure which contained the official rationale that explained the 12 claims of the petition (see Reisigl and Wodak, 2001:

Chapter 4). The intertextual analysis comparing the two texts makes some of the vagueness and many possible readings of a few textual clauses distinctive and clear. Such a move to other related texts in other genres offers important evidence for some of the interpretations and this approach should be followed whenever possible. Moreover, textual chains for some arguments can then be constructed and the recontextualization analysed, as we have proposed in our research programme. Here I will merely summarize some relevant issues of the intertextual analysis.

Frequently, the FPÖ combined in its argumentation the topos of burdening with the topos of threat, and this is also found in the explanation of point 2 of the petition:

A state under the rule of law and order cannot accept these sorts of conditions. The existing problems in the area of the black economy and growing criminality are being further exacerbated through the permanent increase in 'illegals'. Moreover, in Austria the housing shortage is rapidly increasing. [. . .] Because of the lack of adequate housing capacity numerous foreigners are also being forced to take up residence in slums at unreasonably high rates of rent.

Here the mention of the numerous foreigners who are also burdened by housing problems seems to be intended to make the petition more acceptable, apart from the fact that, at this point, one group of so-called 'foreigners' is played off against another group.

In the explanation of point 10, the victim–victimizer reversal is made manifest by combining the topos of threat of hostility to 'foreigners' with the topos of culture and the topos of abuse. To quote just one excerpt:

Specifically in population centres, especially in the federal capital, Vienna, foreigners are increasingly gathering together in associations and clubs. In this area, however, there is a degree of abuse going on that reaches far beyond the legal basis of Austrian association regulations. With increasing frequency, many [such] associations and clubs take the form of eating establishments which fall considerably short of meeting the [relevant] business, sanitary or building codes (lack of sanitary facilities, no closing hours, no noise protection, prohibited gambling, secret prostitution, black market, etc.). Consequently, irritation and justified displeasure are created among indigenous residents and businesses. Only a revised legal code and its strengthened enforcement would be able to re-establish order in

> this area. In the last few years, there has been an increase in the abuse of
> social welfare by foreigners, which makes counter-measures necessary. In
> this context examples include new birth certificates, which allow for the
> premature drawing of pension benefits; children who exist only on paper,
> and who make [foreigners] eligible for family assistance; the feigning of a
> domestic place of residence so that considerable compensatory benefits –
> which cannot be financed through contribution payments – are added to
> minimal pensions.

A whole range of anti-foreigner prejudices are reproduced in this piece
of text. The 'foreigners' are made to feel guilty for the 'Austrians''
negative feelings against them because they are dirty (this prejudice is
implied by 'lack of sanitary facilities') and behave in a deviant manner,
namely conspicuously, noisily and illegally. In consequence, hostility to
'foreigners' seems to be justified. The allegedly justified animosity
mentioned is the displeasure and irritation of the fact that 'foreigners'
have different cultural habits of cooking, eating, dressing, celebrating
and playing music. Instead of conceiving this as cultural enrichment,
many Austrians simply brand such differences as the expression of 'the
foreigners'' desire to resist 'integrating' into 'the Austrian culture' –
'integration' in the majority of cases euphemistically meaning simply
'assimilation' and 'homogenization'.

An even more explicit example of the aim of 'protecting the German
culture' against a potential 'multicultural society' is the explanation
offered for point 6:

> For a number of Socialists, such as Education Minister Scholten, who, as
> always, promote the idea of a multicultural society, our cultural identity is
> practically worthless, indeed politically suspect. This can be read in the
> official writings of the Minister of Education. In order to preserve our
> cultural identity, to achieve the successful integration of children whose
> mother tongue is not German, to be able to continue to finance education,
> but also to guarantee a solid education for our children, the percentage of
> children whose native language is not German must be limited to about
> 30. [. . .] Because the educational authorities – who are dominated by the
> grand coalition – insist specifically that children with inadequate or com-
> pletely lacking proficiency in the German language be immediately integ-
> rated into regular classes within the compulsory educational system, the
> educational level is deteriorating, and difficulties for the entire educational
> community are inevitable.

In this passage, the topos of threat is merged with the topos of burden and the topos of culture into the 'topos of the impending decline of the Austrian cultural identity'.

Already in the first sentence, the Socialist Minister of Education is accused of neglecting 'the Austrian cultural identity' in favour of a multicultural identity. In this context, only a German culture can be implied. And this implication is always associated with German nationalists and politicians who do not respect the sovereignty of the Austrian state and still wish for a great German nation, a unification with Germany. The second argumentative assumption is that the cultural identity is threatened by people who are not native speakers of German; the German language being presupposed to form an indispensable ingredient of the definition of an 'Austrian nation'. This puts the immigrant children into the difficult position of either being required instantly to enculturate linguistically – which for most of the newly immigrant children is clearly impossible – or being segregated and placed, from the very beginning, at a great disadvantage with probable lifelong consequences.

Here, the FPÖ implies – by a topos of burden in combination with a topos of threat and a topos of culture – that for Austrian schools, non-native speakers of German represent a great handicap for the school education of the 'Austrian' children, a burden (because they are assumed to hinder the 'native Austrian children' from learning at school) and, thus, a threat to the 'Austrian children's solid education'. Of course, what the FPÖ means by a 'solid' education' remains unsaid. And it also remains unsaid why the FPÖ assumes 30 per cent to be the absolute limit of non-German natives that should be allowed in a school class. The problem of what is to be understood as a 'mother tongue' is not asked, and the fact that a child may speak more than one native language is not even taken into consideration.

Nobody would argue against the fact that language proficiency does indeed help every school child, but the assumption that the percentage of 'foreign' school children within a class directly correlates with the average educational level of the class is a hasty hypothesis. The statement that the level of education falls if there is a higher percentage of children who do not have German as their native tongue is nowhere explained and nowhere proven. No evidence is given for this prejudiced assumption.

All in all, the whole passage is characterized by declarative sentences, which give the impression that the propositions asserted are factual and objective, although one searches unsuccessfully for any evidence. Instead, many of the current problems in today's schools (many of them due to budget cuts, to reductions in numbers of teachers, of teaching materials and of teaching infrastructures) are simply projected on to 'the foreigners': they are made to feel guilty for problems which do not concern them. Such scapegoat strategies are applied throughout the whole rationale and illustrate typical patterns of argumentation. Similar to the 'Judeus ex machina' strategy (see Reisigl and Wodak, 2001: Chapter 3), we find the 'foreigner ex machina' strategy here.

Conclusions and procedures: a summary

Of course, it is not possible to provide a really extensive application of the discourse–historical approach and all its categories in one short chapter. Nevertheless, I would like to summarize the most important procedures to be used in the analysis of specific texts:

1 Sample information about the co- and context of the text (social, political, historical, psychological, and so on).
2 Once the genre and discourse to which the text belongs have been established, sample more ethnographic information; establish inter-discursivity and intertextuality (texts on similar topics, texts with similar arguments, macro-topics, fields of action, genres).
3 From the problem under investigation, formulate precise research questions and explore neighbouring fields for explanatory theories and theoretical aspects.
4 Operationalize the research questions into linguistic categories.
5 Apply these categories sequentially on to the text while using theoretical approaches to interpret the meanings resulting from the research questions.
6 Draw up the context diagram for the specific text and the fields of actions.
7 Make an extensive interpretation while returning to the research questions and to the problem under investigation.

These steps are taken several times, always coming and going between text, ethnography, theories and analysis. Most importantly, the decisions that are constantly required and taken, have to be made explicit and have to be justified. The mediation between theories and empirical analysis, between the social and the text, will never be implemented totally. A gap exists, and hermeneutics and interpretatory devices are always needed to bridge the gap.

Further reading

Reisigl, M. and Wodak, R. (2001) *Discourse and Discrimination*. London: Routledge.

This book presents the discourse–historical approach and its application in three case studies (anti-Semitic discourse, populist discourse and racist discourse).

Notes

1   I would like to stress that all the research presented here has been developed together with many colleagues in Vienna and elsewhere. Specifically, I would like to thank Rudolf De Cillia and Richard Mitten. The most recent elaborations of these studies and the discourse–historical approach have taken place together with Gilbert Weiss and Gertraud Benke (www.oeaw.ac.at/wittgenstein), in the 'Discourse, Politics, Identity', research centre at the Austrian Academy of Science. This chapter, moreover, integrates very valuable creative discussions with Martin Reisigl and also some of his highly original work on linguistic theory and realizations (see Reisigl and Wodak, 2001, Chapter 2; Reisigl, 2001; Reisigl and Wodak, 2000). The example provided in this chapter is elaborated extensively in Reisigl and Wodak (2000). Because of the textbook requirements, some of the categories and specificities of the analysis had to be neglected or simplified (see Reisigl and Wodak (2001) for the complete overview).

2   In recent years, the discourse–historical approach has increasingly been influenced by other schools and sub-disciplines, especially British discourse analysis in the tradition of Hallidayan systemic functional linguistics (e.g. by Fairclough, 1989, 1992, 1995; Fowler, 1996; Hodge and Kress, 1991 and van Leeuwen, 1993a, 1995 and 1996), by classical and new rhetorics as well as argumentation theory (e.g. by Toulmin, 1969; Perelman, 1976, 1980, 1994; Kopperschmidt, 1980, 1989; Kienpointner, 1992, 1996; Kindt, 1992; Wengeler, 1997) and by German 'politolinguistics' (e.g. Dieckmann, 1964, 1975, 1981; Burkhardt, 1996; Jung et al., 1997; Jarren et al., 1998; Klein, 1998 and Sarcinelli, 1998).

3   See Horkheimer and Adorno, 1991 [1944]; Marcuse, 1980; Horkheimer, 1992; Bonss and Honneth (eds), 1982; Benhabib, 1992; Honneth, 1989, 1990, 1994; Menke and Seel, 1993; Calhoun, 1995; Habermas, 1996, 1998.

4   All these strategies are illustrated by numerous categories and examples in Reisigl and Wodak (2001: Chapter 2). It would be impossible owing to space restrictions to present all these linguistic devices in this chapter. Therefore I will focus on topoi as one central category in discourses of discrimination, and must refer readers to other publications for more information on the other four strategies. The analysis of the petition and the media discourses about it are elaborated extensively in Reisigl and Wodak (2001, Chapter 4).

5   In German: 'Es handelt sich hier um Leute aus Ländern, denen man die Abstammung eindeutig ansieht, und man fürchtet dadurch Rückgänge im Rahmen des Fremdenverkehrs' (Austrian newspaper, *Standard*, 10 March 1990).

6   The original text goes as follows: 'Der ärgste Schaden, den man einem Volk zufügen kann, ist es, seine Identität, sein kulturelles Erbe, die Chancen seiner Jugend fahrlässig aufs Spiel zu setzen. Darum haben wir das Volksbegehren "Österreich zuerst" eingeleitet. Um den Österreichern ihr Recht auf Heimat zu sichern' (*Neue Freie Zeitung*, 16 December 1992).

5

Multidisciplinary CDA: a plea for diversity

Teun A. van Dijk

CONTENTS

In favour of diversity

In this chapter I formulate principles and practical guidelines for doing critical discourse analysis (CDA). This does not mean, however, that I offer a ready-made 'method van Dijk' of doing CDA. I have no such method. Nor do I lead or represent an 'approach', 'school' or other scholarly sect that seems so attractive to many scholars. I am against personality cults. I do not want colleagues or students to 'follow' me – a form of academic obsequiousness that I find incompatible with a critical attitude.

Also in my many years of experience as editor of several international journals, I have found that contributions that imitate and follow some great master are seldom original. Without being eclectic, good scholarship, and especially good CDA, should integrate the best work of many people, famous or not, from different disciplines, countries, cultures and directions of research. In other words, CDA should be essentially diverse and multidisciplinary.

What is CDA?

Let me begin spelling out what CDA is not. CDA is not a direction of research among others, like TG grammar, or systemic linguistics, nor a subdiscipline of discourse analysis such as the psychology of discourse or conversation analysis. It is not a method, nor a theory that simply can be applied to social problems. CDA can be conducted in, and combined with any approach and subdiscipline in the humanities and the social sciences.

Rather, CDA is a – critical – perspective on doing scholarship: it is, so to speak, discourse analysis 'with an attitude'. It focuses on social problems, and especially on the role of discourse in the production and reproduction of power abuse or domination. Wherever possible, it does so from a perspective that is consistent with the best interests of dominated groups. It takes the experiences and opinions of members of such groups seriously, and supports their struggle against inequality. That is, CDA research combines what perhaps somewhat pompously used to be called 'solidarity with the oppressed' with an attitude of opposition and dissent against those who abuse text and talk in order to establish, confirm or legitimate their abuse of power. Unlike much other scholarship, CDA does not deny but explicitly defines and defends its own sociopolitical position. That is, CDA is biased – and proud of it.

Like in any kind of research, there is also bad scholarship in CDA, but not because it is biased. Biased scholarship is not inherently bad scholarship. On the contrary, as many scholars, especially among women and minorities, know, critical research must not only be good, but better scholarship in order to be accepted. No scholarship is attacked as ferociously because of its alleged lacking or deficient methodology as critical scholarship. Specialized also in the critical (and self-critical) analysis of scholarly discourse, CDA of course recognizes the strategic nature of such accusations as part of the complex mechanisms of domination, namely as an attempt to marginalize and problematize dissent.

Precisely because of its combined scholarly and social responsibilities, CDA must be rigorous scholarship. Its multidisciplinary theories must account for the complexities of the relationships between discourse structures and social structures. Without explicit and systematic methods, no socially useful as well as scholarly reliable observations and descriptions can be produced. In CDA, theory formation, description, problem formulation and applications are closely intertwined and mutually inspiring. This means that in CDA theories and analyses not only should be elegant or sophisticated, as well as empirically grounded, but face the toughest test of all – relevance. They should work.

And finally, CDA should be accessible. Esoteric style is inconsistent with the fundamental aims of critical research, namely that it can be shared with others, especially also by dominated groups. Obscurantism promotes blind imitation, instead of insight. CDA must be teachable, and hence comprehensible. If students do not understand us, they can neither learn from us, nor criticize us. Complex theorizing and analysis do not require abstruse jargon and profound insights need no arcane formulations.

The discourse-cognition-society triangle

Following these metatheoretical principles, I propose to formulate and illustrate some of the guidelines that I try to observe when doing CDA. Given my multidisciplinary orientation, the overall label I sometimes use for my way of doing CDA is that of 'socio-cognitive' discourse analysis. Although I dislike labels (because they are reductionist and because I have many times changed my area of research), I have few quarrels with this one, especially since it emphasizes that – unlike many of my colleagues in CDA – I value the fundamental importance of the study of cognition (and not only that of society) in the critical analysis of discourse, communication and interaction.

This label however does not mean that I think that CDA should be limited to social and cognitive analysis of discourse, or to some combination of these dimensions. It only means that (at present) I am personally most interested in the fascinating socio-cognitive interface of discourse analysis. For instance, in my earlier work on racism (van Dijk, 1984, 1987, 1991, 1993), and my current research on ideology (van Dijk, 1998), I have shown that these are both cognitive and social phenomena. It goes without saying, however, that the complex, 'real-world' problems CDA deals with also need a historical, cultural, socio-economic, philosophical, logical or neurological approach, depending on what one wants to know (see for instance the various approaches represented in van Dijk, 1997).

It behoves little argument that given the fundamentally verbal nature of discourse, explicit CDA also needs a solid 'linguistic' basis, where 'linguistic' is understood in a broad 'structural–functional' sense. In other words, whatever other dimensions of discourse CDA deals with, CDA as a specific form and practice of discourse analysis obviously always needs to account for at least some of the detailed structures, strategies and functions of text and talk, including grammatical, pragmatic, interactional, stylistic, rhetorical, semiotic, narrative or similar forms of verbal and paraverbal organization of communicative events.

Having emphasized the necessity of a broad, diverse, multidisciplinary and problem-oriented CDA, I thus limit my own endeavours to the domain defined by the theoretical discourse–cognition–society triangle. Since this is merely a handy label and hence liable to reductionist misinterpretation, it should further be stressed that 'discourse' is here meant in the broad sense of a 'communicative event', including conversational interaction, written text, as well as associated gestures, facework, typographical layout, images and any other 'semiotic' or multimedia dimension of signification. Similarly, 'cognition' here involves both personal as well as social cognition, beliefs and goals as well as evaluations and emotions, and any other 'mental' or 'memory' structures, representations or processes involved in discourse and interaction. And finally, 'society' is meant to include both the local, microstructures of situated face-to-face interactions, as well as the more global, societal and political structures variously defined in terms of groups, group-relations (such as dominance and inequality), movements, institutions, organizations, social processes, political systems and more abstract properties of societies and cultures.

In a more or less informal way we may view the combined cognitive and social dimensions of the triangle as defining the relevant (local and global) context of discourse. Indeed, the sociopolitical and problem-oriented objectives of CDA especially need sophisticated theorization of the intricate text–context relationships. Just an analysis of text or talk added to some cognitive and/or social study will not do. We shall see that adequate discourse analysis at the same time requires detailed cognitive and social analysis, and vice versa, and that it is only the integration of these accounts that may reach descriptive, explanatory and especially critical adequacy in the study of social problems.

It should be stressed that CDA, and discourse analysis in general, are not 'methods' that can simply be applied in the study of social problems. Discourse studies is a cross-discipline with many subdisciplines and areas, each with its own theories, descriptive instruments or methods of inquiry. CDA does not provide a ready-made, how-to-do approach to social analysis, but emphasizes that for each study a thorough theoretical analysis of a social issue must be made, so as to be able to select which discourse and social structures to analyse and to relate. In addition to that, concrete methods of research depend on the properties of the context of scholarly investigation: aims, participants, setting, users and their beliefs and interests.

Which discourse structures should we analyse?

Although we have argued that especially in CDA a text–context theory is crucial, let us briefly make some remarks on discourse structures per se. Decades of specializations in the field have 'discovered' many hundreds, if not thousands, of relevant units, levels, dimensions, moves, strategies, types of acts, devices and other structures of discourse. We may have paraverbal, visual, phonological, syntactic, semantic, stylistic, rhetorical, pragmatic, and interactional levels and structures. This means that in any practical sense there is no such thing as a 'complete' discourse analysis: a 'full' analysis of a short passage might take months and fill hundreds of pages. Complete discourse analysis of a large corpus of text or talk, is therefore totally out of the question.

Hence, also in CDA, we must make choices, and select those structures for closer analysis that are relevant for the study of a social issue. This requires at least some informal ideas about text–context links that tell us which properties of discourse may vary as a function of which social structures. Thus, if we want to study – as would be typical in CDA – the ways some speakers or writers exercise power in or by their discourse, it only makes sense to study those properties that can vary as a function of social power. Thus, stress and intonation, word order, lexical style, coherence, local semantic moves (such as disclaimers), topic choice, speech acts, schematic organization, rhetorical figures and most forms of interaction are in principle susceptible to speaker control. But other structures, such as the form of words and many structures of sentences are grammatically obligatory and contextually invariant and hence usually not subject to speaker control, and hence irrelevant for a study of social power.

But even for those discourse structures that are contextually variable and hence possibly relevant in a critical study of discourse, some are marginally relevant and others much more significantly so, depending of course on the research questions one asks. For instance, a perfectly legitimate and interesting study of informal or institutional conversation between men and women may want to examine how interactional dominance is also enacted by male intonation or volume, including shouting and other forms of intimidation.

However, if one is interested in a critical study of the role of discourse in the reproduction of sexism or machismo in society, one would not typically limit oneself to the rather specific structures of intonation and volume, but probably begin with a study of interaction control on the one hand and with an analysis of 'content', such as choice of topics, propositions and lexical items, on the other hand. The reason is that such forms of meaning seem more directly related to the beliefs and hence the attitudes and ideologies sexist men enact or express when talking to (or about) women. Note though that this is not obviously the case, but a conclusion of a theory of text–context relations, in which specific discourse structures are related to specific context structures such as the socially shared beliefs of speakers.

Levels and dimensions of CDA – an example

By way of example, we shall illustrate our theoretical framework and analytical categories in a brief description of a text of the Centre for the

Moral Defence of Capitalism, 'a petition against the persecution of Microsoft', downloaded from the Internet (www.moraldefense.com). This petition criticizes the US government for its legal battle against Microsoft, and asks readers to sign it:

A PETITION AGAINST THE PERSECUTION OF MICROSOFT

Sign the petition – international version (for non-US residents)

To: Members of Congress, Attorney General Janet Reno, and President Bill Clinton.

Fellow Americans:

The Declaration of Independence proclaims that the government's fundamental purpose is to protect the rights of the individual, and that each individual has an inalienable right to the pursuit of happiness. Throughout America's history, this noble idea has protected the individual's right to pursue his own happiness by applying his energy to productive work, trading the products of his effort on a free market and rising as far as his abilities carry him.

Over the past century, however, this freedom has been under attack, and one notorious avenue of this attack has been the antitrust laws. Under the guise of 'protecting the public', these laws have allowed envious competitors and power-hungry officials to attack successful businessmen for the crime of being successful. It has led to the ugly spectacle of the creative geniuses of the business world – the men who have made this country great – being branded as oppressive tyrants, whose hard-won business empires must be broken to pieces and subjected to the control of government regulators.

The Justice Department's current suit against Microsoft is the latest example of this trend. It is based on envy for the productive ability of Microsoft and its founder, Bill Gates. The result of this suit, if successful, will be to deprive Mr Gates of his right to control his own company, and to deprive the company of its ownership and control of its own products.

The Justice Department's case – and indeed the entire edifice of antitrust law – is based on the bizarrely inverted notion that the productive actions of individuals in the free market can somehow constitute 'force', while the coercive actions of government regulators can somehow secure 'freedom'.

The truth is that the only kind of 'monopoly' that can form in a free market is one based on offering better products at lower prices, since under a free market even monopolies must obey the law of supply and demand. Harmful, coercive monopolies are the result, not of the operation of the free market, but of government regulations, subsidies, and privileges which close off entry to competitors. No business can outlaw its competitors – only the government can.

We hold that Microsoft has a right to its own property; that it has the authority, therefore, to bundle its properties – including Windows 95 and Internet Explorer – in whatever combination it chooses, not by anyone's permission, but by absolute right. We hold that to abridge this right is to attack every innovator's right to the products of his effort, and to overthrow the foundations of a free market and of a free society.

We do not want to live in a country where achievement is resented and attacked, where every innovator and entrepreneur has to fear persecution from dictatorial regulators and judges, enforcing undefined laws at the bidding of jealous competitors. We realize that our lives and wellbeing depend on the existence of a free market, in which innovators and entrepreneurs are free to rise as far as their ability can carry them, without being held down by arbitrary and unjust government regulations.

As concerned citizens, we ask that the Justice Department's case against Microsoft be dismissed. We call for a national debate over the arbitrary and unjust provisions of the antitrust laws and for an end to the practice of persecuting businessmen for their success.

(follow: spaces where address can be written)

Since a single short text obviously does not exemplify the hundreds of possible discourse structures, and since on the other hand even a more or less complete analysis of such a short text would require dozens if not hundreds of pages, it hardly needs to be emphasized that we can do no more than give a very partial analysis. We do this by providing a brief discussion of some of the discourse structures that appear to be relevant in much of my own (and other) CDA research. Apart from showing the practical usefulness that these categories seem to have in analysis, I shall also briefly explain why this is so by describing the theoretical framework in which such structure categories are related to social structures. In other words, the choice of discourse categories in CDA is guided by theory, as well as by the main aims of CDA, namely the critical study of the discursive reproduction of domination in society.

Topics: semantic macrostructures

For discursive, cognitive and social reasons, the topics of discourse play a fundamental role in communication and interaction. Defined as 'semantic macrostructures' derived from the local (micro) structures of meaning, topics represent what a discourse 'is about' globally speaking, embody most important information of a discourse, and explain overall coherence of text and talk (van Dijk, 1980). They are the global meaning that language users constitute in discourse production and comprehension, and the 'gist' that is best recalled by them. Language users are unable to memorize and manage all meaning details of a discourse, and hence mentally organize these meanings by global meanings or topics. Hence also the social relevance of topics in discourse in interaction and social structure: they define what speakers, organizations and groups orient towards and that has most impact on further discourse and action.

Topics defined as global meanings cannot, as such, be directly observed, but are inferred from or assigned to discourse by language users. However, they are often expressed in discourse, for instance in titles, headlines, summaries, abstracts, thematic sentences or conclusions. These may be used by language users as strategic devices for the inference or assignment of topics – as intended by the speaker or writer (van Dijk and Kintsch, 1983). This also allows for influence and manipulation. Speakers and writers may thus emphasize meaning, control comprehension and influence the formation of so-called 'mental models' of the event the discourse is about. These cognitive and social roles of topics will be further explained below.

Because topics have such an important role, and since topical (macrostructural) analysis can also be applied to larger corpora, I usually recommend starting with such an analysis. It provides a first, overall, idea of what a discourse or corpus of texts is all about, and controls many other aspects of discourse and its analysis. Since summaries by definition express macrostructures, we can – for all practical purposes – simply 'list' the topics of a text by summarizing it, a method that can be repeated for various levels of abstraction.

In our sample text, the title, 'A petition against the persecution of Microsoft', expresses not only part of the topic ('the persecution of Microsoft'), but also the self-categorization of the text genre ('petition'). Thus, we may summarize this text by, for example, the following 'macropropositions':

M1   Antitrust laws threaten the freedom of enterprise.
M2   Successful businessmen are being represented as tyrants.
M3   The suit against Microsoft is an example of this trend.
M4   The government should not limit the freedom of the market.
M5   Microsoft has the right to do with its products what it wants.
M6   Innovators should not be punished.
M7   We call that the case against Microsoft be dismissed.

In a further reduction one can summarize these macropropositions with the higher level, overall macroproposition (topic):

The US government is requested to stop its judicial persecution of innovator Microsoft.

We see that these various topics/macropropositions indeed represent very high-level, sometimes abstract principles. In this case, these propositions are a more or less direct expression of some tenets of a classical capitalist ideology about the freedom of enterprise. In other words, the macropropositions express the general neo-liberal principles of the freedom of the market, and then apply these to the special case of Microsoft. We shall see later that this distinction reflects the difference between socially shared representations, on the one hand, and more personal mental models, on the other.

Local meanings

My next analytical choice would be a study of local meanings, such as the meaning of words (a study that also may be called lexical, depending on one's perspective), the structures of propositions, and coherence and other relations between propositions. Again, the reason for such a choice is mostly contextual. Local meanings are the result of the selection made by speakers or writers in their mental models of events or their more general, socially shared beliefs. At the same time, they are the kind of information that (under the overall control of global topics) most directly influences the mental models, and hence the opinions and attitudes of recipients. Together with the topics, these meanings are best recalled and most easily reproduced by recipients, and hence may have most obvious social consequences.

Although there are many ways to study meaning, only some of which are mentioned here. CDA research is often interested in the study of ideologically biased discourses, and the ways these polarize the representation of us (ingroups) and them (outgroups). Both at the level of global and local meaning analysis, we thus often witness an overall strategy of 'positive self-presentation and negative other presentation', in which our good things and their bad things are emphasized, and our bad things and their good things are de-emphasized.

At this local semantic level, we may for instance examine the choice of the word 'persecution' in the title of our sample text, a choice that has various implications that express the ideological perspective of the author (the Centre for the Moral Defence of Capitalism). The action of the government is defined in negative terms, implying a form of morally or legally reprehensible harassment or force, or abuse of power. At the same time the choice of this word implies that Microsoft is represented as the victim of this aggression. In more general terms, lexical selection here shows the familiar form of negative other presentation, and positive self-presentation. As part of the main macroproposition, the choice of the concept of 'persecution' also contributes to the organization of the local meanings in the rest of the text. In more cognitive terms this means that the choice of this word may influence the formation of the macro-nodes of the mental model of the readers of this text.

Similarly relevant is the repeated use of the word 'rights' in the first paragraph, typically associated with 'individual' and 'freedom', all profoundly ideological concepts related to the constitution and prevailing ideology of the US. In order to be able to qualify the legal action of the government in the starkly negative terms of a 'persecution', it needs to be shown that the rights of individuals are being violated, and what these rights are. The emphasis on rights has several other functions, such as associating us and our position with something good and legitimate, and thus preparing the negative evaluation of the US government when it allegedly violates these rights. Apart from polarizing the mental model being construed here, this paragraph at the same time functions as an important premise in the overall argumentation of this text.

Especially interesting for CDA research is the study of the many forms of implicit or indirect meanings, such as implications, presuppositions, allusions, vagueness, and so on. We call information implicit when it may be inferred from (the meaning of) a text, without being explicitly expressed by the text. In theoretical terms (see below) this means that implicit information is part of a mental model of (the users of) a text, but not of the text itself. That is, implicit meanings are related to underlying beliefs, but are not openly, directly, completely or precisely asserted, for various contextual reasons, including the well-known ideological objective to de-emphasize our bad things and their good things.

In our sample text there are many propositions that are implied or presupposed, but not explicitly asserted. When the authors say that antitrust legislation comes 'under the guise of "protecting the public"', the expression 'under the guise' and the quotes imply that it is not true that antitrust laws protect the public. Note also that here in the second paragraph as well as throughout the text, many expressions have ideological presuppositions, such as:

- competitors are envious of successful businessmen
- officials are power hungry
- the business world has creative geniuses
- business empires are hard won.

Apart from further emphasizing the polarization between government and business, the local meanings of the text thus create another polarization between envious competitors and brilliant creators in the business. Notice also that the lexical choice and metaphors further emphasize these polarizations: envious, power-hungry, hard-won, control, regulators, and breaking to pieces and so on are the negative concepts associated with 'them', the government (and some business people), whereas we and those we protect, are associated with successfulness, creative geniuses and by negation (litotes) with 'crime' and 'tyrant'. Again, such words not only contribute to the overall polarization of the conceptual structure of the text, but also to the formation of a biased, polarized model of the events, where the actors are neatly differentiated between the good and the bad.

The first two paragraphs are formulated in general terms, and apply to rights and their violation, as well as to the antitrust laws. The third paragraph begins with the functional move of specification or example: what has been said so far specifically applies to the case of Microsoft. Theoretically this means that the first paragraphs are rather expressions of (general) social representations, such as attitudes and ideologies, whereas the third paragraph describes the current case, Microsoft, and thus sets up the more specific mental model based on these general social representations (see below). Given the ideological slant of the first paragraphs, there is little doubt that this model, as expressed by the Centre, is also ideological biased, and we may expect that the general polarization constructed before will be applied here, as is indeed the case. Notice also that conceptual polarization often is implemented in the text by various forms of hyperboles, as we already have seen in the lexical choice of 'crime', 'tyrants' and 'geniuses'. Such hyperboles may even come close to outright lies, for instance when it is asserted that Bill Gates is deprived of his right to control his own company.

The use of 'his', 'businessmen' and 'the men who have made this country great' suggest that especially or exclusively men, and no women, are involved in business and its success. Thus, apart from expressing a starkly conservative neo-liberal ideology, the Centre also professes a sexist ideology by verbally excluding women, thus contributing to a more overall conservative meta-ideology that also controls the nationalist ideology expressed in the characteristic form of US self-glorification (the 'greatness' of this country).

Finally, among the many other semantic properties of this text, we should also mention the importance of what is being left out in the text. Thus, it is suggested that the success of Microsoft is based on the principle of better products for a lower price, but of course not the well-known practice of forced bundling of products (like Windows and its Internet browser). Nearly trivially then we may formulate the general rule that negative properties of us (or those we defend) are either omitted or downgraded in the text. Note that theoretically omission is only a relevant property of a discourse when it can be shown that the omitted information is part of the mental model (the Centre no doubt knows about the illegal practices of Microsoft), or of more general, shared knowledge that is needed or may be used to produce or understand a text. In this case, the mental model of a critical reader may of course be different from the one that is persuasively expressed by the Centre.

We now have a first impression of some of the theoretically based practical guidelines that may be used to decide which discourse structures to study among many hundreds of others. Of course, this is only an example. The point is that such a choice is twice context-bound: firstly by our own (scholarly) aims, our research problems, the expectations of our readers, as well as the social relevance of our research project and secondly, by the relevance of specific discourse structures studied in their own context, such as the aims and beliefs of the speaker or the recipients, the social roles, positions, and relations of participants, institutional constraints, and so on.

The relevance of subtle 'formal' structures

Besides or instead of the semantic structures just mentioned, critical discourse analysts may be more interested in those structures of text or talk that are much less consciously controlled or controllable by the speakers, such as intonation, syntactic structures, propositional structures, rhetorical figures, as well as many properties of spontaneous talk, such as turn taking, repairs, pauses, hesitation, and so on. These various 'forms' generally do not directly express underlying meanings and hence beliefs, but rather signal 'pragmatic' properties of a communicative event, such as the intention, current mood or emotions of speakers, their perspective on events talked about, opinions about co-participants, and especially interactional concerns such as positive self-presentation and impression formation. Thus men may well be able to hide negative opinions about women, or white people about black people, but indirectly their evaluations, position or face, and hence their identity may be signalled by subtle structural characteristics of talk.

In the same way as I made a distinction between global and local meanings, I distinguish between global and local discourse forms or formats. Global forms or superstructures are overall, canonical and conventional schemata that consist of typical genre categories, as is the case for arguments, stories or news articles. Local forms are those of (the syntax of) sentences and formal relations between clauses or sentences in sequences: ordering, primacy, pronominal relations, active–passive voice, nominalizations, and a host of other formal properties of sentences and sequences.

Of the many formal properties of our sample text, we may thus observe the repeated use of passive constructs that typically hide agents, such as 'this freedom has been under attack', and 'creative geniuses of the business world. . . [are] being branded as oppressive tyrants'. The obvious function is that the Centre may be vague in its accusations by omitting the agents of negative actions, or vaguely identifying them in terms of laws. Besides these and other syntactic structures that realize underlying semantic representations, the most obvious formal structure that would deserve attention in a CDA approach would probably be the complex argumentative framework, in which general norms and values as well as ideological principles function as general arguments, and their application to the Microsoft case, with the conclusions: Microsoft should be able to do what it wants with its products. Of course, this argument is marred by fallacies, and omits vital information, namely that Microsoft abused its power by imposing its products, and thus violating the basic principle of 'freedom' that forms the ideology of this text. There are many other fallacies, such as the 'authoritative' use of the (shared value of the) US Constitution to argue a business case.

In the same way that the semantic and rhetorical polarization of this text expresses and helps construct biased models of the case against Microsoft, its formal style is a marker of its genre: the official petition. This formal style begins with the paraphrase of the Declaration of Independence, but also is lexically expressed in the Centre's own petition, as in the repeated 'We hold that . . .', 'not by anyone's permission, but by absolute right', and so on, signalling something like a declaration of the free market.

The global and local study of discourse meaning and form briefly illustrated above may be much more detailed and sophisticated, and only space limitation prevents me from doing so in this chapter. However, the relevance of such a study (also) in CDA projects should now be clear, especially as part of a systematic account of how ideological discourse represents 'us' versus 'them'. Thus, speakers or writers may emphasize our good things by topicalizing positive meanings, by using positive lexical items in self-descriptions, by providing many details about good actions, and few details about bad actions, by hyperbole and positive metaphors, by leaving implicit our negative properties, or by de-emphasizing our agency of negative acts through passive sentences or nominalizations. As we shall see below, such formal and meaning aspects of dominant discourse not only express and enact power, but are also geared to the construction of desired mental models and social representations, that is, to influence, manipulation or control of the mind.

Context models

As argued above, the critical aims of CDA can only be realized if discourse structures are related to structures of local and global contexts. In my analyses above I have made some informal remarks about mental models, ideologies, situations, aims, and social groups and institutions, but these obviously need to be defined in explicit theories. The rest of this chapter provides some brief fragments of such theories, and illustrates their principles in a broader, and more relevant analysis of some fragments of our sample text.

Whereas we have many theories of text and talk, there is no such thing as an explicit theory of context. Indeed, there is not even a monograph about context. I am working on some fragments of such a theory, of which I present a brief summary here.

As I also distinguished between local and global structures within discourse, we may distinguish between local and global contexts. Global contexts are defined by the social, political, cultural and historical structures in which a communicative event takes place. In CDA, they often form the ultimate explanatory and critical rationale of discourse and its analysis.

Local context is usually defined in terms of properties of the immediate, interactional situation in which a communicative event takes place. Some properties of such a situation are its overall domain (politics, business), an overall action (legislation, propaganda), participants in various communicative and social roles (like the Centre in our example), as well as their intentions, goals, knowledge, norms and other beliefs. Such contexts are said to constrain the properties of text and talk. That is, what we say and how we say it depends on who is speaking to whom, when and where, and with what purposes.

My theory of context recognizes that such an analysis of the cognitive and social properties of communicative events is relevant, but defines (local) contexts in cognitive terms, namely as a form of mental model of a communicative situation, that is, as a context model. This allows subjective interpretations of social situations and differences between language users in the same situation, strategically incomplete models, and in general a flexible adaptation of discourse to the social situation. In other words, not the various properties of the local situation that control and constrain text and talk, but the ways language users interpret or define these properties in their mental context models. For instance, age, gender or profession, as well as aims or knowledge of participants often do influence talk and text, but only if and as defined in the context model of the speaker or writer. Context models allow us to explain what is relevant to the social situation for the speech participants. In other words, a theory of context provides a theory of relevance.

Context models may also be seen as specific cases of the kind of personal, subjective mental models people construct of their many daily experiences, from getting up in the morning to going to bed at night. Communicative events are just a prominent type of such 'models of everyday experience'.

Context models have the same cognitive status and schematic structure as other mental models, to which we shall turn below. At this point it is only relevant to emphasize that context models are the mental representations that control many of the properties of discourse production and understanding, such as genre, topic choice, local meanings and coherence, on the one hand, but also speech acts, style and rhetoric on the other hand. Indeed, style may be defined as the set of formal properties of discourse that are a function of context models, such as lexicalization, word ordering and intonation.

In our example of a petition, the context defining the communicative event is rather obvious. The overall societal domain for this text is that of business or the market, and the overall actions those of advocating the freedom of enterprise, and protecting business against government interference. The local setting of the communicative event is the Internet. The communicative role of the participant is that of speaker/writer, author and originator, the interactional role that of a defender of Microsoft and as an opponent of the government, whereas the societal-economic role is that of an organization advocating the freedom of the market. The other participant, the addressee, is explicitly referred to in the beginning of the text as 'Fellow Americans', thus pragmatically trying to emphasize the unity of the WE-group for which this centre claims to be the defender. It is interesting that although the proposal for the petition is directed at 'Fellow Americans', the proposed petition itself is addressed to the relevant final destinataries: the judge, the Senate Judiciary Committee, the Attorney General, and the President of the US.

The current communicative action is that of publishing a text on the Internet persuading readers to sign a petition. This action is being performed through the speech acts of accusing the government, and defending Microsoft. The (complex) mental structures defining the cognitive dimension of the context, consist of the various ideologies analysed above, as well as the more specific attitudes and opinions (about the legal action of the government against Microsoft) we have found expressed throughout the text. Although expressing group co-membership in addressing 'Fellow Americans', the persuasive structure of the text presupposes that not all Americans may have the same opinion about the practices of Microsoft. Finally, the text is meaningful for its readers only because it presupposes a vast amount of common ground and common-sense knowledge, for example, about the Declaration of Independence, Microsoft, antitrust laws, and so on, as well as specific (model based) knowledge about the current court case against Microsoft.

The important point is that, throughout, this text adapts to this sub-jectively construed context model of the current communicative situation, for example as follows:

- The meanings of the text are all understandable within the broader framework of the three domains of business, justice and government.
- The genre and speech act of the petition is one form of implementing the overall defence of the free market, which is the global aim of the Centre.
- The action of the government is defined as a violation of our rights, and hence a sufficient condition for the successfulness of the current genre and speech act of a petition.
- The overall topic semantically realizes the reason for the speech act and genre of this specific petition: Microsoft's rights have been violated.
- The argumentative structure is organized in such a way as to optimally sustain the communicative function of this text as a form of persuasion.
- The polarization of the opinions at all levels of the text expresses the attitudes and the ideology of the Centre, and tries to influence those of the readers – and final destinataries.
- Lexical choice is appropriate for the genre of a formal, public petition.
- The text presupposes existent general knowledge about what business, laws, governments, and so on are, as well as specific knowledge about the case against Microsoft. However, it does not express or presuppose knowledge that debilitates its defence (for example about the illegal practices of Microsoft).

Why are context models so important? Context models are crucial because they are the interface between mental information (knowledge, and so on) about an event and actual meanings being constructed in discourse. What we know or believe, either about a specific event, thing or person, or more generally, need not all be expressed in discourse, either because it is irrelevant or because it is redundant. Context models thus provide the constraints that allow language users to make situationally relevant selections of information people have, and construe these as meanings to be expressed in talk. As we have seen, such 'pragmatic' constraints of communication are not so much expressed in meanings, but rather in various structures. For instance, difference of status or position between speakers, if represented in the context model, may control the selection of pronouns and a number of other stylistic devices. Thus context models are those representations in (episodic) memory that act as the overall control of a communicative event.

For any kind of CDA research that links text with some social situation, it is important to realize that whatever the broader social or political situation is, it may not 'reach' or impact on discourse simply because a speaker may find it irrelevant and further ignores the relevant information in the construction of the context model. Also the changes that speakers apply in their discourses, for example because of politeness or other forms of persuasion, need to be taken into more explicit attention.

Event models

Language users not only form mental models of the situation they interact in, but also of the events or situations they speak or write about.

We had to use the notion of a mental model above several times to explain various properties of discourse meanings. Thus, local and global coherence of discourse is not only defined in terms of functional relations between its propositions (such as generalization, specification, example, explanation), but especially also by the relations of the 'facts' referred to by these propositions, such as cause–consequence relations. However, psychologically speaking, this is not how coherence should be defined. It is not the facts that define coherence, but rather the ways the facts are defined or interpreted by the language users in their mental models of these facts. These interpretations are personal, subjective, biased, incomplete or completely imaginary.

In other words, discourses are interpreted as coherent relative to the mental models the users have about the events or facts referred to.

Thus, in our example, it is not the Microsoft case, and the actions of the government that form the semantic (referential) basis of the petition text, but rather the (obviously biased) ways the Centre represents this case and the government in its mental model of these events.

It is this mental model of events talked or written about that forms the basis for the production and understanding of a discourse, especially of its meaning. That is, under the control of the context model (see above), those propositions of the event model are selected that are relevant for the current communicative event, for instance those propositions that the recipients do not yet know. In other words, the meaning of a discourse, compared to its mental model, is by definition incomplete: speakers or writers need not include all those propositions recipients already know or can infer for themselves. Mental models feature all personally relevant beliefs about an event, that is, knowledge as well as opinions (and probably also emotions).

In the case of an obvious opinion discourse, as is the case for our example, what is relevantly expressed are the opinions of the writers, for example about the Microsoft case and the government. At the same time, the petition aims to influence the (opinions in the) mental models of the President or of politicians about the Microsoft case. One aspect of persuasion can thus be defined as discursive control of preferred mental models. We shall see below that there is also a broader definition of persuasion in terms of the control of social representations such as knowledge, attitudes and ideologies.

Context models and event models are mental representations in episodic memory, that is, the part of long term memory in which people store their knowledge and opinions about episodes they experience or read/hear about. Mental models probably consist of a schematic representation of the personally and socially relevant dimensions of events, such as setting, participants (in various roles), actions, and so on.

In a rough sense, we may say that context models control the 'pragmatic' part of discourse and event models the 'semantic' part. Understanding a discourse basically means being able to construct a model for it. And in production it is the mental model of events and situation that forms the starting point of all text and talk. What we usually remember of a discourse is thus not so much its meaning, as the mental model we construct during comprehension.

However, model theory of discourse goes much beyond the explanation of meaning and contextually controlled variation in text and talk. Models also form the crucial interface between discourse and society, between the personal and the social. Without such models we are unable to explain and describe how social structures influence and are affected by discourse structures. This is because mental models not only represent personal beliefs, but also (often personal versions of) social representations, such as knowledge, attitudes and ideologies, which in turn are related to the structure of groups and organizations (see below). Thus, mental models of language users are the core interface that theoretically enable the link between social groups, their social representations, the mental models of their members and finally the discourse of their members. Mental models explain how a discourse can exhibit both personal and social properties, and indeed how in the same social situation each discourse is different. It is this complex series of links that theoretically adequate CDA research focuses on. There is no direct link between discourse and society.

Social cognition

Because CDA is interested in power, domination and social inequality, it tends to focus on groups, organizations and institutions. This means that CDA also needs to account for the various forms of social cognition that are shared by these social collectivities: knowledge, attitudes, ideologies, norms and values. Although many books have been written about these 'social representations', we in fact know very little about their precise mental structures, and how exactly these control the production and comprehension of text and talk. I assume that such control takes basically two forms, a direct and an indirect form. Thus, knowledge or attitude items may be expressed directly, in their general, abstract form, for instance in the generic sentences typical of teaching and propaganda.

Thus, our Microsoft text has several of such generic sentences that express general forms of knowledge or opinions, such as 'each individual has an inalienable right to the pursuit of happiness'.

The second way such socially shared representations are expressed in discourse is through mental models, that is through application to a specific event or situation.

Our sample text is a classic example of such an 'application' of general propositions in a specific case, namely the application of neo-liberal norms, values and ideologies to the special case of Microsoft. Nearly all sentences of the text are thus specific 'examples' of the representations shared by neo-liberals.

Theoretically, this means that social representations are 'particularized' in mental models, and it is often through mental models that they are expressed in text and talk. And conversely, it is through mental models of everyday discourse such as conversations, news reports and textbooks that we acquire our knowledge of the world, our socially shared attitudes and finally our ideologies and fundamental norms and values. We now have a very rough picture of the way groups and power are able to affect discourse and vice versa, namely through the social representations shared by groups, and the mental models that in turn are the specific instances of these social representations. The theories involved here are exceedingly complex, and much of this is still obscure, but we have a general picture of the main components and relationships involved. Let us only make a few general remarks on the main forms of social representation involved:

Knowledge   It makes sense to distinguish between different kinds of knowledge, namely personal knowledge, group knowledge and cultural knowledge. Personal knowledge is represented in mental models about specific, personal events, as explained above. Group knowledge is shared by specific social groups, such as professionals, social movements or business companies. Such knowledge may be biased and ideological, and not be recognized as 'knowledge' by other groups at all, but be characterized as mere 'belief'. Of course, the beliefs of some groups have more influence, power and legitimacy than those of others, as is the case for scientific discourse. Cultural knowledge is shared by all competent members of a society or culture, and forms the basis or common ground of all social practices and discourses. Indeed, in principle all culturally shared knowledge may therefore be presupposed in public discourse. Of course, such common ground knowledge constantly changes, and what is common ground yesterday, may be ideological group belief today (as is the case for Christian religion), or vice versa, as is the case for much scholarly knowledge. Discourses are like icebergs of which only some specific forms of (contextually relevant) knowledge are expressed, but of which a vast part of presupposed knowledge is part of the shared sociocultural common ground. Many properties of discourse, such as overall topics, local coherence, pronouns, metaphors and many more require definition in terms of this kind of socially shared cultural knowledge. One of the main theoretical challenges has been the organization of knowledge in memory, for which many proposals have been formulated, for instance in terms of scripts, schemas, scenarios, and many more. These proposals are not only relevant for cognitive science, but also for CDA, because such knowledge structures (directly or through models) also organize the structures of discourse.

Attitudes   Attitudes are socially shared opinions, such as the opinions people share about immigration, abortion or nuclear energy. These are usually complex, that is, consist of a cluster of evaluative propositions. In the same way as general knowledge may influence mental models, the general propositions of attitudes may also be 'particularized' as specific, personal opinions in mental models, as is the case for the Centre's opinions about the Microsoft case.

Ideologies   Finally, I define ideologies as the basic social representations of social groups. They are at the basis of the knowledge and attitudes of groups such as socialists, neo-liberals, ecologists, feminists as well as anti-feminists. They probably have a schematic structure that represents the self-image of each group, featuring membership devices, aims, activities, norms and resources of each group. Ideologies feature the basic principles that organize the attitudes shared by the members of a group. Thus, a racist ideology may organize attitudes about immigration, education or the labour market.

> In our sample text, we find that virtually all general attitudes about the relation between the state and business, as exemplified by the Microsoft case, are organized by a neo-liberal ideology.

Discourse and society

I shall be brief about the third dimension of the theoretical framework: the relation between discourse and society. This relation is being dealt with in more detail in the other chapters of this book. And many of the aspects of discourse and cognition dealt with above (such as knowledge and ideology) are at the same time social.

I have suggested that society may also be analysed in more local and more global terms, firstly at the level of interaction and situations and secondly at the level of groups, social organizations, organizations and institutions. The latter, social structure, may only be related to discourse in two ways: firstly through the social representations of social members about such social structures, and secondly through the instantiation of social structures (such as groups and organizations) through social actors, interactions and situations at the local, micro level. In other words, there is a cognitive and a social way to bridge the famous levels of differentiation in the account of social structure. Thus, CDA may be interested in macro notions such as power and domination, but their actual study takes place at the micro level of discourse and social practices. Let me make some comments on some of these concepts.

Social situations The structure of social situations is especially relevant, as we have seen above, for a theory of context. Discourse is often defined as a communicative event, and occurring in a social situation, featuring a setting, participants in different roles, actions, and so on. We have seen that such situational features are only relevant for discourse when represented in mental representations: context models. In other words, we may have a theory of social situations to account for contexts, but again we need the cognitive interface to transform them into the 'structures of relevance' we call contexts.

In our example, to understand the petition text, one also needs to understand, and hence construct, the communicative situation, featuring an Internet site as communicate medium, the Centre and the user as participants. That is, the petition speech act can only be understood as directed at the/any Internet user who reads this text, and the persuasive language and arguments as directed at that user, but at the same time at the final addressees of the petition, the President and politicians.

Action CDA is not only interested in speech acts, but also in many other actions, interactions and social practices that are accomplished by discourse, or that form conditions or consequences of text and talk and that are a relevant part of what I defined as context above. Thus, a speech in parliament may consist of assertions or accusations against government policies, but also at many levels many other social and political actions are relevantly involved, such as criticizing the government, being in opposition, representing voters and legislation. In other words, to understand what is going on in discourse, we need construct it as an instance of, or as part of many other forms of action at several levels of social and political analysis.

Thus, in the petition text, an organization requests Internet users to sign a petition, but the Centre is doing much more than that – defending Microsoft, attacking the US government, persuading Internet users, and finally advocating neo-liberal business principles. Understanding this text, either as user or as analyst, means understanding these actions, and how they are related to discourse structures. Obviously, as suggested above, such sociopolitical interpretations require socially shared beliefs that are not explicitly expressed but presupposed by this text.

Actors   Similar remarks may be made for actors as we made for actions. They are constituent categories of social situations, and as parts of communicative situations, they have various communicative roles, such as various types of speakers, writers or producers, and various types of recipients. They may be locally defined as individuals or globally in terms of groups, organizations or institutions.

In our example, for instance, the global writer or producer of the Internet text is the Centre, although locally the text is probably written by an employee of the Centre. Similarly, the text is addressed to (any) Internet user, that is to a non-identified individual, and indirectly to the whole Internet community and any other person who has access to the text. These and other roles organize many aspects of the text, such as the forms of address and the request ('Sign the petition'). Note that not only do these actors define the communicative situation, but that also the 'cited' discourse (the petition) has its own addressees (the President, and so on and ultimately the American people). Again, an interesting CDA analysis of this text would need to analyse the complex participant structures of social and political actors involved (both individual as well as collective) and how such situational or semantically represented actors are described or otherwise related to discourse structure.

Societal structures   We have seen that local situations of interaction enact, manifest or instantiate global societal structures. Participants speak and listen as women, mothers, lawyers, party members, or company executives. Their actions, including their discursive actions, realize larger social acts and processes, such as legislation, education, discrimination and dominance, often within institutional frameworks such as parliaments, schools, families, or research institutes.

CDA is mainly interested in the role of discourse in the instantiation and reproduction of power and power abuse (dominance), and hence particularly interested in the detailed study of the interface between the local and the global, between the structures of discourse and the structures of society. We have seen that such links are not direct, but need a cognitive and an interactional interface: social representations, including attitudes and ideologies are often mediated by mental models in order to show up in discourse, and such discourse has social effects and functions only when it in turns contributes to the formation or confirmation of social attitudes and ideologies. And white group dominance can only be 'implemented' when white group members actually engage in such derogating discourse as an instance of discrimination. Racism or sexism are thus not merely abstract systems of social inequality and dominance, but actually 'reach' down in the forms of everyday life, namely through the beliefs, actions and discourses of group members.

Similar remarks have been made in the analysis of our sample text. In order to fully understand and explain (the structures of) this text, we not only need to spell out its cognitive and contextual conditions and consequences, but also the broader societal structures on which such cognitions and contexts are ultimately based, and which at the same time they help sustain and reproduce. We have seen how throughout the text and at all levels the negative opinion about the US government in the Microsoft case is linked with the overall neo-liberal ideology of a free market, in which creative 'businessmen' are the heroes and the government (and its justice system) the enemies, against whose attacks the Centre plays its specific role of 'defender' of capitalist values. That is, the ideology as implemented in the mental models constructed for the Microsoft case and as more or less directly expressed in the text, needs to be linked to societal groups, organizations, structures and relationships of power. Indeed, the current text is in that respect just one of the myriad of (discursive and other) actions of the business community in its power struggle with the state. It is only at the highest level of societal analysis that we are able to fundamentally understand this text, its structures and functions.

Concluding remarks

It is this permanent bottom-up and top-down linkage of discourse and interaction with societal structures that forms one of the most typical characteristics of CDA. Discourse analysis is thus at the same time cognitive, social and political analysis, but focuses rather on the role discourses play, both locally and globally, in society and its structures.

The relevant relationships run both ways. Societal structures such as groups and institutions as well as overall relations such as power or global societal acts such as legislation and education provide the overall constraints on local actions and discourse. These constraints may be more or less strong, and run from strict norms and obligations (for instance as formulated in law, such as the acts of judges or members of parliament), to more flexible or 'soft' norms, such as politeness norms. And the constraints may affect such diverse discourse properties as interaction moves, who controls turn taking or who opens a session, speech acts, topic choice, local coherence, lexical style or rhetorical figures. And conversely, these discourse structures may be interpreted as (count as) actions that are instances or components of such very global societal or political acts as immigration policy or educational reform.

It is precisely in these links that we encounter the crux for a critical discourse analysis. Merely observing and analysing social inequality at high levels of abstraction is an exercise for the social sciences and a mere study of discourse grammar, semantics, speech acts or conversational moves is the general task of linguists, and discourse and conversation analysts. Social and political discourse analyses are specifically geared towards the detailed explanation of the relationship between the two along the lines sketched above.

As we have seen in the partial analysis of our example, the crucial critical dimension of this sociopolitical dimension is finally provided by the specific aims of such research, such as the focus on the way discourse is involved in the reproduction of dominance. This also means that CDA needs an explicit ethics. Dominance defined as power abuse presupposes a definition of abuse, for instance in terms of the violation of norms and human and social rights. These are formulated at the macro level of groups, movements, institutions, and nation states, often in relation to their members. CDA is specifically interested in the discursive dimensions of these abuses, and therefore must spell out the detailed conditions of the discursive violations of human rights, for example, when newspapers publish biased stories about minorities, when managers engage in or tolerate sexism in the company or organization, or when legislators enact neo-liberal policies that make the rich richer and the poor poorer.

Further reading

Caldas-Coulthard, C. and Coulthard, M. (eds) (1996) *Texts and Practices: Readings in Critical Discourse Analysis*. London: Routledge.

This is probably the first collection of papers that appeared with the label CDA. It features fine papers by prominent scholars from many countries (including those from outside Europe or North America), on both written and spoken discourse and in different contexts.

Fowler, R., Hodge, B., Kress, G. and Trew, T. (1979) *Language and Control*. London: Routledge and Kegan Paul.

This is the book that spawned work in critical linguistics and then in CDA. It is regarded as a classic, in conjunction with the work of Tony Trew about the syntactic aspects of negative outgroup description (active versus passive sentences, and so on).

van Dijk, T.A. (1993) *Elite Discourse and Racism*. London: Sage.

This summarizes much of my work on discourse and racism done in the decade before publication, for example on the media and textbooks, and adds results of new research on parliamentary debates, scholarly discourse and corporate discourse, concluding that the most influential (and most denied) form of racism is that of the elites.

van Dijk, T.A. (1998) *Ideology*. London: Sage.

The first instalment of a long project on ideology and discourse, in which the basic framework of a new multidisciplinary theory of ideology is outlined, related to cognition, society and discourse. Illustrations are given of racist ideologies. This book also provides the foundation of the ideology component of a theory of CDA.

Wodak, R. (ed.) (1989) *Language, Power and Ideology. Studies in Political Discourse.* Amsterdam: Benjamins.

This important collection of studies is certainly CDA before its time and definition. It is also important because the work of several German-language scholars is translated into English here. It comprises work on fascism, racism, prejudice, patriarchy, and political discourse.

6

Critical discourse analysis as a method in social scientific research

Norman Fairclough

CONTENTS

My aim in this chapter is to describe critical discourse analysis (CDA) as a method which can be used in social scientific research. I shall refer to necessarily selective aspects of a particular object of research: how language distinctively figures in the new capitalism.

I should declare at once that I have certain reservations about the concept of 'method'. It can too easily be taken as a sort of 'transferable skill' if one understands a 'method' to be a technique, a tool in a box of tools, which can be resorted to when needed and then returned to the box. CDA is in my view as much theory as method – or rather, a theoretical perspective on language and more generally semiosis (including 'visual language', 'body language', and so on) as one element or 'moment' of the material social process (Williams, 1977), which gives rise to ways of analysing language or semiosis within broader analyses of the social process. Moreover, it is a theory or method which is in a dialogical relationship with other social theories and methods, which should engage with them in a 'transdisciplinary' rather than just an interdisciplinary way, meaning that the particular co-engagements on particular aspects of the social process may give rise to developments of theory and method which shift the boundaries between different theories and methods (Fairclough, 2000a). Put differently, each should be open to the theoretical logics of others, open to 'internalizing' them (Harvey, 1996) in a way which can transform the relationships between them.

I shall first describe the theoretical position of this version of CDA. Secondly, I shall then describe the analytical framework – the 'method' – and the view of critique. Finally, I shall illustrate it with respect to one particular issue within the broad research object of language in the new capitalism – representations of change in the 'global economy'.

Theoretical position of CDA: discourse as a moment of social practices

In this section I shall set out a framework for CDA which tries to incorporate the view of language as an integral element of the material social process (see Chouliaraki and Fairclough, 1999; Fairclough, 2000a). This version of CDA is based upon a view of semiosis as an irreducible part of material social processes. Semiosis includes all forms of meaning making – visual images, body language, as well as language. We can see social life as interconnected networks of social practices of diverse sorts (economic, political, cultural, and so on). And every practice has a semiotic element. The motivation for focusing on social practices is that it allows one to combine the perspective of structure and the perspective of action – a practice is on the one hand a relatively permanent way of acting socially which is defined by its position within a structured network of practices, and a domain of social action and interaction which both reproduces structures and has the potential to transform them. All practices are practices of production – they are the arenas within which social life is produced, be it economic, political, cultural, or everyday life.

Let us say that every practice includes the following elements:

- productive activity;
- means of production;
- social relations;
- social identities;
- cultural values;
- consciousness;
- semiosis.

These elements are dialectically related (Harvey, 1996). That is to say, they are different elements but not discrete, fully separate, elements. There is a sense in which each 'internalizes' the others without being reducible to them. So for instance social relations, social identities, cultural values and consciousness are in part semiotic, but that does not mean that we theorize and research social relations for instance in the same way that we theorize and research language – they have distinct properties, and researching them gives rise to distinct disciplines.

CDA is analysis of the dialectical relationships between semiosis (including language) and other elements of social practices. Its particular concern is with the radical changes that are taking place in contemporary social life, with how semiosis figures within processes of change, and with shifts in the relationship between semiosis and other social elements within networks of practices. We cannot take the role of semiosis in social practices for granted; it has to be established through analysis. And semiosis may be more or less important and salient in one practice or set of practices than in another, and may change in importance over time.

Semiosis figures in broadly three ways in social practices. Firstly, it figures as a part of the social activity within a practice. For instance, part of doing a job (such as being a shop assistant) is using language in a particular way; so too is part of governing a country. Secondly, semiosis figures in representations. Social actors within any practice produce representations of other practices, as well as ('reflexive') representations of their own practice, in the course of their activity within the practice. They 'recontextualize' other practices (Bernstein, 1990; Chouliaraki and Fairclough, 1999) – that is, they incorporate them into their own practice, and different social actors will represent them differently according to how they are positioned within the practice. Representation is a process of social construction of practices, including reflexive self-construction – representations enter and shape social processes and practices. Thirdly, semiosis figures in the 'performances' of particular positions within social practices. The identities of people who operate in positions in a practice are only partly specified by the practice itself. People who differ in social class, in gender, in nationality, in ethnic or cultural membership, and in life experience, produce different 'performances' of a particular position.

Semiosis as part of social activity constitutes genres. Genres are diverse ways of acting, of producing social life, in the semiotic mode. Examples are: everyday conversation, meetings in various types of organization, political and other forms of interview, and book reviews. Semiosis in the representation and self-representation of social practices constitutes discourses. Discourses are diverse representations of social life which are inherently positioned – differently positioned social actors 'see' and represent social life in different ways, different discourses. For instance, the lives of poor and disadvantaged people are represented through different discourses in the social practices of government, politics, medicine, and social science, and through different discourses within each of these practices corresponding to different positions of social actors. Semiosis in the performance of positions constitutes styles.

For instance, doctors, teachers or government ministers do not simply have semiotic styles as a function of their positions in practices; each position is performed in diverse styles depending on aspects of identity which exceed the construction of positions in those practices. Styles are ways of being, identities, in their semiotic aspect.

Social practices networked in a particular way constitute a social order – for instance, the currently emergent neo-liberal global order of the new capitalism, or at a more local level, the social order of education in a particular society at a particular time. The semiotic aspect of a social order is what we can call an order of discourse. It is the way in which diverse genres and discourses are networked together. An order of discourse is a social structuring of semiotic difference – a particular social ordering of relationships amongst different ways of making meaning, that is different discourses and genres. One aspect of this ordering is dominance: some ways of making meaning are dominant or mainstream in a particular order of discourse; others are marginal, or oppositional, or 'alternative'. For instance, there may be a dominant way to conduct a doctor–patient consultation in Britain, but there are also various other ways, which may be adopted or developed to a greater or lesser extent in opposition to the dominant way. The dominant way probably still maintains social distance between doctors and patients, and the authority of the doctor over the way interaction proceeds; but there are others ways which are more 'democratic', in which doctors play down their authority. The political concept of 'hegemony' can be usefully employed in analysing orders of discourse (Fairclough, 1992; Forgacs, 1988; Laclau and Mouffe, 1985) – a particular social structuring of semiotic difference may become hegemonic, become part of the legitimizing common sense which sustains relations of domination, but hegemony will always be contested to a greater or lesser extent, in hegemonic struggle. An order of discourse is not a closed or rigid system, but rather an open system, which is put at risk by what happens in actual interactions.

Critical discourse analysis, as I indicated earlier, oscillates between a focus on structure and a focus on action – between a focus on shifts in the social structuring of semiotic diversity (orders of discourse), and a focus on the productive semiotic work which goes on in particular texts and interactions. In both perspectives, a central concern is shifting articulations between genres, discourses, and styles – the shifting social structuring of relationships between them which achieve a relative stability and permanence in orders of discourse, and the ongoing working of relationships between them in texts and interactions. The term 'interdiscursivity' is reserved for the latter: the 'interdiscursivity' of a text is a part of its intertextuality, a question of which genres, discourses and styles it draws upon, and how it works them into particular articulations.

Analytical framework for CDA

An analytical framework for CDA is represented schematically below. It is modelled upon the critical theorist Roy Bhaskar's concept of 'explanatory critique' (Bhaskar, 1986; Chouliaraki and Fairclough, 1999):

1   Focus upon a social problem which has a semiotic aspect.
2   Identify obstacles to it being tackled, through analysis of
   a   the network of practices it is located within
   b   the relationship of semiosis to other elements within the particular practice(s) concerned
   c   the discourse (the semiosis itself)
     • structural analysis: the order of discourse
     • interactional analysis
     • interdiscursive analysis
     • linguistic and semiotic analysis.
3   Consider whether the social order (network of practices) in a sense 'needs' the problem.
4   Identify possible ways past the obstacles.
5   Reflect critically on the analysis (1–4).

A key feature of the framework is that it combines relational (2) and dialectical (4) elements – negative critique in the sense of diagnosis of the problem, positive critique in the sense of identification of hitherto unrealized possibilities in the way things are for tackling the problem.

Stage 1 shows that this approach to CDA is problem-based. CDA is a form of critical social science, which is envisaged as social science geared to illuminating the problems which people are confronted with by particular forms of social life, and to contributing resources which people may be able to draw upon in tackling and overcoming these problems. Of course, this begs a question: a problem for whom? Like critical social science generally, CDA has emancipatory objectives, and is focused upon the problems confronting what we can loosely refer to as the 'losers' within particular forms of social life – the poor, the socially excluded, those subject to oppressive gender or race relations, and so forth. But this does not provide a clearly defined and uncontroversial set of social problems. What is problematic and calls for change is an inherently contested and controversial matter, and CDA is inevitably caught up in social controversy and debate in choosing to focus on certain features of social life as 'problems'.

Stage 2 of the critique approaches the diagnosis of the problem in a rather indirect way, by asking what the obstacles are to it being tackled – what is it about the way in which social life is structured and organized that makes this a problem which is resistant to easy resolution? The diagnosis considers the way social practices are networked together, the way semiosis relates to other elements of social practices, and features of discourse itself. Since the latter constitutes the particular focus of discourse analysis, I should discuss it in more detail.

I have discussed above the oscillation within CDA between a focus on structure and a focus on action – a focus on the structuring of orders of discourse, and a focus on what goes on in particular interactions. The obstacles to tackling a problem here are in part to do with the social structuring of semiotic differences in orders of discourse (for example, the way in which managerial discourse has colonized public service domains such as education). They are also in part a matter of dominant or influential ways of interacting, ways of using language in interaction. This means that we need to analyse interactions. ('Interaction' is used in a broad sense: a conversation is a form of interaction, but so too, for instance, is a newspaper article, even though the 'interactants' are distant in space and time. Written as well as, for instance, televisual or email texts are interactions in this extended sense.)

Interactional analysis has two aspects. Firstly there is interdiscursive analysis: how do particular types of interaction articulate together different genres, discourses and styles? The assumption here is that an interaction (or text) is typically hybrid in terms of genres, discourses, and styles – part of the analysis is unpicking the particular mix characteristic of particular types of interaction. The second aspect is linguistic and other forms of semiotic analysis (for example, analysis of visual images). I shall just say a little about linguistic analysis.

One problem facing people who are not specialists in linguistics is that there are many different aspects of the language of an interaction which may be relevant to critical analysis. There are however checklists of linguistic features which tend to be particularly worth attending to in critical analysis (for example, Fairclough, 1992: Chapter 8; Fowler et al., 1979: Chapter 10). This version of CDA draws upon a particular linguistic theory, systemic functional linguistics (Halliday, 1994), which has the virtue of being 'functional' – it sees and analyses a language as shaped (even in its grammar) by the social functions it has come to serve. This makes it relatively easy to see how categories of social analysis connect with categories of linguistic analysis (see Chouliaraki and Fairclough, 1999: Chapter 8 for an appreciation and critique of this type of linguistic analysis).

Stage 3 of the analysis, considering whether the social order 'needs' the problem, is an indirect way or linking 'is' to 'ought'. If one can establish through critique that the social order inherently generates a range of major problems which it 'needs' in order to sustain itself, that contributes to the rationale for radical social change. The question of ideology also arises here: discourse is ideological in so far as it contributes to sustaining particular relations of power and domination.

Stage 4 of the analysis moves from negative to positive critique – identification of hitherto unrealized or not fully realized possibilities for change within the way things are. This may be a matter of showing contradictions or gaps or failures within the domination in the social order (for instance contradictions in dominant types of interaction), or a matter of showing difference and resistance.

Finally, Stage 5 is the stage at which the analysis turns reflexively back on itself, asking for instance how effective it is as critique, whether it does or can contribute to social emancipation, whether it is not compromised through its own positioning in academic practices which are nowadays so closely networked with the market and the state.

Example: representations of change in the 'global economy'

The example I have chosen to illustrate this approach to CDA is representations of change in the 'global economy'. The significance of such representations for critical social science emerges within the broader area of research I alluded to earlier: language in the new capitalism. I shall therefore begin by framing the former within the latter.

The new capitalism can be seen as a re-networking of social practices. According to Jessop (2000), it involves both a 'restructuring' and a 're-scaling'. New structural relations are being established between domains of social life – between networks of practices, or in Bourdieu's terminology (for example, 1979) 'fields'. Notably, there is a restructuring of relations between economic and non-economic fields which involves an extensive colonization of the latter by the former. Re-scaling is a matter of new relations being established between different scales of social life (and between networks of social practices on different scales): between the global, the regional, the national, and the local. From this point of view, the phenomenon widely referred to as 'globalization' is not simply a move from a mainly national to a mainly global scale of economic organization and processes: globalization has a long history and what is involved rather is new relations between scales.

Language and semiosis are of considerable importance in the restructuring and re-scaling of capitalism. For instance, the whole idea of a 'knowledge-based economy', an economy in which knowledge and information take on a decisive new significance, entails a discourse-based economy: knowledge is produced, circulates, and is consumed as discourses – discourses which are operationalized as new ways of acting and interacting (including new genres), and inculcated as new ways of being, new identities (including new styles). An example would be knowledge of new ways of managing organizations. The restructuring and re-scaling of capitalism is partly a semiotic process – the restructuring and re-scaling of orders of discourse, involving new structural and scalar relationships between genres, discourses and styles.

Language is also important in bringing about this restructuring and re-scaling of capitalism. The term 'neo-liberalism' can be understood as referring to a political project aimed at removing obstacles (such as states with strong welfare programmes) to the full development of the new capitalism (Bourdieu, 1998). As Bourdieu has pointed out, neo-liberal discourses are a significant part of the resources which are deployed in pursuing the neo-liberal project. That is where my example comes in: a particularly important aspect of neo-liberal discourse is the representations of change in the 'global economy' which are pervasive in contemporary societies – representations of economic change as inevitable and irresistible, and something we must simply learn to live with and adapt to.

The new capitalism, then, is a distinctive network of practices part of whose distinctiveness is the way language figures within it – its genres, discourses and styles. We can distinguish three interconnected analytical concerns: dominance, difference and resistance.

Firstly, we need to identify which genres, discourses, and styles are the dominant ones. Examples would be the genres which regulate action and interaction in organizations (for example, the sort of language which constitutes 'teamwork', 'consultation', 'partnerships', or 'appraisals'); the neo-liberal economic discourses (including representations of change) which are internationally disseminated and imposed by organizations like the International Monetary Fund and the World Trade Organization (including keywords and phrases like 'free trade', 'transparency', 'flexibility', 'quality'); and the styles of key figures in the new order – entrepreneurs, managers, political leaders, and so on. We also need to consider how these genres, discourses, and styles are disseminated internationally (re-scaled), and across areas of social life (restructured, for example how the discourse and genre of 'negotiation' so to speak 'flows' between economic, political, military, and family life).

Secondly, we need to consider the range of difference, diversity, in genres, discourses and styles – and the social structuring and restructuring of that difference. One issue is access: who does or does not have access to dominant forms? Another is relationships between dominant and non-dominant forms – how other genres, discourses and styles are affected by the imposition of new dominant ones. For instance, mainstream political discourse has widely converged around neo-liberal discourse – what has happened for instance to radical and socialist political discourses? How have they been marginalized? How do they continue to sustain themselves? An error which must be avoided is assuming that dominant forms are the only ones that exist.

This brings us now to the third concern: resistance. Dominant genres, discourses and styles are colonizing new domains – for instance managerial genres, discourses and styles are rapidly colonizing government and public sector domains such as education, and rapidly moving between scales. But colonization is never a simple process: the new forms are assimilated and combined in many cases with old forms. There is a process of appropriating them, which can lead to various outcomes –

quiescent assimilation, forms of tacit or more open resistance (for example, when people 'talk the talk' in a consciously strategic way, without accepting it), or indeed the search for coherent alternatives.

As I said earlier, the sort of representations of change in the global economy which I am concerned with are pervasive – one finds them in economic, political and educational media and other sorts of texts. In another paper (Fairclough, forthcoming) I have traced how such representations of change move between such different types of discourse. I have also shown (Fairclough, 2000b) that they are a salient feature in the discourse of the 'third way' in the political language on New Labour in Britain. The first text I shall discuss has been selected as a rather typical example – it could be supplemented by many others, and in a fuller study it would be. It is the Foreword written by the British Prime Minister Tony Blair to the Department of Trade and Industry's White Paper on competitiveness in 1998 (DTI, 1998). This is reproduced as Appendix 1. I shall follow the five-point analytical framework introduced above.

Focus upon a social problem which has a semiotic aspect

For this part of the analysis, we need to go outside the text, using academic and non-academic sources to get a sense of its social context. One's sense of what the major contemporary social problems are comes from a broad perspective on the social order – see the discussion above on language in the new capitalism. I shall focus on what I take to be one social problem manifested in this text, which can be summed up in Margaret Thatcher's notorious claim: 'There is no alternative' (since widely referred to as 'TINA'). Global capitalism in its neo-liberal form is pervasively constructed as external, unchangeable, and unquestionable – the simple 'fact of life' which we must respond to. The social problem here is that feasible alternative ways of organizing international economic relations which might not have the detrimental effects of the current way (for instance, in increasing the gap between rich and poor within and between states) are excluded from the political agenda by these representations.

Identify obstacles to it being tackled

I shall begin with the network of practices which texts such as this one are located within. The text comes from a White Paper, which is a British governmental policy document – it is located in one practice within the network of practices which constitute government. However, national governments are increasingly incorporated within larger networks of practices which include not only other governments but also intergovernmental and government-sponsored international agencies (such as the European Union, the World Bank, the International Monetary Fund), business networks, and so forth. Governments according to Castells (1998) are increasingly coming to function as 'nodes' within a transnational network based upon a business–government complex, whose central 'functions' are focused on creating the conditions (the financial, fiscal and legal structures, the 'human capital', and so on) for successful competition in the 'new global economy' – which is simply taken as given. Given that the particular practice at issue here is locked into this powerful network, there is a substantial obstacle to tackling the problem.

In terms of the second aspect of obstacles to the problem being tackled, the relationship of semiosis to other elements within the network of practices, semiosis plays a crucial role as I said above in imposing, extending and legitimizing the 'new global economy'. Bourdieu (1998) has emphasized the importance of this role of 'the discourse of power', as one significant element in a range of resources deployed by those with an interest in extending and consolidating the new neo-liberal order. This means that such representations of the new economy and of economic change are by no means lightly dispensable. One might also refer here to changes in government and 'governance' – what New Labour refers to as the 'modernization' of government – which include a dual movement of dispersal or devolution of governance, and strengthening the centre in certain respects, especially in co-ordinating different arms of government, and in 'managing perception'. 'Managing perception' is partly what is now widely referred to as 'spin', and it puts a premium on the language of government and the careful monitoring of that language. On different levels, therefore, the relationship of semiosis to other elements in the network of practices constitutes a formidable obstacle to tackling the problem.

The third aspect of obstacles to the problem being tackled brings us to discourse, semiosis, per se, in both structural (order of discourse) and interactional terms. One thing which makes the problem at issue difficult to tackle is recontextualization (Bernstein, 1990; Chouliaraki and Fairclough, 1999). Representations of the 'new global economy' and economic change very similar to the example are, as I have said, pervasively present in economic, political, media, educational, and so on, discourse, both in Britain and internationally. Such representations 'flow' through the transnational business–government network, and are recontextualized (and, as the concept entails, transformed) from genre to genre, from one domain of discourse to another.

Turning now to interactional analysis, I shall comment first on linguistic features of the text in its representation of economic change, then come to interdiscursivity. At this stage in the analysis I shall have to use some linguistic terminology, though I shall keep it to a minimum. The framework for linguistic analysis is based, as I said earlier on systemic functional linguistics (Halliday, 1994). Dominant representations of 'the new global order' have certain predictable linguistic characterics: processes in the new economy are represented without responsible social agents; they are represented in a timeless, ahistorical present; in terms of modality, statements about the new economy (which are often very familiar truisms) are represented categorically as unmodalized truths, and authoritatively, and there is a movement from this 'is' of the economic to an 'ought' of the political – from what is categorically the case, to what 'we' ought to do in response; the new economic reality is represented as universal, indifferent to place; and series of evidences or appearances of the new economy are represented paratactically as lists. I have shown elsewhere (Fairclough, forthcoming) that these features are sustained through recontextualization, appearing in economic texts (for example, texts of the World Bank), political texts, educational texts, and so forth. They are present in Blair's text.

In the representation of economic change, change in 'the modern world', there is an absence of responsible social agents. Agents of material processes are abstract or inanimate. In the first paragraph ('The modern world is swept . . .'), 'change' is the agent in the first (passive) sentence, and 'new technologies' and 'new markets' are agents in the second – agents, notice, of intransitive processes ('emerge', 'open up') which represent change as happenings, processes without agents. The third sentence is existential – 'new competitors' and 'new opportunities' are merely claimed to exist, not located within processes of change. Notice also that in the third paragraph it is the inanimate 'this new world' that is the agent of 'challenges'. By contrast, when it comes to national responses to these implacable and impersonal processes of world change, social agents are fully present – business, the government, the DTI, and especially 'we'.

Turning to time, tense and modality, world change is represented in the ahistorical present, as indeed are national processes in response, and, in terms of modality, through authoritative categorical assertions of truisms (for example, 'The modern world is swept by change' – as we all know – and indeed all five statements in the first paragraph). The only historical reference to the past is to the old (indeed 'old-fashioned') system in paragraph 4 ('Old-fashioned state intervention did not and cannot work.'). There is a movement from 'is' to 'ought'. 'Ought' is implicit in paragraphs 2 and 3: 'our success depends on how well we exploit our most valuable assets' implies we should exploit them, 'this new world challenges business to be innovative', and so on and 'government: to create', and so on implies that business and government should do these things. From paragraph 5 onwards, 'ought' is explicit and recurrent – the modal auxiliary verb 'must' occurs six times. The domain of 'is' is world change; the domain of 'ought' is national responses to world change: a divide is textually constructed between economics and politics, fact and value, which excludes the former from the latter – in contrast with the social democratic tradition from which New Labour has come. In contrast with economic processes, political processes do have responsible social agents: the agent in processes modalized with 'must' is in five cases 'we' and in one case 'the government'. Summing up, world change is a present process without a history which 'we' must respond to. Moreover, the process of world change is implicitly represented as indifferent to place (in other texts this may be explicit, in expressions like 'Wherever we look in the contemporary world') – there are no place expressions in the first paragraph or in the third paragraph.

The syntax is paratactic, both in relations between sentences and relations between phrases in sentences. Take for instance the first two paragraphs. The first paragraph consists of three paratactically related sentences (the second and third also have internally paratactically related clauses), listing evidences of world change. The same is true of the second paragraph, though the sentences are thematically related (hence the anaphoric pronominal themes in the second and third sentences); the second contains paratactically linked phrases. Notice that the sequencing of these sentences is not significant – the sequence is changeable (with some minor rewording in the case of paragraph 2 because of the anaphora) without any substantive meaning effect. Indeed, what is included or excluded from this list of evidences is somewhat arbitrary, for instance the second sentence of the first paragraph might equally have been 'Huge amounts of money move across the globe in a fraction of a second, and even our family cat, Socks, has his own homepage on the World Wide Web'. The second clause is fanciful only in that Blair does not have a cat called Socks. It was actually included in a very similar list in a book by US President Bill Clinton. What is significant, rhetorically, is the relentless accumulation of evidences of change – what Clarke and Newman, 1998 call 'the cascade of change' – which firmly establishes the new economy as simple fact; what we must live with and respond to.

Summing up, change is authoritatively represented in this text as lists of known appearances (and truisms) in the present which are indifferent to place and whose social agency is effaced, and which must be responded to in certain ways. These features together construct the new economy as simple fact to which there is no alternative.

Let me turn to interdiscursivity. This is a recontextualization of the sort of developmental economic language which appears in texts of organizations such as the World Bank, which means that it is inserted into a different context, and therefore is combined with a different sort of language, a political and governmental language. This manifests itself in various features of the text. For instance, the text belongs to a particular governmental genre, the (prime) ministerial Foreword to an official document, which predicts the heading, the signature at the end, the photograph of the Prime Minister, but also the rhetorical organization of the text as a whole. This is a political text, which is primarily designed to make a persuasive case, whereas a World Bank text would be primarily oriented to analysis (see Fairclough, forthcoming for an actual example) – which does not preclude a more covert persuasive intent. The Blair text has familiar features of political rhetoric – it is more heavily oriented towards 'ought' than towards 'is', towards prescriptions and injunctions for action; the agent of these projected actions is mainly the first-person pronoun 'we', which characteristically oscillates in its reference between an exclusive 'we the government' ('we must also invest in British capabilities when companies cannot alone') and an inclusive 'we the British' ('we must compete more effectively'), though the exact reference of inclusive 'we' is characteristically vague. There are a number of anti- theses which set up neat and striking contrasts ('new competitors but also great new opportunities', 'a long-term vision in a world of short- term pressures', 'compete . . . in today's tough markets . . . prosper in the markets of tomorrow'). 'But' is a favoured paratactic conjunction, used sentence initially in paragraphs 3, 4 and 5, and again setting up anti- theses. The text begins and ends with short, dramatic, metaphorical sentences which would serve well as soundbites ('The modern world is swept by change', 'We must put the future on Britain's side'). The vocabulary of process includes words which highlight the will and energy of agents in projected actions ('build', 'create', 'promote', 'forge', 'foster', 'seize'), as do words which represent affective states ('prepared to', 'committed to'). The text is a call to collective, inclusive, committed, action.

Recontextualization entails such hybridity, such mixing of different discourses, in this case the discourse of economic development and political discourse. Recontextualization entails transformation – repre- sentations of the new economy are not identical in a World Bank report and a political preface; they are inflected by the discourse it is recon- textualized into. For instance, in the first paragraph of Blair's text the representation of change is stripped down to three short sentences which incorporate the features of political rhetoric I have referred to (the dramatic metaphor of the first sentence, the antithesis of the third) and which constitute a stark, blunt and dramatic basis for persuasive political rhetoric of the text. Analogous material would be likely to be fuller and more elaborate in a World Bank report (see Fairclough, forthcoming for an actual comparison). Recontextualization implies transformation to suit the new context and its discourse.

The interactional analysis shows how the 'new economic order' is constructed textually as an inevitable fact of life. If texts with such con- structions are as I have suggested common and pervasive in various types of discourse, and moreover 'domesticated' through recontextua- lization within different types of discourse and different genres, one can appreciate that the 'drip effect' of such representations in many texts and interactions is also an obstacle to the problem being tackled.

Does the social order (network of practices) in a sense 'need' the problem?

I have effectively already answered this question above: representations of economic change and the 'new global economy' as inevitable are an important legitimizing part of the new social order. This is also the question of ideology. These are partial representations and misrepresentations: concretely, the inevitability and inexorableness of the new economy rests to a significant extent on intergovernmental agreements, for instance on world trade and the deregulation of financial markets, which are reversible; more generally, although on one level markets do have an impersonal logic to which all involved in them are subject, there is nothing that has been socially created that is incapable of being socially changed. These representations are misrepresentations which clearly contribute to sustaining unequal relations of power – they are ideological.

Identify possible ways past the obstacles

At this point I shall introduce another text which is in Appendix 2, an extract from a book (Brown and Coates, 1996) written by two long-standing members of the Labour Party, Ken Coates (who is a Member of the European Parliament) and Michael Barratt Brown (they are now operating within the Independent Labour Network). They are writing here about New Labour's view of what they call 'capitalist globalization' ('the new global economy' in New Labour terms).

The point of introducing another text at this stage is to move, in the terms I introduced earlier, from the dominant to difference and resistance: the sort of representation of the new economy I have been discussing so far is not the only one in contemporary texts and interactions, though it is the dominant one. There is difference, but there is also resistance: these authors are writing against New Labour from a left position within the Labour movement. There are also resistant texts in for instance the anti-capitalist organizations which have recently come into prominence, in events such as the protests at the meeting of the World Trade Organization in Seattle in 1999. As in the case of the Blair text, I am selecting one text here to typify many others – a fuller study would analyse more. These alternative representations are located within an emergent counter-network of social practices which at least constitutes a possible resource for countering the obstacles I have discussed, though it is currently relatively marginal. How substantive a resource is rather difficult to assess at this stage – and a detailed assessment is beyond the scope of this chapter. I shall limit myself here to interactional analysis focusing on the same features as I identified in the Blair text to demonstrate how this representation of change differs from the dominant one.

The agents in this extract are different from those in the Blair text – they are social agents: 'the big transnational companies', 'British-based companies', 'foreign-based companies', 'the European Union', 'the European Commission', and so forth. (New Labour representations of the new economy virtally never refer to transnational corporations.) 'Capital' is used in two senses, first as a social agent equivalent to 'capitalist business' ('Capital has always been global'), second in the sense of money as capital ('capital is more mobile'). These social agents are in some cases agents of material processes in the economy: 'capital . . . moving internationally', 'companies operating transnationally . . . operating in the UK', 'the European Union . . . reinforces their status as clients', 'the European Commission . . . providing a better organized clientele for the transnationals'. But there are also material processes which might have had social agents but do not: 'capital is more mobile . . . it can be moved quicker by electronic means' (the former former clause is relational, but one might see it as a grammatical metaphor (Halliday, 1994) for a material clause – 'capital can more easily be moved', 'companies can more easily move capital').

Rather than a timeless, ahistorical present, present tense clauses are in some cases given temporal specification ('governments now increasingly require' – and 'increasingly' constructs the present as a process of becoming – 'the present aim of the European Commission'), present tense is combined with present perfect ('such transnational companies have become more dominant') which gives historical depth to the present, framing the present in relation to the past and in terms of a process linking past to present. Moreover, economic change is partly specified in terms of place rather than being represented as indifferent to place ('peculiar to the UK', 'Europe').

In terms of modality, we do not here have the division between 'is' and 'ought' characteristic of dominant representations, but there is a significant shift at the end from 'is' to 'could be' which represents the current economic set-up as not the only possible one, as open to change initiated by social agents (by implication, 'the European states' governments'). The modality of statements is categorical and authoritative, as in the Blair text, but the statements are not such obvious truisms.

The syntax of the extract is also different from that of the Blair text. It does not have the paratactic listing of the latter, the building up of lists of evidence to establish rhetorically the inexorable reality of change. The extract is more argumentative – one indication of this is the nature of the cohesive linkages between sentences, which include conjunctives ('in other words', 'indeed', 'but'), comparatives ('more importantly', 'further', 'other, better orders'), an anaphoric pronoun with a clausal antecedent ('that').

One might say that this is a different discourse, and its features also include vocabulary which New Labour does not use (for example, 'capital' in the sense of 'capitalist business', 'transnationals', 'clientism'), as well (elsewhere in the same chapter) as representations of governments and capital (for example, governments 'challenging the power of international capital').

Reflect critically on the analysis

How can analyses such as this contribute to tackling problems such as the one I have focused upon? How can we connect academic papers to for instance campaigns against neo-liberalism, or more concretely to some aspects of the World Trade Organization's attempts to extend 'free trade'? Academic life is organized as a distinct network of practices, indeed as a distinct market, and critical research which stays within its confines is unlikely to have much effect. It may have some: people who spend some of their time in higher education can 'carry' ideas and approaches into other parts of their lives. But I think we have to keep rethinking how we research, how and where we publish, and how we write. With respect to how we research, what I have said above about representations of the new economy does not link directly with activists campaigning around issues like 'free trade' – why not work with activists in designing and carrying out research, tying it for instance to the campaigns of disabled people over welfare reform? How and where we publish – why not seek to publish pamphlets, articles in newspapers and magazines, popular books, or on the Web? With respect to how we write: is it possible to develop ways of writing which are accessible to many people without being superficial? (For an attempt at writing a popular book, on the language of New Labour, see Fairclough, 2000b, and see the *Daily Telegraph* of 2 March 2000 for a feature article on the same theme.)

Further reading

Chouliaraki, L. and Fairclough, N. (1999) *Discourse in Late Modernity: Rethinking Critical Discourse Analysis*. Edinburgh: Edinburgh University Press.

This book gives a more systematic account of the version of CDA presented in this chapter.

Fairclough, N. (1989) *Language and Power*. London: Longman.

This is the first version of this approach to CDA, with a broad treatment of questions of language and power.

Fairclough, N. (1992) *Discourse and Social Change*. Cambridge: Polity Press.

An earlier version of CDA, linked to research on social change.

Fairclough, N. (2000) *New Labour, New Language?* London: Routledge.

A popular introduction to analysis of political discourse, based upon the version of CDA presented in this chapter.

APPENDIX 1: BUILDING THE KNOWLEDGE DRIVEN ECONOMY

Foreword by the Prime Minister

The modern world is swept by change. New technologies emerge constantly; new markets are opening up. There are new competitors but also great new opportunities.

Our success depends on how well we exploit our most valuable assets: our knowledge, skills, and creativity. These are the key to designing high-value goods and services and advanced business practices. They are at the heart of a modern, knowledge driven economy.

This new world challenges business to be innovative and creative, to improve performance continuously, to build new alliances and ventures. But it also challenges government: to create and execute a new approach to industrial policy.

That is the purpose of this White Paper. Old-fashioned state intervention did not and cannot work. But neither does naïve reliance on markets.

The government must promote competition, stimulating enterprise, flexibility and innovation by opening markets. But we must also invest in British capabilities when companies alone cannot: in education, in science and in the creation of a culture of enterprise. And we must promote creative partnerships which help companies: to collaborate for competitive advantage; to promote a long-term vision in a world of short-term pressures; to benchmark their performance against the best in the world; and to forge alliances with other businesses and with employees. All this is the DTI's role.

We will not meet our objectives overnight. The White Paper creates a policy framework for the next ten years. We must compete more effectively in today's tough markets if we are to prosper in the markets of tomorrow.

In government, in business, in our universities and throughout society we must do much more to foster a new entrepreneurial spirit: equipping ourselves for the long term, prepared to seize opportunities, committed to constant innovation and enhanced performance. That is the route to commercial success and prosperity for all. We must put the future on Britain's side.

The Rt Hon. Tony Blair MP, Prime Minister

APPENDIX 2

Capital has always been global, moving internationally from bases in the developed industrial countries. What has changed is not that capital is more mobile . . . but that the national bases are less important as markets and production centres. In other words, the big transnational companies are not only bigger but more free standing . . . the European Union, far from offering a lead and a challenge to the nation-states of Europe, reinforces their status as clients of the transnational companies. Indeed, this clientism applies not only to companies based in Europe . . . While it is true that a national capitalism is no longer possible in a globalized economy, it is not true that national governments – and by extension the European Union – are totally lacking in powers to employ against the arbitrary actions of transnational capital. There is much that governments can do in bargaining – in making or withholding tax concessions for example . . . But such bargaining has to have an international dimension or the transnational companies can simply continue to divide and conquer . . . New Labour appears to have abandoned what remained of Labour's internationalist traditions . . . Yet the ICFTU, the European TUC and the Geneva trade groups all offer potential allies for strengthening the response of British labour to international capital. (Brown and Coates, 1996: 172–4)

7

Action and text: towards an integrated understanding of the place of text in social (inter)action, mediated discourse analysis and the problem of social action

Ron Scollon

CONTENTS

Social problems in our contemporary world are inextricably linked to texts. From television and newspaper stories about unemployment, international military interventions, or the restructuring of identities in nations undergoing sociopolitical change to public discourse campaigns promoting safe sex or discouraging drug use, social problems are couched in public and private discourses that shape the definition of these problems as well as inhibit productive social change. Our actions are frequently accompanied by language and, conversely, much of what we say is accompanied by action. Critical Discourse Analysis (CDA) is a programme of social analysis that critically analyses discourse – that is to say language in use – as a means of addressing problems of social change.

The programme of CDA is founded in the idea that the analysis of discourse opens a window on social problems because social problems are largely constituted in discourse. Nevertheless, it remains problematical to this programme to establish the links between discourses and social actions. Jones (1999, 2000) for example, has shown that there is an all but unbridgeable gap between what public media say about AIDS/ HIV or about drug use and the actions and identities of social actors engaged in non-safe sex behaviour or drug use. This gap makes these public health discourses largely irrelevant in producing effective changes in behaviour.

Mediated Discourse Analysis (MDA) shares the goals of CDA, but strategizes to reformulate the object of study from a focus on the discourses of social issues to a focus on the social actions through which social actors produce the histories and habitus of their daily lives which is the ground in which society is produced and reproduced. That is, MDA is focused on social action rather than on discourse or language. This is not to say that MDA takes no interest in discourse. On the contrary, MDA takes it as one of its central tasks to explicate and understand how the broad discourses of our social life are engaged (or not) in the moment-by-moment social actions of social actors in real time activity.

In addition to the work of Jones on public discourses of AIDS/HIV and drug use in Hong Kong and China cited above, projects in this programme of MDA have studied the ways in which university students in Hong Kong have appropriated in their day-to-day lives the multiple public discourses of sociopolitical change as political sovereignty over Hong Kong changed from Britain to China (Jones et al., 1997; R. Scollon, 1999a; R. Scollon et al., 1999a; Scollon and Scollon, 1997; Yung, 1997), the effects of the Taiwan Missile Crisis on a social structure of a group of friends who exercise together in Hong Kong (S. Scollon, 1996, 1998, 1999, 2000a,b,c,d), public discourses on unemployment in the European Union and the training of long-term unemployed youth in a training centre in Belgium (de Saint-Georges, 2000b), the writing of committee papers and the restructuring of a large charitable entertainment organization in Hong Kong at a time of sociopolitical change (Boswood, 2000), and the dialectic tensions among personal, regional, national, and European identities during the present post-Soviet, Europeanization period (de Saint-Georges and Norris, 1999).[1]

Critical discourse analysis and mediated discourse analysis

Fairclough and Wodak (1997) have put forward an eight-point programme to define critical discourse analysis as follows:

1 CDA addresses social problems.
2 Power relations are discursive.
3 Discourse constitutes society and culture.
4 Discourse does ideological work.
5 Discourse is historical.
6 The link between text and society is mediated.
7 Discourse analysis is interpretative and explanatory.
8 Discourse is a form a social action.

Perhaps no contributors to the programme of CDA would take up each and all of these points and they would, no doubt, also wish to add points not elaborated by Fairclough and Wodak. Mediated discourse analysis is no different in this. MDA takes the analysis, interpretation and explanation of social problems as its central concern – hence the focus in MDA on social action. It is this very point, however, which provides at least one partial departure from CDA. MDA takes it that power relations in society are not only discursive or just discursive but are grounded, instead, in practice. MDA, therefore, sees discursive practice as one form of social practice, not the foundational or constitutive form of practice out of which the rest of society and the resulting power relations arise. As a result, MDA also does not take Fairclough and Wodak's third point as stated. MDA takes it that discourse is among the means by which society and culture are constituted. MDA also argues that society and culture are constituted in the material products of that society as well as in its non-discursive practices. Having said that, MDA does take the points of the Fairclough/Wodak programme that discourse is ideological and historical and that discourse is a form of social action as central to its own agenda.

The programme of CDA (and therefore also of MDA) is sometimes taken as being 'critical' in a simply negative sense of the word. Kant, to my knowledge, innovated the use of the terms clustering about 'critique' in his *Critique of Pure Reason* (1781) on the basis of the more general meaning of offering severe or even injurious judgement. He said the following about his work:

> From all that has been said, there results the idea of a particular science, which may be called the *Critique of Pure Reason* . . . Such a science must not be called a doctrine, but only a *critique of pure reason*; and its use, in regard to speculation, would be only negative, not to enlarge the bounds of, but to purify, our reason, and to shield it against error – which is not little gain. (p. 20, emphasis in original)

In the 'Preface to the Second Edition, 1787' Kant comments on the accusation that his criticism is negative as follows:

> To deny the positive advantage of the service which this criticism renders us would be as absurd as to maintain that the system of police is productive of no positive benefit, since its main business is to prevent the violence which citizen has to apprehend from citizen, that so each may pursue his vocation in peace and security. (p. 9)

Further on in that preface he refers to his *Critique of Pure Reason* as a 'critical science':

> This critical science is not opposed to the *dogmatic procedure* of reason in pure cognition; for pure cognition must always be dogmatic, that is, must rest on strict demonstration from sure principles *a priori* – but to *dogmatism*, that is, to the presumption that it is possible to make any progress with a pure cognition, derived from (philosophical) conceptions, according to the principles which reason has long been in the habit of employing – without first inquiring in what way and by what right reason has come into the possession of these principles. Dogmatism is thus the dogmatic procedure of pure reason *without previous criticism of its own powers*, and in opposing this procedure, we must not be supposed to lend any countenance to that loquacious shallowness which arrogates to itself the name of popularity, nor yet to scepticism, which make short work with the whole science of metaphysics. On the contrary, our criticism is the necessary preparation for a thoroughly scientific system of metaphysics. (p. 11, emphasis in original)

That is, the philosophical/analytical words 'critique' and the adjectival form 'critical' are Kant's (as well as the noun 'criticism'). They are characterized by him as 'negative' in the sense that they clear away the debris of dogmatism through an a priori examination of the principles by which reason will be understood to operate. That is, rational process is understood as limited in that it cannot understand its own foundations without prior critique of those limits. This, of course, is the foundation of Enlightenment thinking and, perhaps, all philosophy and science since Kant.

This first critique was followed, of course, by Kant's *Critique of Practical Reason* (1788) and then his *Critique of Judgement* (1790). In the introduction to the latter he notes, 'With this, then, I bring my entire critical undertaking to a close' (p. 462).

Kant's usage of these terms, 'critique', 'negative', 'criticism', and 'critical' within what is the fundamental philosophical work of the modern period supports and justifies our continued use when discussing theoretical questions of discourse analysis, even though all of these have continued in their more popular and non-philosophically negative senses of providing severe or injurious judgements.

MDA, in the version I put forward shares with CDA, as it does with Kant many years earlier, this understanding of the critical enterprise. MDA seeks not only to examine the ideological positioning within the discourses of abusive power in contemporary society – though it has a central interest in that. MDA seeks to examine the limits of its own theory and method. In what follows, I will try to put forward the methodology we have used in first identifying the significance of social actions, not only for the analyst but for the participants in those social actions, and then, briefly, outline how we use a necessarily broad and interdisciplinary approach to the study of the operations of discourse within those social actions.

Neo-capitalism, neo-liberalism and a cup of coffee: a mediated action

As a small contribution to the programme of CDA and to illustrate the concepts I will use, here in this chapter I will argue that we can begin to shed light on the dialectic between the broad contemporary neo-liberal, neo-capitalist discourses (Fairclough, 2000b) and day-to-day social action in the study of something as mundane and apparently irrelevant as having a cup of coffee in a coffee shop. Through this illustrative example, which is admittedly only sketched out here, I hope to show that MDA offers a programme for capturing the broad sociopolitical issues of our time in the simple daily actions of our lives.

Social actions are called mediated actions within MDA to highlight the idea that all social actions are mediated by cultural tools or mediational means. The most salient and perhaps most common of these mediational means is language, or to use the term we prefer, discourse. What this means for MDA in relationship to Critical Discourse Analysis (CDA) is that language (or discourse) is not the central focus of MDA, but rather it is social action which is the focus, whether or not language (or discourse) is involved in the action. To put this another way, discourse in MDA is just one of the mediational means by which social action may be taken; it is never considered the central or defining aspect of a MDA project.

Many theories of language and of discourse start out with a focus on 'social action' such as speech act theory, pragmatics, interactional sociolinguistics, and CDA but then somehow in practice tend to become focused only on text. Other aspects of social action and other mediational means than language and discourse are backgrounded as 'context'. Unfortunately, this can lead to a distorted understanding of the relationship between discourse and social action. This may well be a problem produced by the technology of representation we most commonly use in reporting our analyses, the printed text. For example, if I

FIGURE 7.1

try to make this same point with a cartoon (Figure 7.1) we might see (and think) differently about the issues.

The cartoon in Figure 7.1 is another way of representing the statement, 'Many theories start out with "social action", but then somehow in practice tend to become focused only on text'. In this cartoon, as poorly drawn as it is, we see much more than the statement. Here the statement is polarized into two distinct voices, one of which is suggested as more aggressive than the other. We see this in the bold typeface in the speech balloon of the figure on the left, in the squared speech balloon, and in the physical stance taken in making the statement. The weaker and some-what defensive figure on the right is positioned as making an adversative statement through the adversative conjunction 'but', while at the same time the posture, the weaker typeface, and the oval speech balloon undermine the strength of this confrontation.

I do not wish to suggest that this cartoon is an analogy with any theoretical positions. I only want to suggest that what we see in the cartoon is very different from what we see in lines of text alone. In what I will write below in this chapter, I will use lines of text, not cartoons, to develop my argument. What I would like to keep in mind, however, is that the focus of MDA is on social action, even when we must use text as the means of illustrating this action, and that these representations in text will always under-represent the meanings present in the actions.

There is a further reason why MDA does not take discourse and language as its central focus. In this we[2] follow Kant's 'critiques' (*Critique of Pure Reason, Critique of Practical Reason,* and *Critique of Judgement*) as well as the thinking of Nishida (1958), Bateson (1972) and Bourdieu (1977, 1990) in believing that social action is based in practice (habitus, will, judgement) not in rational, logical, or objective analysis. That is to say, MDA takes the position that whatever it is that people say in and about their social actions, these discourses are not likely ever to grasp the bases in habitus for these actions which are largely outside the awareness of social actors.

This different focus makes the relationship between MDA and CDA problematical. MDA begins with the social action and only takes up the analysis of language (discourse, texts) when those are understood to be significant mediational means for the mediated actions under analysis. The a priori base of MDA, then, is action, not text (or language or discourse). Therefore, the methodological problem to be solved for MDA is not how to accomplish an analysis of any text – although that is often a necessary aspect of a MDA – but how to accomplish an analysis of a social – mediated – action. In this sense, MDA is not a branch or aspect of CDA, because the purpose is not the critical analysis of discourse or text. In another sense, however, because MDA often must incorporate a critical analysis of discourse as that discourse is used in undertaking social action, MDA is closely linked in most cases to CDA. The difference is a difference in focus.

Mediated discourse analysis is not called mediated action analysis (Wertsch, 1991, 1998), however, because there remains a central interest in discourse. MDA takes the position that while discourse cannot be directly and uniquely linked to social practice or social action and social action does not have a unique or fixed discursive manifestation, nevertheless, the vast majority of social actions within which we have a critical interest do involve discourse in an important way (Chouliaraki and Fairclough, 1999; Fairclough and Wodak, 1997; R. Scollon, 2000a, c). The central problem of MDA is to examine and to theoretically elucidate the often indirect and always complex linkages between discourse and action. We neither assume that social action can be 'read off' the discourses which may accompany it, nor that any social action will give direct rise to a predictable discourse. That is, MDA takes the position that we cannot take a transcript of a conversation, a newspaper article, an advertisement or a commercial and draw any obvious or direct 'reading' of the social actions which have led to its production on the one hand nor can we make any direct assumptions about how they will be 'read' by any subsequent social action in taking any particular social action.

MDA is organized about six central concepts:

1 mediated action;
2 site of engagement;

3   mediational means;
4   practice and mediational means;
5   nexus of practice;
6   community of practice.

I will use the mundane example which we could call 'having a cup of coffee' – in the sense of going to a café for a conversation with a friend – to illustrate these concepts.

Mediated action

As I have noted above, the unit of analysis of MDA is not the discourse or text or genre, but the mediated action. The central concern is upon social actors as they are acting. The term 'mediated action' highlights the unresolvable dialectic between action and the mediational means (see below) by which actions are accomplished (Wertsch, 1991, 1998).[3] In the narrowest sense, having a cup of coffee is a sequence of mediated actions – queuing, ordering, paying, picking up the coffee, selecting a table, sitting, chatting, collecting one's things when leaving, and the rest. Each of these mediated actions constructs a higher level mediated action 'having a cup of coffee'.

1   MEDIATED ACTION

A mediated action is defined as a social action taken with or through a mediational means (cultural tool). All social actions are construed as mediated actions, it being definitional that 'social' means socially mediated. The principal mediational means (or cultural tool) of interest is language or discourse, but the concept includes all objects in the material world including other social actors. Within MDA there is no action (agency) without some mediational means (that is, the semiotic/material means of communicating the action) and there is no mediational means without a social actor (agency).

Site of engagement

The concept of the 'site of engagement' (R. Scollon, 1997, 1998b, 1999b) is intended to capture the real-time nature of the mediated action. A mediated action is not a class of actions but rather the moment in real time when multiple social practices intersect to form a unique moment in history that is identified by participants as a social action.[4] The site of engagement is constructed out of linkages among the practices of queuing, service encounter, discursive exchanges, handing of objects such as coins, ordering in one place and picking up in another place and the like (see Figure 7.2).

2 SITE OF ENGAGEMENT

A site of engagement is defined as the convergence of social practices in a moment in real time which opens a window for a mediated action to occur. While the concept of the mediated action focuses upon the unresolvable dialectic between agency and mediational means, the concept of the site of engagement focuses upon the social practices which enable the moment of the mediated action. A site of engagement may be momentary – reading the exit sign from a fast trunk road in a second or so – or somewhat extended as in a conversation with a friend, viewing a film or theatre production, or reading a novel on a bus ride.

FIGURE 7.2   The site of engagement – multiple practices intersecting in real time

Mediational means

In MDA, a mediated action is understood to be carried out through the use of a variety of mediational means (or cultural tools) which include both semiotic or psychological tools such as language as well as material tools such as word processors, tables and chairs, and even in some cases other persons (Randolph, 2000). These mediational means are always multiple in any particular action and carry with them historical affordances and constraints. That is, the use of a particular mediational means (English, for example) will support or even foster certain actions and constrain others. Mediational means are also understood to be inherently polyvocal, intertextual, and interdiscursive. Among the mediational means used in mediated actions are a large variety of texts, both spoken and written. It should be clear that while texts play an important role in MDA as mediational means which are sometimes employed in social action, texts are not privileged as the central focus of analysis.[5] The mediational means involved in having a cup of coffee range from the language used in ordering and conversing to the money, the cash register, the cups and coffee, the logos and other texts printed on the coffee cup, the menus behind the cash register, and the tables which provide the means of arranging to have a conversation.

3 MEDIATIONAL MEANS

A mediational means (a term in either the singular or plural) is defined as the semiotic means through which a mediated action, that is any social action, is carried out (communicated). In this definition 'semiotic' is intended to convey not just abstract or cognitive systems of representation such as languages or systems of visual representation, but also any and all material objects in the world which are appropriated for the purposes of taking a social action. This would include, for example, the layout and design of the room as well as the grammatical structure of any utterances made by the social actors. In MDA, mediational means are construed as the carriers of social, cultural, and historical formations.

Practice and mediational means

A mediated action occurs as the intersection of social practices and mediational means which in themselves reproduce social groups, histories, and identities. From the point of view of MDA a mediated action is only interpretable within practices. Practices are conceived within MDA as narrowly defined, concrete, and specific – handing an object, greeting, paying for an item.

4 PRACTICE

Practice is defined as a count noun – practices – within MDA. A practice is a historical accumulation within the habitus/historical body of the social actor of mediated actions taken over his or her life (experience) and which are recognizable to other social actors as 'the same' social action. A practice predates the social actor; that is, we mostly learn the practices of our society, but rarely initiate them. A practice, because it is an accumulation of mediated actions, carries with it a constellation of appropriated mediational means. Examples are 'handing' (of an object from one person to another), 'queuing' (standing in an order line while waiting), 'the question/answer adjacency sequence' (recognizing that a question has been asked and an answer is required), 'greeting' (answering 'How are you?' with 'I'm fine'), 'deductive topic ordering' (saying your main point first), 'paying a bus fare' (using a coin, bill, token, fare ticket, or handing money to the driver). The social world, as construed by MDA, consists of myriads of practices.

The actions of queuing and ordering, for instance, reproduce a social structure that is replicated not just in having a cup of coffee, but also in buying theatre tickets or in cashing a cheque in the bank. A mediational means is an object in the world as it has been appropriated within a practice. That is, it is not just the coffee cup as material object, but also my practice–history–habitus with a paper coffee cup that is the mediational means as Figure 7.3 suggests.

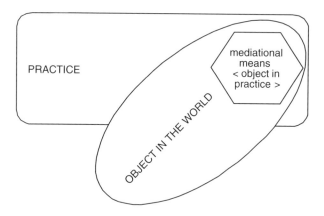

FIGURE 7.3 Practice and mediational means

Nexus of practice

As I have just noted, MDA takes a narrow view of social practice as composed of social practices (count nouns, not a mass noun). When these practices are linked to other practices (both discursive ones and non-discursive ones) MDA uses the term 'nexus of practice' for the linked practices which social actors recognize in the actions of others (Gee, 1999; Gee et al., 1996). That is, the cashier can read from my actions whether or not I am within a nexus of practice of regular customers. The concept of the nexus of practice should not be taken as simply an alternative to the term 'community of practice' (Lave and Wenger, 1991; Wenger, 1998; R. Scollon, 1998b, 1999b) but is defined within MDA at a 'lower' level of social organization in being rather loosely structured. Any linkage of practices that is recognized by members of a social group as a repeatable set of linkages might be a nexus of practice; we would reserve the term 'community of practice' for the analysis of relatively fixed and bounded social groups. Whenever there are a number of people who share practices and the linkages among them, that is, to the extent that there is a *we* who know how to have a cup of coffee, how to catch a bus, or how to send an email message, there is a nexus of practice. A nexus of practice is any group who can and do engage in some action.

5 NEXUS OF PRACTICE

A nexus of practice is defined as the intersection or linkage of multiple practices such that some group comes to recognize 'the same' set of actions. Nexus of practice is in this sense a recognizable grouping of a set of mediated actions. Since mediated actions are an undissolvable dialectic of agent and mediational means, a nexus of practice is also at some minimal level a group of social actors and an archive of mediational means. 'Having coffee in Starbucks' might be analysed as a nexus of practice consisting of the mediated actions of buying coffee and having a conversation. To this extent the concept of the nexus of practice simultaneously signifies a genre of activity and the group of people who engage in that activity.

Community of practice

A nexus of practice in many cases begins to be more explicitly recognized as a group. MDA prefers to use 'community of practice' when explicit membership in a group becomes the focus of attention. Wertsch (forthcoming) has used the distinction between an 'implicit' community and an 'imagined' community to capture this distinction. While I might

be quite familiar to the waiters and even to other customers in a particular café, it would remain a nexus of practice to the extent this remained
an implicit identification. On the other hand, if the café began offering
specials to regular customers, set up a separate faster service queue for
regulars, or in any other way began to produce the nexus of practice as a
social group which is identified both to other members and to those
outside the group, we would refer to this process in general as technologization (because the linkages and so forth are being made regular
enough that they can in themselves be recognized and used as mediational means in taking other actions) and the resulting groupness as a
community of practice. If I regularly visit More Uncommon Grounds, the
student-owned and run café at my university, I might be recognized
within a nexus of practice. If I begin to say, 'I'm an "Uncommon
Grounds" person', I am working towards producing a community of
practice.

6 COMMUNITY OF PRACTICE

A community of practice is defined as a group of people who regularly
interact with each other towards some common purpose or goal. The term
has been much used, perhaps overused, in management, 'virtual
community' development on the Internet, family medicine, industrial
marketing, community psychiatry, dispute resolution, and in religious or
quasi-religious groups. Its oldest versions appear to be within New Age
Buddhist communities in North America and elsewhere. In MDA we
reserve the use of community of practice to these cases in which some
nexus of practice somewhat self-consciously produces itself as such a
community. This process we refer to as the technologization of a nexus of
practice.

Figure 7.4 below captures this difference by indicating that the lines of
practice extend indefinitely outward to other actions and other nexus of
practice though for some purposes, a grouping of these practices may be
defined by members as constituting a community of practice.

Objectives and strategies of the method

The methodological problem of MDA is that of all ethnography. How
does the researcher know what is significant to focus upon in the first
place since the focus is broadly upon social action and not specific or

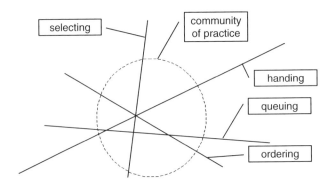

FIGURE 7.4   *Nexus of practice and community of practice*

concrete texts, and once the significance of particular actions is determined, how can the researcher sharpen the focus to take into account the main elements of a social action without wresting it from the historical, sociocultural world of real-time social activity? The objective of method in MDA is to provide a set of heuristics by which the researcher can narrow the scope of what must be analysed to achieve an understanding of mediated actions even knowing that mediated actions occur in real time, are unique and unrepeatable and therefore must be 'caught' in action to be analysed. In a real sense it is a matter of structuring the research activities to be in the right place at the right time.

It must be stressed that MDA makes no a priori assumptions about what kinds of texts or discourses will ultimately be relevant to the analysis. Nor does MDA make any a priori assumptions about what social actions will emerge from these initial strategies as the significant ones for analysis. What may seem extremely important or interesting to the analyst may well turn out to be of no significance to the social actors involved in the actual life and world of the research problem. It is the purpose of what follows to show how we can systematically begin to determine what actions are significant and what texts or discourses are relevant from the point of view of the social actors we are analysing.

Three major principles are followed in MDA methodology to establish the significance of the sites of engagement and mediated actions under study. These are triangulation among different types of data, participants' definition of significance, and issue-based analysis.

Triangulation in MDA is achieved, following Ruesch and Bateson (1968 [1951]) and elaborated also in S. Scollon (1995), and Scollon and Scollon (forthcoming), by seeking to construct four main types of data:

1   members' generalizations;
2   neutral ('objective') observations;

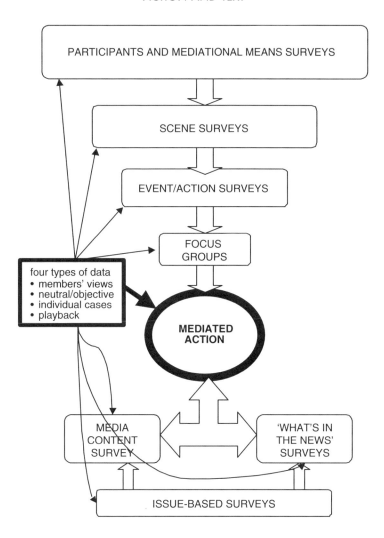

FIGURE 7.5   *Methodology for identifying the significant mediated action*

3   individual member's experience;
4   observer's interactions with members.

These four types of data are sought for all of the specific elements of the method as indicated in Figure 7.5 which will be explicated in what follows.

Members' generalizations are those statements and claims members of the group under study will make about their own actions, ideologies and motives ('We usually have coffee at Starbucks', or 'We tip in the university café because we're students and all the waiting staff there are also students'). Members' generalizations can be found in many places. A major and important source are media and consumer products intended for consumption by a particular group. A television sitcom which makes reference to contemporary public discourse, to common idioms, and to current events makes the indirect generalization that 'this is our contemporary world as we (and you) see it'. Health warnings on products reflect the generalization within the society that produces them that 'we' are concerned with the health of consumers in the use of consumer products. Of course, members' generalizations are virtually always stereotypical and based on ideology and should never be taken as representing the 'truth' of that society or social group. Opinion surveys are a particularly common way of eliciting members' generalizations.

Neutral ('objective') observations are those observations made by the researcher for which some level of reliability (multiple observations would produce the same 'facts') and validity (the observations represent an objective 'truth') are claimed ('Professor Scollon bought coffee at More Uncommon Grounds at about 9:50 on Mondays and Wednesdays during the Spring semester'). MDA recognizes the constructed and ideological nature of all observations, but nevertheless also recognizes that data which is photographed, audio- or video recorded, or otherwise instrumentally subjected to recording procedures can serve as a check on the overgeneralizations of members as well as on the subjectivity of the researcher as participant-observer. In themselves, these data can be problematical, but in the contrast or dialectic between such 'neutral' or 'objective' data on the one hand and the other types of more subjective data on the other can be seen points of divergence and contradiction for further analysis.

An individual member's experience is often claimed to depart from that of the group ('We all go to Starbucks, but I like to go to small independent cafés'). It is not at all unusual for a participant in a research project to say, 'We usually do X, but even though I am a member of this group, I usually do Y'. That is, MDA believes that there is much to be learnt in the self-claimed contradictions of members. Individual members' experiences often retain a richness of concrete detail that undercuts excessive stereotyping and generalization because these experiences include concrete historical detail about the habitus of the individual. Interviews and life histories are the fullest source of such data.

An observer's interactions with members are part and parcel of the methodology of participant observation, of course. But here we want to go beyond just the common give and take of fieldwork. To the greatest extent possible, we want to bring our own analyses back to participants to get their reactions and interpretations. A conversational version of this aspect of triangulation would be to say, 'You said that you always go to Starbucks, but that you yourself prefer small independent cafés; I've observed you actually going to the Borders coffee shop quite often.

Isn't that a rather large, international company?' The gist is to uncover divergences and contradictions between one's own analysis of the mediated actions one is studying and those of participants.

Obviously, it will be difficult in any particular study to develop data of all four types to the fullest extent. Good triangulation, however, requires that no study would rely on just one or two of these types of data for its interpretation. Contradictions among these multiple types of data should be searched for and then accounted for in the final interpretation.

Participants' definition in MDA is achieved through a sequence of studies, each somewhat independent of each other, which focus on separate aspects of the situation under study. It should be obvious that the triangulation I have just discussed is carried out through the studies of the participants' definitions and through the issue-based studies, not independently. Here the central question is this: 'How do participants themselves define the key actions and within what scenes do these actions take place and with what mediational means?'

Normally we have tried to arrive at participants' definitions by including four studies:

1   participants and mediational means surveys;
2   scene surveys;
3   event/action surveys;
4   focus groups.

Participants and mediational means surveys are designed first to identify the main participants in the research and then to identify the primary mediational means which will be examined. Note that it is the mediational means we are seeking to identify, not the contents of specific media products. Often the participants will be defined within the definition of the research problem. For example, if one wants to know how unemployment is affecting urban youth, the participants are already broadly specified. In that case, one's first survey would be to find out what are the broad public and media discourses to which urban youth are responding. I will clarify below in writing about issue-based analysis that this part of the task is to identify not all of the places where this issue is being discussed, but those specific media to which one's participants are paying attention. We found in our Hong Kong research in a survey of university youth (Jones et al., 1997; Scollon and Yung, 1996; R. Scollon et al., 1999a; R. Scollon et al., 1999b), for example, that even though there were at that time over 50 daily newspapers published in Hong Kong, only three of these were read at all commonly by the participants in our study. More important than these newspapers, however, were two weekly magazines, and more important than these was a nightly infotainment television programme. Such a study, then, tells one that whatever analysis one might develop of one of the leading political newspapers, this analysis is likely to be quite irrelevant to the population one is studying.

On the other hand, close attention to the nightly infotainment programme would be essential.

7 A NOTE ON SURVEYS

A wide variety of 'surveys' may be used as long as care is taken to match the survey to the purpose. In trying to establish 'who reads what?', for example, as long as the population is clearly and accurately sampled rather open-ended questions may be asked. The concern here is not with close-grained analysis of the meaning of 'read' in answering these questions as the goal is simply to make a list of popular magazines or newspapers. Your only concern is to narrow the field and to eliminate relatively insignificant media sources. On the other hand, if you are trying to analyse ideological positions towards those sources, the questions must be very tightly framed with cross-checking questions as follow-up, and even so, further checking must be done through other means such as interviews and participant observation.

We used several techniques to conduct these surveys (Yung, 1996, 1997; R. Scollon, 1998a). Beginning with a broad and relatively loose survey of large groups of the population will narrow down the range. We asked such questions as: 'What media do you regularly read, listen to, or see?' We followed this with diary/journal studies of a subset of this population. Participants were asked to write down over the period of a week all of the media they used, times of day, and the places along with who was present at the same time. We then conducted focus groups going both through the survey results and through examples of the media they had selected to see in detail how they spoke of the specific examples. The net result of such surveys is to have a fairly clear idea of how the participants select among media in addition to being a good beginning on knowing what issues are of interest to them.

Scene surveys are designed to narrow down the scope of the research to a few highly salient places or scenes, in which the actions we are interested in are taking place – talking about 'the news', buying brand name consumer goods, using new media technology and the like. It is impossible to follow participants everywhere in their daily lives and so it is essential to develop a motivated focus on just a few of the most common or most important places where social actions of interest are taking place. We have found, for example, that our university students in Hong Kong spend the vast bulk of their time in one of just four places:

- at the university in classes or working on assignments;
- at home in crowded family flats;

- on public transport;
- in small fast-food restaurants (noodle shops).

We were able to find this out by a system of random paging of a representative group of university students over the period of a week which established the four key scenes and then through focus groups verifying the salience of these scenes. Once the four scenes were established, participant-observation could focus on just these four scenes. In fact, one can often narrow the focus even further. If the participant media survey has identified a particular television programme as the central media source of interest, then one might be able to focus more carefully on just those scenes where students are watching this programme – principally at home. On the other hand, if the action of interest is face-to-face peer interaction, the university and small fast-food restaurants would be the preferred scenes for research. In any event, once the pivotal scenes are identified, we have studied them through the conventional ethnography of communication research strategies (Saville-Troike, 1989; Scollon and Scollon, forthcoming).

8 SCENE AND ACTION SURVEYS

The word 'survey' can cover a wide range of investigative techniques. Here we mean not a questionnaire survey but a pager survey combined with the subjects making notations of the times of the calls along with their activities at that time. We recommend in each particular case that, first, the researcher should determine the type of information needed, and then consult any of the many sources on survey techniques. Within MDA our only concern is to be certain that the type of survey taken matches the purposes of the survey as much time can be wasted in excessive rigour on the one hand or carelessness on the other.

Event/action surveys are designed to identify the specific social actions taking place within the scenes we have identified which are of relevance to the study of mediated action. In this sense, the event/action surveys are ethnographically continuous with the scene surveys, though now the focus is internal to the scene, not upon identifying the key scenes. At this stage, we are not yet ready to do a close study of the practices and mediational means but simply to identify the main actions taking place within a particular scene. If, for example, we have decided that our interest is in neo-capitalism, and we want to address this through the study of the consumer consumption of mass-marketed products; and if within that, we want to study having a cup of coffee at an international chain such as Starbucks, we would then position ourselves ethnographically to isolate the particular actions I have noted above – entering, queuing, ordering, receiving the order, selecting a place to sit and so forth.

Focus groups are often employed at this stage of the analysis, though the use of the term 'focus group' is, perhaps, not entirely correct (Jones et al., 1997; Yung, 2000). The intent of such groups in this case is not to get user reactions to specific consumer products or public issues as it often is in marketing or opinion research. The purpose of such groups at this stage is twofold. Firstly, the researcher wants to know to what extent the identification of specific scenes, media, and actions have reliability and validity for members of the group under study, and secondly the researcher wants to understand how important or salient the categories which have been identified are for the population being studied.

To give an example from our Hong Kong research, we were studying the change of political sovereignty from Britain to China which occurred in July 1997 (R. Scollon, 1997). We had identified a wide variety of semiotic symbols of this political change, from label buttons which would play the Chinese national anthem to new designs for coins and post boxes which would substitute new images for those of the Queen of England. In focus groups with students we discovered, however, that among the most salient objects (and its images) was the newly constructed Tsing Yi bridge. This bridge had nothing directly to do with the political change (in our view) and we had rated flags, coin images, and other such more overtly political symbols much above it in salience. Focus groups at this stage are useful in setting priorities for the research focus on mediated actions which follows and is the centre of the research agenda.

9 FOCUS GROUPS

Care should be taken in using focus groups. The literature on social interaction shows that almost every variable can change not only the dynamics but also the topics, attitudes, and conclusions reached by the participants in a focus group. We found in our 'focus groups', for example, that many common assumptions made in the North American and European focus group literature do not apply to equivalent groups in Hong Kong and China. For example, Yung (2000) has noted that in the Western literature it is assumed that:

1   Strangers who are put together in the same situation will want to talk to each other.

2 If people are seated around a common centre such as at a round table, they will more easily engage each other in conversation.

3 People who are seated around a table will principally talk to each other as a single group, rather than converse with people beside them.

The Hong Kong participants in our 'focus groups' operated on the basis of the following assumptions:

1 Strangers will not talk to each other. Therefore, a focus group should always consist of people who know each other.

2 People around a common centre will either avoid a central conversation or that central conversation will be dominated by traditional patterns of deference to age and authority. Therefore, the best focus group would avoid such seating arrangements.

MDA takes the position that each 'technology' of research must itself be examined as potentially embedding the beliefs and ideologies of the analysts and therefore prejudicing the analysis towards the analysts' preconceptions.

Of course I have outlined these four types of studies as a chronological sequence but, in practice, much of this work of achieving a participants' definition of the research objects (practices, actions, and mediational means) may be conducted simultaneously. One type of 'focus group' we conducted in the Hong Kong studies, for example, was to ask a group of student research assistants to conduct whatever group studies they felt would be useful in discovering how other students viewed the political change in Hong Kong. In this we learnt not only from the participants in the focus groups, but we also learnt from our research assistants how they saw the issue when it was seen within a rather different task structure. The central question driving this aspect of the methodology is: how do participants themselves define the key social actions? This, of course, includes a definition of the scenes in which these actions take place and the mediational means.

Issue-based analysis in MDA begins in the broad public discourses within which the research takes place. Like CDA, MDA has a central concern with the social issues of contemporary life. Much of the work of MDA in this respect is little different from work in CDA. Nevertheless, MDA takes the position that it is a methodological problem to identify the central issues of concern to the participants in the study and not to simply presuppose them. That is to say, MDA takes it that whatever the importance an issue might have on a broad social scale, it remains to be made clear how this issue is being taken up by some identified members of society.

There are two forms of survey used in identifying the significant social issues being addressed, as indicated earlier in Figure 7.5:

1   media content surveys and
2   'What's in the news?' surveys.

In our Hong Kong research, for example, we were concerned to see if we could explicate the link between broad social issues and the day-to-day talk and writing of university students. To do this we collected a large sample of the public media discourses over a two-week period. While we did not achieve total collection, we did collect all of the newspapers and magazines (as identified in our earlier participant and media surveys), all of the main news bulletins in radio and television versions, and a full sampling of television infotainment broadcasts for a period of two weeks.

Simultaneously, we conducted 'What's in the news?' surveys of four populations: our City University students, university students from other universities in Hong Kong, City University non-students, and non-City University non-students. These surveys conducted daily over the two weeks asked, roughly, what were the main events currently happening and how those surveyed had come to know about them.

These surveys clarified two main points. Firstly our students (as well as other university students) learnt of the main news events through word of mouth and only went to news sources after 'knowing' the story. The sources they used were television first, and then later, magazines and then newspapers. The television programmes of greatest salience for them were not the main news bulletins but the infotainment programmes. In other words, our students primarily knew what was happening from talking to others and from watching infotainment shows. Secondly, the big story of that two-week period – the so-called 'Taiwan missile crisis' in which the mainland government tested missiles in the waters between the Chinese mainland and Taiwan just before the Taiwan election – was sidelined for many days by two stories of the tragic killing of children, one in Dunblane, Scotland, the other in Fanling, Hong Kong.

These surveys of issues showed us that an analysis of the Taiwan missile crisis in the texts of the elite newspapers or even the populist newspapers would remain at a great distance from any actions undertaken by City University students. On the whole they had no direct contact with these texts of public discourse. Any link between the stories of the missile crisis and student talk or writing would be highly indirect, recontextualized and inferential. Thus we learnt that if our interest is in coming to understand how our university students in Hong Kong appropriate such texts in their own social actions, we need not only an analysis of the texts of public discourse (though we do need that), and not only an analysis of the social actions of the students (our central focus), but also an analysis of the indirect and complex linkages of texts of public discourse, the scripts and images of infotainment shows, and processes of word-of-mouth transmission of ideas.

Mediated action in sites of engagement: the central focus

All of the methodological work to this point is in a sense preliminary, though absolutely necessary, in that it is designed to locate and to establish the significance of the mediated actions in particular sites of engagement which are the focus of research in MDA. In this respect, my interest in studying having a cup of coffee is not simply because it is a whimsical, common event that the reader is likely to be able to grasp in some detail through his or her own experience. The existence of national and international chains of cafés and bookshops or, often as not, cafés/bookshops is centrally located in the late capitalist/neo-capitalist developments of our period of history. An MDA analysis would locate the apparently casual action of having a cup of coffee with a friend within this economic, social and political restructuring of global society. It would argue that, at least in North America, to have coffee in one of the relatively new 'designer' cafés is to participate in, and to that extent at least, to legitimate the worldwide production of neo-capitalist business options. One does not have coffee in a particular place on Wisconsin Avenue in Washington, DC without in some way supporting the presence of a franchised shop in Oxford Street, London or in Xidan District, Beijing. If we ask how the neo-capitalist enterprise supports, legitimates, and extends itself, then the MDA answer would be that in part it does so when I have a cup of coffee with a friend at Starbucks.

I hope that in what I have written up to this point I will have made it clear how one might proceed from such broad social issues as the Taiwan missile crisis or the spread of neo-capitalist, globalist 'choice' to a focus on specific actions within concrete scenes. Having a cup of coffee has emerged from such a study as a scene within which such broad social discourses are engaged in a common day-to-day action. We might equally have taken for our focus purchasing groceries at an international chain supermarket or using a word processor/email software package to send a message to other scholars in protest at the spread of neo-capitalism around the world. The MDA question to which we now will turn is: how do we study an actual social action in a specific, real-time instance?

Now I will organize the analysis of a specific action 'having a cup of coffee' around a set of heuristic questions which might be asked within any site of engagement, taking up each of the central concepts of MDA in turn. It will be understood, I hope, that this set of questions is merely suggestive of the sort of analysis that must be done. In particular cases, certain questions would be more central than others.

Action

Once having a cup of coffee and conversation with a friend has been identified as the mediated action in which we are interested, the following questions should be asked:

1   What is the action?
2   What chain or chains of mediated actions are relevant?
3   What is the 'funnel of commitment'?
4   What narrative and anticipatory discourses provide a metadiscursive or reflective structure?

What is the action?   As I have suggested above, having a cup of coffee could be viewed at multiple levels simultaneously (Lemke, 1999). At one level it is constituted by a chain of mediated actions. We enter the café, we queue, we order, we pay, we wait for the coffee to be delivered, we select a place to sit, we sit and chat, we return our cups when we have finished, and we leave the café. Each of these is constituted by a lower level of actions. 'Entering' is constituted in certain practices of approaching a door, pulling it open with one or the other hand, going first or allowing the other to go first, and so forth. Paying is constituted in taking out money, counting out a certain amount, handing money to a cashier, receiving change. Each of the 'actions' at one level is constituted by lower level actions and in turn constitutes or at least is constrained by (Lemke, 1999) actions at a higher level.

For example, we could equally have said there were just two actions here – getting the coffee and sitting for a chat. Above that we have said we are 'having a cup of coffee' which itself is part of a chain of actions at that level such as making an invitation to have coffee and going for coffee. The level above that could be said to be the action of maintaining a friendship, but also the action of supporting and legitimating the global neo-capitalist ideology of choice, as I have suggested above and as roughly plotted below (see Figure 7.6).

The point I wish to make here is that we will never discover simply one action upon which to focus, but we must necessarily conceive of any mediated action as one which is constituted by lower level actions and which, in turn, constitutes higher level actions. The micro level action of handing several coins to a cashier simultaneously constructs the actions of handing, of paying, of having a cup of coffee, of consumer choice, of sociopolitical support for a global economic system and, of course, many other actions as viewed in relation to other research questions. In a MDA the guiding question is not 'What is the action here?' The guiding question is, 'How is this action (at its multiple levels) linked to the broad

getting a cup of coffee							
selecting a consumer product				buying a cup of coffee			
entering a café				ordering		paying	
opening a door	allowing someone to pass	locating a queue	queuing	selecting from a menu	placing an order	handling money	handing money

FIGURE 7.6 *Getting a cup of coffee*

social issues with which we are concerned?' Put in another way, 'How does this action participate in, legitimate, challenge, or contest higher and lower level actions by which it is constituted and which in itself it participates in constituting?'

From this point of view, within MDA a social action is meaningful – it makes sense – as a constituent action of higher level action and at the same time makes sense of lower level actions. Handing coins to another person makes sense as an action within the higher level action of paying for a cup of coffee. This in turn makes sense of taking coins out of my pocket at that time. The semiosis or sense making aspect of social action is seen here as paradigmatically located in these levels of social action. Here, then, the primary methodological concern is to identify the levels at which the action upon which we are focusing is operating for the participants and within our analysis.

What is the action?

Members' generalization – that is, strategies for discovering what members say is the action are:

- Find member's vocabulary: 'No, I haven't paid yet' shows that 'paying' is a member's category of a particular kind of action.
- Use this in further elicitation: 'When you paid, did you use coins or notes?' or 'Where do you pay?'
- Look for signs, displays, promotional materials.
- Interview, listening for categorical or classificatory statements: 'Why do you come to this shop?' 'I like the way you order here.' 'Ordering' is a potential action.
- Make audio tape recordings wherever possible of interviews, casual conversations.

Neutral observations – that is, strategies for making objective observations:

- Spend time in cafés.
- Make field notes, particularly focusing on divergences from members' generalizations.

- Discuss your field notes with others to get members' generalizations and individual members' experiences. 'I've been studying cafés and found X.' 'Really, I always thought Y.'
- Take photographs or videos. Often you can take pictures of friends with what you want as the 'background'. That is, a company might not want you to photograph their floor plan directly but would be very happy for you to celebrate a birthday with a friend, take some photos of that, and incidentally get the floor plan.

Individual member's experience:

- Talk about your fieldwork project to everyone you know (formal or informal interviews).
- Interview key social actors – customers, waiters, former employees.

Observer's interactions with members:

- Discuss your analysis (in progress) with members.
- Show your photographs to members.
- Play back audio tapes in interviews and focus groups.

What chain or chains of mediated actions are relevant? An action such as paying for coffee makes sense paradigmatically within a hierarchy of actions as I have just mentioned. An action must also make sense syntagmatically as part of a sequence or chain of mediated actions. In the particular café I have in mind, the sequence of actions is: order – pay – pick up order. In another shop (which, incidentally is a franchise of the same company) the chain of actions is: order – pick up order – pay. The methodological question to be asked here, then, is: 'What is the chain or what are the chains of mediated actions within which the action takes place?' This is normally a straightforward methodological issue which is quite amenable to observation but should not be ignored. Ascriptions of identity, or of competence or incompetence are often constructed around different chains of mediated actions. One may be entirely competent and practised in queuing, in ordering, in paying and the rest, but trying to do them in an order that is not the one expected may suggest incompetence or non-membership – non-recognition in Gee's (1999) term – to other participants in the situation. We would argue that ascriptions of identity, of membership or of strangeness are more likely to take place at the level of the syntax of actions than at the more micro level of the constituent actions.

 Perhaps it is obvious, but should be said nevertheless, that these chains of mediated actions will not be the same for all participants in a mediated action. The chain of mediated actions that is relevant for the cashier/order taker is rather different. For her/him at a minimum this chain would consist of taking an order, calling the order over to the preparer, turning back to the customer to ask if there is a further order, if so, dealing with that, if not, asking for payment, moving on to the next customer in the queue. It might further include various acts of provisioning, cleaning, or stocking, all of which fit into a longer chain of the work day. For a particular cashier and for a particular customer, only the few moments that they are engaged with each other form intersecting chains of mediated actions. Thus, the chains of mediated actions must be determined and analysed separately for the various relevant participants in a mediated action.

10 CHAINS OF MEDIATED ACTION AND PRACTICE

A practice, as defined above, is a historical accumulation within the habitus/historical body of the social actor of mediated actions taken over his or her life (experience) and which are recognizable to other social actors as 'the same' social action. The analyst discovers what is a practice using the same four types of data: What do members say is a practice? What does the analyst observe is a repeated type or class of action? How does the individual participant's definition clarify or challenge both of these? How is the resulting analysis understood by participants?

- 'We mark the order on the paper cup with a black felt pen.'
- 'Yesterday, he used a blue felt marker to mark the order.'
- 'I usually like to use a different colour so my orders don't get mixed up with hers.'
- 'You actually use different colour pens and it doesn't really matter.'
- 'Yes, actually, what I meant to say was that we mark the order on the cup with a felt pen. The colour doesn't really matter.'

This set of comments gives us a fair idea that we can talk about the practice of marking the order on the paper cup.

- 'Well first I get the order from the person in the queue. Then I give the order to the one making up the orders. Then I collect the money.'

This is the member's generalization of a sequence of actions (practices) which can then be checked out objectively through observation and the other types of triangulation.

There is a possible confusion between the concept of 'chains of mediated actions' and the concept of practice as both consist in the historical

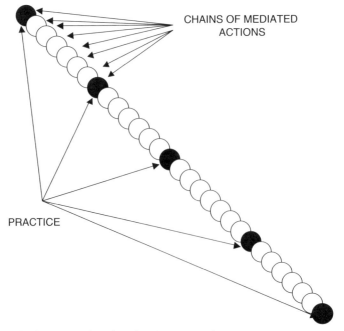

FIGURE 7.7   *Practice and mediated actions across time*

sequence of mediated actions. When we speak of 'chains of mediated actions', we have in mind the close chronological sequence of actions – entering, queuing, paying, and so on – which constitute the higher level action of 'buying a cup of coffee'. When we speak of the practice of 'handing coins', for example, we have in mind the discontinuous historical sequence of all of the occasions when a particular person undertakes this action. Each case will be embedded within some close sequence of mediated actions, of course, as Figure 7.7 illustrates.

What is the 'funnel of commitment'?   Not only do mediated actions make sense in relationship to a hierarchy of action (paradigmatic meaning) and to sequences of action (syntagmatic meaning), some actions are more or less reversible than others. When I enter the café, that action has narrowed the range of cafés from which I will be buying that cup of coffee but just what coffee I will order, where I will sit, and the rest are still open. I might, in fact, decide at that point that I want to leave and go elsewhere – perhaps because it is too crowded – and so, in a sense, 'undo' this action of entering. Likewise, when I stand in the queue I might be examining the menu of options posted above the counter, but at this point I am not committed to any particular type or quantity or style of coffee. Once I have ordered (but not yet paid), however, it is much less likely that I will say, 'No, not a latte; I'd rather have a cappuccino.' After paying for a latte it is highly unlikely that I will change my order. And when the latte arrives for me to pick it up, if I decide that I would rather have a cappuccino, I believe it would be understood that it would be more appropriate for me to get back in the queue to 'reverse' my earlier actions. And, in fact, I would not be reversing them, but starting a new sequence. This is what we are trying to capture with the idea of the 'funnel of commitment'. Some actions are placed in a hierarchy of significance that operates somewhat independently of the other structures of meaning. That is, not only is there a chain of mediated actions, but some of these are more easily 'undone' than others. Methodologically, then, a third task in analysing mediated actions is coming to understand the significance or importance of the situatedness of actions in a sequence. Entering, queuing, and ordering are, in this sense, preparatory to paying for the coffee. Put another way, buying a cup of coffee (a higher level action) is more centrally defined by the moment of purchase than by the preliminary ordering and queuing.

Of course, this funnel of commitment must be understood within an action view of social action, not a purely discursive one. While I might have spoken my order, the order is reversible (though perhaps with some irritation) up until the preparer has actually taken up the process of making the item, whether it is paid for or not. The action of making a cup of coffee, to be reversed, would involve more than discourse. It would involve wastage of materials, and so it is likely that to some extent the reversibility of some actions and the irreversibility of others is tied to the material world.

Finally, the funnel of commitment can be seen in some quite long chains of mediated actions. In getting dressed for the day, I might well check my wallet to be certain that I have the money on hand to buy a cup of coffee later on in the day. Even more likely is that I would not check for the specific amount to buy a cup of coffee, but that I would check to have a larger than necessary amount so that, if I should meet a friend in the course of the day, I would feel free to make the invitation to have a coffee together. That is, the opening actions might be extremely general – one could think of this as starting the day by putting together an action kit of certain clothing or certain grooming that at that point might not at all be directed down any particular funnel of commitment, but is, rather, constructed for maximal freedom of choice of action in the course of the day which is anticipated.

What narrative and anticipatory discourses provide a metadiscursive or reflective structure? Not only are many social actions begun as rather wide open preparations for action. They are also linked to each other in either preparatory chains of discourse (what we might call anticipatory discourse) or retrospective chains of discourse (narrative and other forms of discursive reconstructive work) in which Goffman (1974, for example) or the discursive psychologists (Boswood, 2000; Edwards, 1992; Harré and Gillett, 1994; Harré, 1998) have had an interest. Having a cup of coffee is defined to a certain extent as a social action by the invitation, 'Let's go and have a cup of coffee.' It is significant that one does not always or often say, 'Let's go and patronize, and therefore legitimate, the worldwide neo-capitalist enterprise.' Retrospectively, one might say, 'I had coffee with Gary the other day', where what would be understood was that I had had a casual and extended conversation with Gary. More rarely might one hear, 'Last semester when I was having coffee one morning with Ruth, we talked about whether such actions as having a cup of coffee were useful or not in trying to understand global, neo-capitalism.' These anticipatory and retrospective discourses occur largely outside of the site of engagement within which the actions we are studying occur, but are nevertheless extremely important in the analysis of the meanings of those actions. They are important both for what they say and for what they do not say, as I have suggested. The significance of the higher levels of social meaning is likely to be subsumed within more trivialized and conventional characterizations of action.

11   WHAT DISCOURSES?

Any social action may have linguistic or textual elements embedded within the action – I speak my order to the cashier and so take that social action largely through the linguistic action – or it might be anticipated in earlier discourse or retrospectively constructed in following discourse. I might say to my friend, 'I suppose I'll have a latte'; I might say to the cashier, 'Please give me a cappuccino'; and then, when my friend says, 'But I thought you were going to have a latte', say, 'Well I changed my mind when I saw that other customer's order.' Also appropriated in this action are the sign-boards with the names of the styles and their prices, the denominations on the coins and notes, the company logos and other texts on the coffee cup, and the waiter's felt-marked indication of the order. MDA asks first, which discourses are relevant both in taking and in reflecting upon this action, and then what is the most effective form of linguistic and discursive analysis to understand how these discourses are being appropriated. (See 'What mediational means?' below.)

Methodologically, these anticipatory and retrospective discourses are hard to capture, occurring as they do outside the actions in which we are interested. Focus groups and interviews are particularly useful to capture retrospective discourses as are playback sessions (Tannen, 1994), or photographic elicitation (de Saint-Georges, 2000a; Yung, 2000; Johnston, 2000). It remains a task of MDA to develop a workable methodology for capturing the richness of anticipatory discourses. This should not make us forget the considerable importance of such discourse.

Practice

A mediated action is understood in MDA to take place at the intersection of several practices in real time. This intersection, if viewed as an action is referred to as a 'mediated action'; if viewed as a moment in time, it is referred to as a 'site of engagement'. The organizing concept is the concept of social practice, defined in a narrow and restrictive sense. Thus practice can be methodologically pinned down through asking the following questions:

1   What are the practices which intersect to produce this site of engage-ment?
2   What histories in habitus do these practices have; that is what is their ontogenesis?
3   In what other actions are these practices formative?

What are the practices which intersect to produce this site of engagement? At the broader level, having a cup of coffee is an intersection of conversational practices (initiation, turn-taking, topic control, repair sequences), eating/ drinking practices (speaking with or without your mouth full, alter-nating speaking and drinking, slow sipping, quick gulping), practices concerning being in public social spaces (civil inattention, ecological proximity and so forth) for those who are socially together – Goffman's 'with' (1963, 1971) consumer purchasing practices, and the like. The narrower level, say buying the coffee, is an intersection of practices such as handing, counting money, eye-contact, and the discursive practices of service encounters (such as saying 'thank you' or not), tipping, and the like.

MDA takes the position that it is more useful methodologically and analytically to take this narrow view of practice rather than speaking vaguely of 'conversational practice' or 'consumer practice' as these rather broad categories are ultimately difficult to specify on the one hand, but worse, they tend to result in an objectivist analysis. There are, of course, no a priori assumptions either about which practices or how many practices are relevant to the analysis of any site of engagement. This must emerge from the analyst's work as well as from the views of the participants through a triangulation of types of data as I have outlined above. It is likely, for example, that the participants would be extremely vague about what practices are involved in buying a cup of coffee and might not be able to articulate much beyond 'ordering' and 'paying'. The analyst, however, would be able to articulate, as we have here, matters of posture, eye-contact, handling money and handing money to another person and so forth.

What histories in habitus do these practices have, that is what is their onto-genesis? It is important, though not often studied, to know the history of practices in the habitus of the participants in social actions. To give a simple example, my history of the practice of handling money is strongest for US coins, quite strong for Hong Kong coins, and relatively weak for pounds sterling. Thus, paying for a cup of coffee in London, though it is at a franchised branch of Starbucks and I am comfortable with many of the other practices in such a site of engagement, encounters a rough spot when I begin to search around in my hand for the right coins. Unlike the practice of handling coins in the US where the simple feel of the coins is enough to count out the right amount, in the UK I need to examine the coins quite carefully. This entails having my glasses on to read the denominations as the feel, size and weight of the coins are not sufficient.

12   WHAT PRACTICES?

The specific practices which intersect in a specific site of engagement to produce a mediated action may be many. Just which practices are involved must be identified by triangulating across the four types of observations: members' views, objective observations, individual experiences, and the dialectic between the analyst's views and members' responses to the analysis.

Cues for the identification of practices are:

- lexical and formulaic;
- discursive;
- non-verbal;
- normative statements;
- material objects, structures, layouts.

Many practices have lexicalizations; that is, they have names. 'Paying', 'ordering', 'standing in a queue'. There are also formulaic utterances: 'Thanks', 'please', 'I'd like an X'. Many have fixed sequences of utterances: 'May I help you?', 'Who's next in the queue?'

Discursive practices may include more complex structures or 'archi-tectures' of language. Jokes may begin with, 'Have you heard the one about', but we know they are not finished until we reach the punchline. News stories begin with a summary lead and give less significant detail progressively towards the end.

Non-verbal cues of practices include particular gestures, stances, clothing such as uniforms. In a restaurant we may order from a person in one type of uniform but expect a person in a different uniform to clear away dishes.

> Normative statements may also cue practices that are not otherwise made explicit. 'Don't do it that way!' 'Why not?' 'That's just not how we do it.'
>
> Material objects may indicate practices such as the 'tipping' cup or box next to the cash register.

In what other actions are these practices formative? In MDA we take the position that no action or no site of engagement is defined by a unique practice. On the contrary, one major position we take is that any practice occurs across a wide number of actions, sites of engagements and nexus of practice. To put this more concretely, a social practice such as handing of coins from one person to another may occur as part of the site of engagement in buying a cup of coffee or in paying a telephone bill, or in giving a child pocket money to spend. The handing itself, as I have argued elsewhere (R. Scollon, 2000c) is the same practice embedded in the habitus of the person. What is different from action to action is the linkage of this practice with other practices (saying certain words or phrases, engaging in a certain kind of eye-contact, its placement in a chain of mediated actions).

This characteristic of practices that they cut across actions, or sites of engagement, allows a methodological affordance for study. Once we have identified the significant practices in a particular action, then we can study those separate practices at other sites of engagement as a way of isolating them. Perhaps there is little need to expand on this as it is among the more common research strategies. The main difference in the methodology of MDA is that in other social interactionist research, the goal is often to arrive at an objectivist, rule-based description of an abstract behaviour or class of actions. Within MDA, the goal is to arrive at a richer understanding of the history of the practice within the habitus of the participants in that particular social action. The focus is not on the practice as a characteristic of a social group but on the action as a point of social change in the habitus of the participants.

Mediational means

I have said earlier that the place of text – of discourse, spoken or written – in MDA is as mediational means which are used by participants to undertake a social action. I have also said that these mediational means may cover a large range of physical objects and semiotic tools from the cup in which our coffee is served to the language we use to place the order. Thus the following five questions finally come closest to the materials most commonly analysed in CDA – the texts.

1 What mediational means are used in this action?
2 What specific forms of analysis should be used in analysing the mediational means?
3 How and when were those mediational means appropriated within practice/habitus?
4 How are those mediational means used in this action?
5 How are the semiotic characteristics of those mediational means constraints on action or affordances for action?

What mediational means are used in this action?   If we approach having a cup of coffee from the direction of mediated actions, the mediational means are many. In the broadest sense we would need to include the door to the café, the overall physical arrangement – objects, layout, and design – the space in which the queue is formed, the menus above the counter upon which the options for purchase and prices are displayed, the cash register, the money used for the transaction, the machines which are used to make the coffee, the coffee cups, the counter space on which the coffee is delivered, and the tables where the conversationalists sit as well as the background Brazilian jazz which is playing, not to mention the coffee or tea or other drinks themselves.

13 WHAT MEDIATIONAL MEANS?

Mediational means are inseparable from the definition of the mediated action. These may include almost anything that is accessible to the social actors either as objects in their immediate environment from cups and tables and other such actual physical tools for action to internalized psychological or semiotic mediational means such as symbolic systems of number, language, and visual semiotics.

Most CDA focuses on texts which in MDA are taken to be among the mediational means available for appropriation in any particular mediated action. Like the mediated actions and practices, the mediational means must be analysed on the basis of members' views, independent and objective observation by the analyst and so forth. No one source of analysis is sufficient.

Mediational means are likely to have different significance for different participants within the same site of engagement. The logo on the coffee cup may have very little significance for the customer in taking the action of having a cup of coffee, but much significance for the marketing specialist within the company who is concerned with branding and brand identification.

From the point of view of texts, there are many of them (R. Scollon, 2000a), but it remains a problem for methodological analysis to determine which texts are relevant within which mediated actions. There are the menu texts, the texts embedded in wall designs, pricing texts on the cash register, the cups themselves are covered in text, and the conversation which is the social focus is an extended text. Shorter spoken texts are the service encounter ordering sequences as well as the texts involved when the person who takes the order calls the order to the coffee maker. In addition there are multiple side-sequence texts among customers in the queue between customers and waiters, and among waiters.

A MDA view would not assume a priori that any particular texts or any particular mediational means, speaking more generally, are significant, but use the overall research problem to guide the selection of mediational means for analysis. If our interest is in the spread of globalist neo-capitalism, for example, and particularly if we are trying to distinguish between neo-capitalism and the more well-established industrial capitalism, we would probably not focus on the money exchanges as these are likely to be about the same whether one buys coffee at Starbucks or at Frost Diner. On the other hand the sentence, 'a tall latte, please', is an impossible utterance at the latter where there is one type of coffee. There a more likely utterance would be, 'coffee'. The difference between these two actions might be said to lie in the difference between a single mediational means – standard, diner-style coffee – and what we might call 'standardized, designer coffee choice'. A Starbucks with only one style of coffee would not be a Starbucks. Thus, we can say, that for a particular mediated action to take place, not only are certain mediational means appropriated, but also the choice among multiple mediational means is significant.

What specific forms of analysis should be used in analysing the mediational means? The variety of things in the world which may be appropriated as mediational means is, in fact, nearly limitless and so there is, as I have said, no a priori means of knowing what kind of analysis or what analytical framework will be most useful in analysing the mediational means in any specific case. We may expect that mediational means will fall largely into the following seven classes:

1 conversational interactions (with gestures, etc.);
2 extended monologues or discourses (narratives, lectures, news presentations, also with gestures);
3 texts;
4 visual holophrastic discourse;
5 images;
6 sounds;
7 material objects, three-dimensional spaces and layouts.

Conversational interactions can be studied using methods developed in conversational analysis, interactional sociolinguistics, and ethno-methodology, though from an MDA point of view it is important to keep the focus on the problem of the mediated actions being taken and not simply to follow out the usual research agendas of these research frameworks. That is, if we have identified the social problem we are interested in as the development of neo-capitalism and its attendant discourse of neo-liberalism, we might find we have a conversation occurring as part of the mediated action of 'having a cup of coffee', but from the point of view of that research problem and the mediated action of supporting a neo-capitalist enterprise, the substance of that conversation is actually quite incidental. It may or it may not be incidental, of course. A tape recording of the conversation will tell us whether or not we need to pay further attention to the conversation as such. It may well be the case that it is not the substance of the conversation so much as its existence as a social action that is important. For that degree of analysis, simply to document that there was a conversation would be sufficient.

Alternatively, during the conversation the topic of the conversation itself, or the company within which it is being held, or the company marketing practices on the cup and so forth may become relevant. In that case, a close analysis of the conversation using methods of conversational analysis or interactional sociolinguistics would be significant, particularly if our interest then became in the question of whether or not these social actors were claiming identities for themselves in that conversation which would support the neo-liberal discourse.

Extended monologues have been studied such as narratives or lectures or news presentations and the like. CDA is often a most useful tool in this analysis, particularly in bringing to light the ideological framing of both topics and social actors. Narrative analysis is often a useful research tool when a conversation shifts modes and all participants focus on the narrative of a single participant. Often conversational analysis and the analysis of extended spoken discourses interact as when two people in a conversation talk about a lecture they have both been to. In fact, virtually any other form of discourse or any other mediational means may be appropriated or recontextualized within another form. We might have a conversation about a film or news broadcast we have seen. We might quote a conversation fragment within a text. The logo or brand name (visual holophrastic discourse) might be used conversationally as in saying, 'Let's go to Starbucks for coffee.' From an MDA point of view it may be necessary to carry out a CDA analysis of an original speech given by a public figure, a second CDA analysis of the news report on that speech, and then a conversational analysis of how that speech and the news report are integrated into a conversation as a narrative about how someone spent last evening after dinner. All of that might then become entirely irrelevant at another level if the focus of analysis is on how brand names reproduce a globalized neo-capitalist economy through producing a favouring of one brand of café over another for that con-versation. The essential point in MDA is to continually seek to link the discourses studied to the originating research questions.

Texts are probably the most fully studied form of discourse within CDA. For MDA it is crucial to see how and when texts are appropriated in sites of engagement to take mediated actions. An ideological analysis of a newspaper story advocating exclusionary employment practices may be essential to an understanding of how that story is appropriated by social actors in taking a mediated action. But it is also possible that that analysis is irrelevant. It depends on the social action taken. A strong neo-liberal statement in a business section editorial is not a text for the purposes of MDA if the paper is used as a surface for cleaning fish. Other practices (fish cleaning ones) in that site of engagement have pre-empted a reading of the text. But if the fish seller notes the content and brings up the subject with a neighbouring vendor, then it becomes most relevant to know how the text is structured and how the ideological positioning is accomplished.

In addition to CDA analysis of texts, MDA often makes use of con-trastive rhetorical analysis of text structures as well as argument structuring. Such text structures orient the reader to the significance of portions of the text. In addition to orienting the reader, text structures may also distract the reader or mislead the reader if the reader comes to the text with different expectations for reading (S. Scollon et al., 2000).

Visual holophrastic discourse may be defined as any of the rapidly increasing number of texts which would include brand names, logos, shop signs, street signs, traffic directional or prohibitional signs, and other forms of discourse in public. In addition to these are images, sounds and material objects, three-dimensional spaces and layouts. The analysis of such mediational means is really in its infancy and there is little that can be said about it here. The work of Kress and van Leeuwen (1996) makes a major contribution to the analysis of visual mediational means including three-dimensional layouts and van Leeuwen (1999) has set out principles by which an integrated study of sound can also be made.

How and when were those mediational means appropriated within practice/ habitus? Within MDA, a mediational means is understood as being appropriated over time within the habitus of a person. That is, a medi-ational means is not simply an external object in the world, nor is it an entirely internal psychological schema or disposition. A mediational means is a dialectic between the material world and the habitus. Some mediational means such as the coffee cup are largely external but, nevertheless, are objects that one has learnt to use in particular ways. One knows, for example, to hold a paper cup without squeezing, some-thing that most of us have forgotten we once needed to learn how to do as a child. Other mediational means such as the phrase, 'a tall latte' are largely internalized language structures. Nevertheless, the word 'tall' has had to be internalized recently as a word meaning 'the smallest cup available for sale', a meaning which departs significantly from the expected meaning of the word 'tall'.

The methodological question here is: 'how do we come to know how and when mediational means have been appropriated within a person's habitus?' This can be approached in one of two ways. first of all, one can study longitudinally the development of particular mediational means in the habitus of particular individuals. This is limited, of course, in that the researcher is then constrained to the study of the mediated actions of just these particular individuals. A seond means is through retrospective interviewing. More can be learnt about a broader range of participants, but the researchers' knowledge is constrained by the problems of historical recontextualization and 'genesis amnesia' (Bourdieu, 1977). That is, we often forget, do not know, or reconstruct our pasts to suit our own present or anticipated purposes.

How are those mediational means used in this action? This question could be said to be the central and focal question in a large number of studies of texts and of social actions. A person who goes into Starbucks and says, 'a tall latte', positions himself or herself as a participant in the nexus of practice of having coffee at a designer café. A person who goes into the Frost Diner and says, 'I don't suppose I could get a tall latte, could I?' positions himself or herself as seriously or ironically commenting on the class or historical place of that kind of restaurant. A marketing analysis might study the branding accomplished with the logos on the cup as well as here and there about the café. A CDA might focus on ways in which the conversation positioned the participants as supporting or critiquing the global, neo-capitalist economy. More often than not, however, the texts themselves would be studied and the question of how they are being used in this particular action would be set aside as a question of context. Thus it is this question which forms the central difference between MDA and many other versions of discursive analysis.

One might find among the mediational means in having this cup of coffee a sentence written on the cardboard insulating sleeve:

> This insulating sleeve is made from 60 per cent post-consumer recycled fibre and uses approximately 45 per cent less material than a second paper cup (Starbucks insulating sleeve, San Diego, California: March 9, 2000)

It would not be hard to develop a critical analysis of this sentence which positions itself, and therefore the company, as an environmentally friendly organization. Keywords 'post-consumer' and 'recycled' indicate the discourse of conservation. The percentages given '60 per cent' and '45 per cent' also signal the scientism of this conservationist discourse. This environmental message is further conveyed in the 'natural' brown colour of the cardboard and in this use of cardboard, not styrofoam. But even though such an analysis could be made, ethnographic observations suggest that users of these insulating sleeves make no direct use of this discourse in the action of having their cup of coffee. This is not to say that they do not make any use at all. It could be argued that it is just these backgrounded discourses of choice, or environmentalism – what is often labelled 'gentrification' or 'yuppification' – that give this café its cachet as a site in which social actors can enact membership in the global, neo-capitalist enterprise. The methodological question MDA seeks to keep in mind is: 'how do we know just how social actors are appropriating the mediational means they are using in taking social actions?'

How are the semiotic characteristics of those mediational means constraints on action or affordances for action? MDA seeks to broadly include under the notion of 'semiotics' all of the meaning-making potentials from the lexico-grammar of the language used as mediational means to the layout, design, colour schemes, and the rest of images, three-dimensional objects and of the spaces within which social actions take place. From this point of view, not only would we be interested in the sentence above, but also in the material upon which it is written (brown, 'natural' cardboard), the design of the insulating sleeve, its placement on the cup and further, the placement of the cup within the broader scheme of a café and a con-versation among friends at a table. The environmental discourse signalled by the colour of the sleeve as well as by the message printed on it both afford (enable, support, encourage) the 'gentrification' of this café and constrain other interpretations. The choice to use this colour scheme is a choice not to use a double cup, a styrofoam cup or sleeve, or any other of the possible means of insulating a hot drink that might be regarded within the environmental discourse to be more intrusive or destructive of ecological balance. Thus this choice affords one reading and constrains other, contrary readings.

Nexus of practice

What linkages among practices form nexus of practice? The first time I enter one of the speciality cafés I rely on a variety of practices within my habitus to buy a cup of coffee and to have my conversation. I have at this time bought many objects. I have queued, read menus and made selec-tions. I have had conversations in public places and I have returned my own objects in fast-food restaurants. In this sense all of the practices upon which I rely are familiar to me as I have a history with them, some of that going back many years. Nevertheless there are specifics about the sequencing of the actions and the linkages among them that make having a cup of coffee in one of these cafés a unique nexus or constellation of practices. I am likely to make mistakes, probably not in any one of these practices, but in making the linkages and sequences operate smoothly.

Having had a cup of coffee several times, these linkages and sequences begin to operate more smoothly – so much so that the waiter begins to 'recognize' me as a regular customer. At this stage it seems useful to introduce the idea of the 'nexus of practice'. This nexus is the regular, smoothly working set of linkages and sequences among practices that can be recognized by someone else in the vague sense of 'doing the right thing'. It is often not difficult to elicit this recognition from members of a nexus of practice. The methodological problem is to determine exactly what are the linkages among practices and the sequences of chains of mediated actions that give rise to this members' recognition. This is a problem because, as I have said, virtually all of the practices are recognizable as working across a much wider range of actions and sites of engagement. What is unique is the constellation, not any of the specific practices out of which this constellation or nexus is constituted.

How might the nexus of practice be recognized? This leads to the next methodological issue of identifying just which practices, linkages among them, and sequences of mediated actions are being used by members to make this identification. In a particular café we might hear someone say to a friend after they have picked up their order, 'Let's go upstairs.' The other might say, 'Oh, are there tables up there?' and from this draw the preliminary judgement that the first has more familiarity than the second with the mediational means in that case which includes the physical layout of that café. The first person would be, at least apparently, more within that particular nexus of practice than the second.

To what extent is there a useful distinction between nexus of practice as group, as situation, and as genre? Within MDA the concept of the nexus of practice depends upon it remaining loosely defined. What we are trying to capture is the lowest level at which there is regularity in the linkages among practices and sequences of actions. Practices 'reside' in the habitus of persons. Actions are taken when particular practices are linked in real-time sites of engagement. A nexus of practice is the regular occurrence of such actions and linkages of practices. We might say that nexus of practice is to the social group what habitus is to the person. That is, the nexus of practice is the largely out-of-awareness production of similar or recognizably 'the same' actions and events. Since practices reside in the habitus, a nexus of practice is really a set of linkages among people through their linkages of practices. Thus the nexus of practice could be thought of as a fledgling social group.

Similarly, however, we could think of a nexus of practice somewhat more objectivistically as fledgling genres or situations. That is, we might focus on the recognizability of the type of action, for example having a cup of coffee in a designer café, and not focus particularly on the persons involved. We might also focus on the situation which would largely be a focus organized around the mediational means. This would be the source of the meaning behind someone saying, 'Oh, it looks like we could get a latte in here', on seeing a café while travelling in a city one has not been in before. That is, one has recognized a constellation of designs, layouts, spaces and the rest that 'look like' situations and spaces one has seen in carrying out similar actions in the past.

The methodological question here is focused on coming to understand to what extent the linkages among practices and the sequences of mediated actions are recognizable to participants as defining groups or genres or situations. To the extent they are recognizable they might well be moving toward definition as communities of practice, genres and situations more familiar in the literature.

Community of practice

Perhaps enough has been said above to indicate the significance of the community of practice within MDA. Methodologically the central questions to ask are:

- To what extent has a nexus of practice become 'technologized'?
- What are the identities (both internal and external) which are produced by community of practice membership?

To what extent has a nexus of practice become 'technologized'? This question organizes a cluster of questions which focus on discovering to what extent group identity, fixed genres and situation are important for the mediated actions being taken. Having a cup of coffee in Starbucks is an action that is relatively little technologized. Attending a meeting of The Jacques Ellul Society produces oneself as joining in or at least supporting the goals and purposes of that community of practice. The technologization consists in having a named society, letterhead stationery, an office with a staff, and somewhat regular meetings. This community of practice itself then has become a cultural tool (hence the term 'technologization') or mediational means which can be used for other actions. For example, I could list the presentation of a brief report at the meeting on my curriculum vitae in a career-building action whereas I would not imagine putting a conversation over coffee on my CV, however intellectually significant the conversation might have been.

What are the identities (both internal and external) which are produced by community of practice membership? A mediated action may or may not be taken within a community of practice. Thus it is an empirical question to be sorted out methodologically whether or not any particular mediated action that one is studying is produced by the social actors as an action within a community. Is the waiter at the café acting as an employee or is he or she acting as a non-aligned social actor? Duties might include taking an order, managing the payment and calling the order to the person preparing the coffee. These actions might be conceived as taking place within a particular formal structure and thereby producing identity within that structure. At the same time, however, the waiter might recognize a friend or family member and so produce an array of asides in and around the employee actions which place him or her within either other communities of practice or simply within other nexus of practice.

In the past two decades or so, in North America at least, there has been an increasing erosion of the distinction between institutional and non-institutional actions. That is, waiters have come to be expected to treat their customers as if they were not only customers but friends or family. To put this another way, what one person might treat as a nexus of practice – a loosely linked set of practices – another might try to produce as a community of practice. That is, there may not be agreement among the participants in a social action about whether or not their actions are taken within a community of practice and so this must remain open to empirical investigation.

Thus, I recently bought a cup of coffee in a café in San Diego where the transaction went something like this:

Waiter: Could I help you?
Me: A tall latte, please.
Waiter: Sure, what's your name?
Me: Uh, (long hesitation) Ron.
Waiter: (says the price and the transaction is completed.)

When the coffee was ready the preparer called me by name to deliver my coffee.

This transaction was far enough outside my expectations and those of several others about my age and generation in the queue that I hestitated in co-operating with the request for my name. One of the other customers, after receiving her coffee, walked past me and said, 'Howya doin', Ron' with heavy irony in her voice.

Methodological assumptions

The theoretical programme of MDA as well as the methodology we have adopted to carry out this programme are predicated on several methodological assumptions which have been elaborated above. These are as follows:

- Social action takes place in real time, therefore, the focus of research is on real-time actions.
- The meaning of any concrete, real-time action is predicated on the history of that action in the habitus of the participants and in the social formations which the action instantiates.
- Participant-observation is the primary research tool for eliciting the data needed for MDA.
- Because of the involvement of the researcher as a participant-observer, clear triangulation procedures are essential in drawing inferences about observations and in producing interpretations.

For our purposes, then, it should be clear now that the texts which are used within mediated actions are signficant, but are often not even central in the production of a mediated action by social actors. This raises the question of whether or not MDA should be called discourse analysis at all. I would argue that it should for two reasons. Firstly MDA does not eliminate the interest in texts or language at all, but only places these texts into a framework of complex interactions with other mediational means. An MDA would be incomplete without taking into account the language used in mediated actions, and it would be equally incomplete without taking into account the other mediational means which are germane to the mediated action under study. Secondly, MDA takes the meaning of 'discourse' in the broadest sense (Gee, 1999; Gee et al., 1996; Fairclough and Wodak, 1997) of whole systems of the possibility of producing meanings, with or without language. Thus MDA would take a discourse such as that of urban traffic regulation as a discourse of interest, even though the vast number of instances of this discourse might be displayed in lines painted on street surfaces, lights of various colours placed at intersections, and colour schemes for authorized and prohibited behaviours.

Preferred fields of application and restrictions

I hope in what I have written that it is now clear how MDA strategizes to see broad social issues in the common actions of our daily lives. Working within this analytical framework and methodology allows the researcher to find a place where these social issues and discourses are grounded in the actions of our lives. This means, of course, that MDA is much more appropriate to certain kinds of data or fields of applications than to others. MDA is most amenable to the analysis of the intersection of the day-to-day common practices of social actors and the broad issue-based public discourses of our societies. It is, in fact, to address these broad public issues in the day-to-day world that we have tried to construct this theoretical and methodological position. That is to say, MDA is relatively useful in coming to understand how social and public issues of our society are instantiated in the ordinary actions of social actors. At the same time, of course, we must be cautious in drawing grand conclusions about the broader social formations of institutions, organizations, nations and cultures. Interdisciplinary work with scholars who specialize in the analysis of texts, institutions, organizations, and cultures is not only welcomed but necessary in MDA.

Acknowledgements

This chapter developed in many discussions with colleagues and students about how to try to 'methodize' mediated discourse analysis. While this is certainly not yet a final view of such things, I want to specifically thank Tom Randolph for his usual meticulous attention to wordings but also to the overall tone, Sigrid Norris for her insistence that the chapter include clarifying diagrams, Ingrid de Saint-Georges, Philip Levine and Vicki Yung for other useful suggestions and to Suzanne Wong Scollon for thirty years of ongoing discussions of methodology.

Further reading

Bourdieu, P. (1990) *The Logic of Practice*. Stanford, CA: Stanford University Press.

This book is the revision of Bourdieu's earlier book *Outline of a Theory of Practice*. The central ideas of a theory of practice including the concept of the habitus are laid out here. Mediated discourse analysis like most critical discourse analysis makes important use of the concept of practice.

Gee, J.P. (1999) *An Introduction to Discourse Analysis: Theory and Method*. London: Routledge.

Gee's term 'Discourse with a capital "D" is becoming widely used to capture what others such as Fairclough have referred to as an order of discourse or a discursive formation. The book is a very readable and useful introduction to the study of discourse as an ideological question.

Scollon, R. (1998b) *Mediated Discourse as Social Interaction: A Study of News Discourse*. New York: Longman.

The first sketch of mediated discourse analysis was made in this book using data from telephone calls, photography practice, and news broadcasting as analytical examples. The central thesis is that when discourse is mediated by texts, the primary social interactions are those among the producers of the text on the one hand or among the readers/viewers on the other hand.

Scollon, R. (2001) *Mediated Discourse: The Nexus of Practice*. London: Routledge.

This book is a fuller treatment of ideas from two papers cited in this volume (R. Scollon (2000a) 'Mediated discourse: an integrated theory of sociolinguistic action'. Paper presented in the colloquium 'Mediated discourse: an integrated theory of sociolinguistic action' at Sociolinguistics Symposium 2000, Bristol, 27–29 April, and R. Scollon (2000c) 'On the ontogenesis of a social practice'. Paper given at a workshop on Theory and Interdisciplinarity in Critical Discourse Analysis, Institute on Discourse, Identity and Politics, University of Vienna, 6–7 July 2000 as a pre-session to the seventh International Pragmatics Conference in Budapest (9–14 July 2000)).

Wertsch, J.V. (1998) *Mind as Action*. New York: Oxford University Press.

Wertsch sets out the main arguments of his neo-Vygotskian theory of mediated action. Mediated discourse analysis uses and extends this psychological paradigm to encompass the analysis of discourse.

Notes

1 These projects have all been undertaken within the MDA framework. Other projects, of course, share in many aspects of this research agenda. The editor has called to my attention Muntigl et al.'s (2000a, b) study of employment discourses in the EU as an example of work which is broadly ethnographic while also paying close attention to the analysis of discourse.
2 In addition to the works cited in the text of this chapter, MDA is being developed by Boswood (2000); Johnston (2000); Jones (1999, 2000); Norris (2000); Randolph (2000); S. Scollon (1996, 1998, 1999, 2000a, b, c); Scollon and Scollon (2000) and Yung (1997, 2000).
3 In this MDA shares much with Goffman's interest in the social interaction without privileging talk as such (1981) though MDA departs from Goffman in taking as well a strong interest in not only social interaction but also the physical spaces and the texts used in taking social actions.
4 The concept of the site of engagement is much like Goffman's social situation in the focus on lived, real-time experience but departs from this concept in that it is based in practice theory and leaves open the proper analysis of the situation to be derived from an analysis of the practices and actions taken.
5 The concept of the mediational means is rooted in Vygotskian psychology (Vygotsky, 1978) as currently explicated in the work of Wertsch (1991, 1998).

References

Albert, H. (ed.) (1971) *Werturteilsstreit*. Darmstadt: Wissenschaftliche Buchgesellschaft.

Altheide, D.L. and Johnson, J. (1994) 'Criteria for assessing interpretive validity in qualitative research', in N.K. Denzin and Y.S. Lincoln (eds), *Handbook of Qualitative Research*. Thousand Oaks: Sage, pp. 485–99.

Anthonissen, C. (2001) 'On the effectiveness of media censorship: linguistic, paralinguistic and other communicative devices of media regulation'. PhD thesis, University of Vienna.

Atkinson, P. and Coffey, A. (1997) 'Analysing documentary realities', in D. Silverman (ed.), *Qualitative Research. Theory, Method and Practice*. London: Sage, pp. 45–62.

Bailer-Galanda, B. and Neugebauer, W. (1993) 'Die FPÖ: vom Liberalismus zum Rechtsextremismus', in DöW: *Handbuch des österreichischen Rechtsextremismus*. Vienna: Deuticke, pp. 327–428.

Bailer-Galanda, B. and Neugebauer, W. (1997). *Haider und die 'Freiheitlichen' in Österreich*. Berlin: Elefanten Press.

Bakhtin, M. (1981) *The Dialogic Imagination*. Austin: University of Texas Press.

Bakker, C. (1997) 'Membership categorization and interview accounting', in D. Silverman (ed.), *Qualitative Research. Theory, Method and Practice*. London: Sage, pp. 130–43.

Balke, F. (1998) *'Was zu denken zwingt'. Gilles Deleuze, Felix Guattari und das Aussen der Philosophie*, in J. Jurt, (ed.), *Zeitgenössische Französische Denker: Eine Bilanz*, Freiburg: Rombach Litterae, pp. 187–210.

Bateson, G. (1972) *Steps to an Ecology of Mind*. New York: Ballantine.

Bauman, Z. (1998) *Globalization – The Human Consequence*. Cambridge: Polity Press.

Becker, F., Gerhard, U. and Link, J. (1997) 'Moderne Kollektivsymbolik. Ein diskurstheoretisch orientierter Forschungsbericht mit Auswahlbibliographie', *Internationales Archiv für Sozialgeschichte der deutschen Literatur (IASL)*, 22 (1): 70–154.

Bellah, R.N. (1973) *Emile Durkheim: On Morality and Society, Selected Writings*. Chicago: University of Chicago Press.

Benhabib, S. (1992) *Kritik, Norm und Utopie. Die normativen Grundlagen der Kritischen Theorie*. Frankfurt: Fischer.

Benke, G. (2000) 'Diskursanalyse als sozialwissenschaftliche Untersuchungsmethode', *SWS Rundschau*, 2: 140–62.

Bernstein, B. (1990) *The Structuring of Pedagogic Discourse*. London: Routledge.

Bhaskar, R. (1986) *Scientific Realism and Human Emancipation*. London: Verso.

Billig, M. (1991) *Ideology and Opinions*. London: Sage.

Billig, M. and Schegloff, E.A. (1999) 'Debate: critical discourse analysis and conversation analysis', *Discourse and Society*, 10 (4): 543–82.

Blommaert, J. and Bulcaen, H. (2000) 'Critical discourse analysis. An overview', *Annual Anthropological Review* (forthcoming).

Blommaert, J. and Verschueren, J. (1999) *The Diversity Debate*. London: Routledge.

Bonss, W. and Honneth, A. (1982) *Sozialforschung als Kritik. Zum sozialwissenschaftlichen Potential der Kritischen Theorie*. Frankfurt: Suhrkamp.

Boswood, T. (2000) 'Strategic writing and organizational identities'. PhD dissertation, City University of Hong Kong.

Bourdieu, P. (1977) *Outline of a Theory of Practice*. Cambridge: Cambridge University Press.

Bourdieu, P. (1979) *La distinction. Critique sociale du jugement*. Paris: Les éditions de minuit.

Bourdieu, P. (1990) *The Logic of Practice*. Stanford: Stanford University Press.

Bourdieu, P. (1998) 'A reasoned utopia and economic fatalism', *New Left Review*, 227: 25–30.

Brown, B.M. and Coates, K. (1996) *The Blair Revelation: Deliverance for Whom?* Nottingham: Spokesman.

Bublitz, H. (1999) *Foucaults Archäologie des kulturellen Unbewussten. Zum Wissensarchiv und Wissensbegehren moderner Gesellschaften*. Frankfurt and New York: Campus.

Burkhardt, A. (1996) 'Politolinguistik. Versuch einer Ortsbestimmung', in J. Klein and H. Diekmannshenke (eds), *Sprachstrategien und Dialogblockaden. Linguistische und politikwissenschaftliche Studien zur politischen Kommunkation*. Berlin and New York: de Gruyter, pp. 75–100.

Caborn, J. (1999) 'Die Presse und die "Hauptstadtdebatte". Konstrukte der deutschen Einheit', in U. Kreft, H. Uske and S. Jäger (eds), *Kassensturz. Politische Hypotheken der Berliner Republik*. Duisburg: DISS, pp. 61–84.

Calhoun, C. (1995) *Critical Social Theory. Culture, History, and the Challenge of Difference*. Oxford, UK and Cambridge, USA: Blackwell.

Castells, M. (1998) *The Information Age: Economy, Society and Culture*, 3 vols. Oxford: Blackwell.

Chomsky, N. (1957) *Syntactic Structures*. s-Gravenhage: Mouton.

Chouliaraki, L. and Fairclough, N. (1999) *Discourse in Late Modernity: Rethinking Critical Discourse Analysis*. Edinburgh: Edinburgh University Press.

Clarke, J. and Newman, J. (1998) *A Modern British People? New Labour and the Reconstruction of Social Welfare*. Department of Intercultural Communication and Management, Copenhagen Business School: Occasional Paper.

Cleve, G. (1997) 'Völkisches Denken im Alltag', in A. Disselnkötter, S. Jäger, H. Kellershohn and S. Slobodzian (eds), *Evidenzen im Fluss. Demokratieverluste in Deutschland*. Duisburg: DISS, pp. 244–60.

Connerton, P. (1976) *Critical Sociology. Selected Readings*. Harmondsworth: Penguin.

de Beaugrande, R.A. and Dressler, W.U. (1981) *Einführung in die Textlinguistik*. Tübingen: Niemeyer.

de Saint-Georges, I. (2000a) 'Discussing images: pictures reception and appropriation in focus groups'. Paper presented at the Georgetown University Roundtable, Washington, DC.

de Saint-Georges, I. (2000b) 'Discourse, practice, and social change: manual work and discourse practice in a vocational training centre for long-term unemployed'. Unpublished PhD thesis, Georgetown University, Washington DC.

de Saint-Georges, I. and Norris, S. (1999) 'Nationality and the European Union: competing identities in the visual design of four European cities'. Paper presented at the International Visual Sociology Association Conference, Antwerp, Belgium.

Deleuze, G. (1992) *Foucault*. Frankfurt: Suhrkamp.

Denzin, N.K. (1970) *The Research Act in Sociology*. London: Butterworth.

Denzin, N.K. and Lincoln, Y.S. (eds) (1994) *Handbook of Qualitative Research*. Thousand Oaks: Sage.

Department of Trade and Industry (1998) *Building the Knowledge-Driven Economy*. London: Stationery Office.

Dieckmann, W. (1964) *Information oder Überredung. Zum Wortgebrauch der politischen Werbung in Deutschland seit der Französischen Revolution*. Marburg: N.G. Elwert.

Dieckmann, W. (1975) *Sprache in der Politik. Einführung in die Pragmatik und Semantik der politischen Sprache. Mit einem Literaturbericht zur 2. Auflage*. Heidelberg: Carl Winter.

Dieckmann, W. (1981) *Politische Sprache – Politische Kommunikation. Vorträge, Aufsätze, Entwürfe*. Heidelberg: Carl Winter.

Disselnkötter, A., Jäger, S., Kellershohn, H. and Slobodzian, S. (eds) (1997) *Evidenzen im Fluss. Demokratieverluste in Deutschland*. Duisburg: DISS.

DöW (1993) *Handbuch des österreichischen Rechtsextremismus*. Vienna: Deuticke.

Drews, A., Gerhard, U. and Link, J. (1985) 'Moderne Kollektivsymbolik. Eine diskurstheoretisch orientierte Einführung mit Auswahlbibliographie', in *Internationales Archiv für Sozialgeschichte der deutschen Literatur (IASL)*, 1st special edition, Tübingen: Forschungsreferate, pp. 256–375.

Durkheim, E. (1933) *The Division of Labour in Society*, translated by George Simpson. New York: The Free Press.

Duveen, G. and Lloyd, B. (eds) (1990) *Social Representations and the Development of Knowledge*. Cambridge: Cambridge University Press.

Eagleton, T. (ed.) (1994) *Ideology*. London: Longman.

Eco, U. (1985) *Lector in fabula: la cooperazione interpretativa nei testi narrativi*. Milano: Bompiani.

Edwards, D. (1992) *Discursive Psychology*. London: Sage.

Ehlich, K. (1983) 'Text und sprachliches Handeln. Die Entstehung von Texten aus dem Bedürfnis nach Überlieferung', in: A. Assmann, J. Assmann and C. Hardmeier (eds), *Schrift und Gedächtnis. Beiträge zur Archäologie der literarischen Kommunikation*. Munich: Fink, pp. 24–43.

Fairclough, N. (1985) 'Critical and descriptive goals in discourse analysis', *Journal of Pragmatics*, 9: 739–63.

Fairclough, N. (1989) *Language and Power*. London: Longman.

Fairclough, N. (1992) *Discourse and Social Change*. Oxford, UK and Cambridge, MA: Polity Press and Blackwell.

Fairclough, N. (1995) *Critical Discourse Analysis: the Critical Study of Language*. London: Longman.

Fairclough, N. (1996) 'A reply to Henry Widdowson's discourse analysis: a critical view', *Language and Literature*, 5: 1–8.

Fairclough, N. (2000a) 'Discourse, social theory and social research: the case of welfare reform', *Journal of Sociolinguistics*, 4 (2).

Fairclough, N. (2000b) *New Labour New Language?* London: Routledge.

Fairclough, N. (forthcoming) 'Representations of change in neo-liberal discourse', to appear in *Relaciones Laborales*, 2000.

Fairclough, N. and Kress, G. (1993) 'Critical discourse analysis'. Unpublished manuscript.

Fairclough, N. and Wodak, R. (1997) 'Critical discourse analysis', in T. van Dijk (ed.), *Discourse Studies: A Multidisciplinary Introduction*. Volume 2. London: Sage, pp. 258–84.

Fassmann, H. and Münz, R. (1992) *Einwanderungsland Österreich? Gastarbeiter – Flüchtlinge – Immigranten*. Vienna: Dachs-Verlag.

Fassmann, H. and Münz, R. (eds) (1996) *Migration in Europa. Historische Entwicklung, aktuelle Trends, politische Reaktionen*. Frankfurt and New York: Campus.

Fassmann, H., Münz, R. and Seifert, W. (1997) 'Die Arbeitsmarktposition ausländischer Arbeitskräfte in Deutschland (West) und Österreich', in K.M. Bolte et al. (eds), *Mitteilungen aus der Arbeitsmarkt – und Berufsforschung*, 30. Jg/ 1997. Stuttgart: Kohlhammer, pp. 732–45.

Fay, B. (1987) *Critical Social Science*. London: Polity Press.

Firestone, W.A. (1993) 'Alternative arguments for generalizing from data as applied to qualitative research', *Educational Researcher*, 22: 16–23.

Forgacs, D. (1988) *Gramsci Reader*. London: Lawrence and Wishart.

Foucault, M. (1978) '"Wahrheit und Macht", Interview mit Michel Foucault von Alessandro Fontana und Pasquale Pasquino', in M. Foucault (ed.), *Dispositive der Macht. Über Sexualität, Wissen und Wahrheit*. Berlin: Merve, pp. 21–54.

Foucault, M. (1983) *Der Wille zum Wissen. Sexualität und Wahrheit Bd. 1*. Frankfurt: Suhrkamp.

Foucault, M. (1988) *Archäologie des Wissens*, third edn. Frankfurt: Suhrkamp.

Foucault, M. (1989) *Überwachen und Strafen. Die Geburt des Gefängnisses*, eighth edn. Frankfurt: Suhrkamp.

Foucault, M. (1992) *Was ist Kritik?* Berlin: Merve (frz. 1990, lecture and discussion 1978).

Foucault, M. (1996) *Diskurs und Wahrheit. Berkeley Lectures 1983*. Berlin: Merve.

Fowler, R. (1991) 'Critical linguists', in K. Halmkjaer (ed.), *The Linguistic Encyclopedia*. London, New York: Routledge, pp. 89–93.

Fowler, R. (1996) *Linguistic Criticism*, second edn. Oxford: Oxford University Press.

Fowler, R., Hodge, G., Kress, G. and Trew, T. (eds) (1979) *Language and Control*. London: Routledge and Kegan Paul.

Gee, J.P. (1999) *An Introduction to Discourse Analysis: Theory and Method*. London: Routledge.

Gee, J.P., Hull, G. and Colin L. (1996) *The New Work Order: Behind the Language of the New Capitalism*. Boulder, CO: Westview Press, Inc.

Girnth, H. (1996) 'Texte im politischen Diskurs. Ein Vorschlag zur diskursorientierten Beschreibung von Textsorten', *Muttersprache*, 106 (1): 66–80.

Glaser, B.G. and Strauss, A.L. (1967) *The Discovery of Grounded Theory. Strategies for Qualitative Research*. Chicago: Aldine.

Goffman, E. (1963) *Behaviour in Public Places: Notes on the Social Organization of Gatherings*. New York: Free Press.

Goffman, E. (1971) *Relations in Public*. New York: Harper and Row.

Goffman, E. (1974) *Frame Analysis*. New York: Harper and Row.

Goffman, E. (1981) *Forms of Talk*. Philadelphia: University of Pennsylvania Press.

Graefen, G. (1997) *Der wissenschaftliche Artikel – Textart und Textorganisation*. Frankfurt: Lang.

Gruber, H. (1991) *Antisemitismus im Mediendiskurs. Die Affäre 'Waldheim' in der Tagespresse*. Wiesbaden: Deutscher Universitätsverlag (WDV).

Grünalternative Jugend (ed.) (1998) *Der Schoss ist fruchtbar noch . . . NSDAP (1920–1933) – FPÖ (1986–1998) Kontinuitäten, Parallelen, Ähnlichkeiten*. Vienna: Grünalternative Jugend.

Habermas, J. (1969) *Technik und Wissenschaft als Ideologie*. Frankfurt: Suhrkamp.

Habermas, J. (1971) *Theorie und Praxis*. Frankfurt: Suhrkamp.

Habermas, J. (1977) *Erkenntnis und Interesse*. Frankfurt: Suhrkamp.

Habermas, J. (1996) *Die Einbeziehung des Anderen. Studien zur politischen Theorie*. Frankfurt: Suhrkamp.

Habermas, J. (1998) *Die postnationale Konstellation. Politische Essays*. Frankfurt: Suhrkamp.

Hall, S. (1996) 'Introduction: who needs identity?', in S. Hall and P. du Gay (eds), *Questions of Cultural Identity*. London: Sage, pp. 1–17.

Halliday, M.A.K. (1970) *The Linguistic Sciences and Language Teaching*. London: Longman.

Halliday, M.A.K. (1978) *Language as Social Semiotic*. London: Arnold.

Halliday, M.A.K. (1985) (1994) *Introduction to Functional Grammar*, first and second edns. London: Arnold.

Harré, R. (1998) *The Singular Self: An Introduction to the Psychology of Personhood*. London: Sage.

Harré, R. and Gillett, G. (1994) *The Discursive Mind*. Thousand Oaks: Sage.

Harvey, D. (1996) *Justice, Nature and the Geography of Difference*. Oxford: Blackwell.

Hodge, R. and Kress, G. (1991) *Social Semiotics*. Cambridge: Polity Press and Ithaca, NY: Cornell University Press.

Honneth, A. (1989) *Kritik der Macht. Reflexionsstufen einer kritischen Gesellschaftstheorie*. Frankfurt: Suhrkamp.

Honneth, A. (1990) *Die zerrissene Welt des Sozialen. Sozialphilosophische Aufsätze*. Frankfurt: Suhrkamp.

Honneth, A. (1994) *Kampf um Anerkennung. Zur moralischen Grammatik sozialer Konflikte*. Frankfurt: Suhrkamp.

Horkheimer, M. (1992) *Traditionelle und Kritische Theorie. Fünf Aufsätze*. Frankfurt: Suhrkamp.

Horkheimer, M. and Adorno, Theodor W. (1991 [1944]) *Dialektik der Aufklärung. Philosophische Fragmente*. Frankfurt: Fischer.

Hymes, D. (1972) 'Models of interaction of language and social life', in J.J. Gumperz and D. Hymes (eds), *Directions in Sociolinguistics – The Ethnography of Communication*. New York: Holt, Rinehart and Winston, pp. 35–71.

Iedema, R. (1997) 'Interactional dynamics and social change; planning as morphogenesis'. Unpublished PhD thesis, University of Sydney.

Iedema, R. (1999) 'Formalizing organizational meaning', *Discourse and Society*, 10 (1): 49–66.

Jäger, M. (1996) 'Fatale Effekte. Die Kritik am Patriarchat im Einwanderungsdiskurs'. Unpublished PhD thesis, Duisburg.

Jäger, M., Cleve, G., Ruth, I. and Jäger, S. (1998) *Von deutschen Einzeltätern und ausländischen Banden*. Duisburg: DISS.

Jäger, M., Jäger, S., Ruth, I., Schulte-Holtey, E. and Wichert, F. (eds) (1997) *Biomacht und Medien. Wege in die Biogesellschaft*. Duisburg: DISS.

Jäger, S. (1993) *Kritische Diskursanalyse. Eine Einführung*. Duisberg: DISS.

Jäger, S. (1996a) *Brandsätze. Rassismus im Alltag*, fourth edn. Duisburg: DISS.

Jäger, S. (1996b) 'Diskurstheorien', in Helmwart Hierdeis and Theo Hug (eds), *Taschenbuch der Pädagogik*, revised and enlarged edn. Hohengehren: Schneider, pp. 238–49.

Jäger, S. (1999) *Kritische Diskursanalyse. Eine Einführung*, second revised and enlarged edn. Duisburg: DISS.

Jäger, S., Kretschmer, D., Cleve, G., Griese, B., Jäger, M., Kellershohn H., Krüger, C. and Wichert, F. (1998) *Der Spuk ist nicht vorbei. Völkisch-nationalistische Ideologeme im öffentlichen Diskurs der Gegenwart*. Duisburg: DISS.

Jarren, O., Sarcinelli, U. and Saxer, U. (eds) (1998) *Politische Kommunikation in der demokratischen Gesellschaft. Ein Handbuch*. Opladen: Westdeutscher Verlag.

Jessop, B. (2000) 'The crisis of the national spatio-temporal fix and the tendential ecological dominance of globalizing capitalism', *International Journal of Urban and Regional Research*, 24 (2): 323–60.

Johnston, A.M. (2000) 'Making history in real time: agents and cultural tools in interaction'. Paper presented at the Sociolinguistics Symposium 2000, Bristol.

Jones, R.H. (1999) 'Mediated action and sexual risk: searching for "culture" in discourses of homosexuality and AIDS prevention in China', *Culture, Health and Sexuality*, 1 (2): 161–80.

Jones, R.H. (2000) 'Mediated discourse in drug abuse education and counselling'. Paper presented at the Georgetown University Roundtable.

Jones, R., Scollon, R., Yung, V., Li, D. and Tsang, W.K. (1997) 'Tracing the voices of Hong Kong's transition with subject-run focus groups'. Paper presented at the Second Symposium on Intercultural Communication, Beijing.

Jung, M., Wengeler, M. and Böke, K. (eds) (1997) *Die Sprache des Migrationsdiskurses. Das Reden über 'Ausländer' in Medien, Politik und Alltag*. Opladen: Westdeutscher Verlag.

Jurt, J. (ed.) (1998) *Zeitgenössische Französische Denker: Eine Bilanz*. Freiburg: Rombach Litterae.

Jurt, J. (1999) *Von Michel Serres bis Julia Kristeva*. Freiburg: Rombach Litterae.

Kant, I. (1952 [1781]) *Critique of Pure Reason. Great Books of the Western World*, in M.J. Adler (ed.), Chicago: Encyclopaedia Britannica, Inc.

Kant, I. (1952 [1788]) *Critique of Practical Reason. Great Books of the Western World*, in M.J. Adler (ed.), Chicago: Encyclopaedia Britannica, Inc.

Kant, I. (1952 [1790]) *Critique of Judgement. Great Books of the Western World*, in M.J. Adler (ed.), Chicago: Encyclopaedia Britannica, Inc.

Kargl, M., Wetschanow, K., Wodak, R. and Perle, N. (1997) *Kreatives Formulieren. Anleitungen zu geschlechtergerechtem Sprachgebrauch*. Vienna: Bundesministerium für Frauenangelegenheiten und Verbraucherschutz.

Kienpointner, M. (1992) *Alltagslogik. Struktur und Funktion von Argumentationsmustern*. Stuttgart-Bad Cannstatt: Frommann-Holzboog.

Kienpointner, M. (1996) *Vernünftig argumentieren. Regeln und Techniken der Diskussion*. Hamburg: Rowohlt.

Kienpointner, M. and Kindt, W. (1997) 'On the problem of bias in political argumentation: An investigation into discussions about political asylum in Germany and Austria', *Journal of Pragmatics*, 27: 555–85.

Kindt, W. (1992) 'Argumentation und Konfliktaustragung in Äusserungen über den Golfkrieg', *Zeitschrift für Sprachwissenschaft*, 11: 189–215.

Klein, J. (1998) 'Politische Kommunikation – Sprachwissenschaftliche Perspektiven', in O. Jarren et al. (eds), *Politische Kommunikation in der demokratischen Gesellschaft. Ein Handbuch*. Opladen: Westdeutscher Verlag, pp. 186–210.

Klemperer, V. (1987 [1947]) *LTI. Notizbuch eines Philologen*, fourth edn. Cologne: Röderberg.

Klemperer, V. (1995) 'Ich will Zeugnis ablegen bis zum Letzten', *Diaries* 1933–1945, Berlin: Aufbau.

Kopperschmidt, J. (1980) *Argumentation. Sprache und Vernunft 2*. Stuttgart: Kohlhammer.

Kopperschmidt, J. (1989) *Methodik der Argumentationsanalyse*. Stuttgart: Frommann-Holzboog.

Kreft, U., Uske, H. and Jäger, S. (eds) (1999) *Kassensturz. Politische Hypotheken der Berliner Republik*. Duisburg: DISS.

Kress, G. (ed.) (1976) *Halliday: System and Function in Language*. Oxford: Oxford University Press.

Kress, G. (1989) 'History and language: towards a social account of linguistic change', *Journal of Pragmatics*, 13 (3): 445–66.

Kress, G. (1990) 'Critical discourse analysis', *Annual Review of Applied Linguistics*, 11: 84–97.

Kress, G. (1993) 'Against arbitrariness: the social production of the sign as a foundational issue in critical discourse analysis', *Discourse and Society*, 4 (2): 169–91.

Kress, G. and Hodge, B. (1979) *Language as Ideology*. London: Routledge.

Kress, G. and van Leeuwen, T. (1996) *Reading Images: The Grammar of Visual Design*. London: Routledge.

Krings, H. et al. (1973) *Handbuch philosophischer Grundbegriffe*. Munich: Kösel.

Kriz, J. and Lisch, R. (1988) *Methodenlexikon*. Munich: Psychologie-Verlags-Union.

Labov, W. (1972) *Language in the Inner City*. Philadelphia: University of Pennsylvania Press.

Laclau, E. (1981) *Politik und Ideologie im Marxismus. Kapitalismus-Faschismus-Populismus*. Berlin: Argument.

Laclau, E. and Mouffe, C. (1985) *Hegemony and Socialist Strategy*. Verso.

Lave, J. and Wenger, E. (1991) *Situated Learning: Legitimate Peripheral Participation*. Cambridge: Cambridge University Press.

Lemke, J.L. (1995) *Textual Politics: Discourse and Social Dynamics*. London: Taylor and Francis.

Lemke, J.L (1999) 'Opening up closure: semiotics across scales'. Paper presented at Closure: emergent organizations and their dynamics, University of Ghent, Belgium, http://academic.brooklyn.cuny.edu/education/jlemke/papers/gent.htm.

Leontjew, A.N. (1982) *Tätigkeit, Bewusstsein, Persönlichkeit*. Cologne: Pahl-Rugenstein.

Levinson, S. (1983) *Pragmatics*. Oxford: Oxford University Press.

Levinson, S.C. (1988) 'Putting linguistics on a proper footing: explorations in Goffman's concepts of participation', in P. Drew and A. Wootton (eds), *Erving Goffman: Exploring the Interaction Order*. Boston: Northeastern University Press, pp. 161–227.

Link, J. (1982) 'Kollektivsymbolik und Mediendiskurse', *kultuRRevolution*, 1: 6–21.

Link, J. (1983) 'Was ist und was bringt Diskurstaktik', *kultuRRevolution*, 2: 60–6.

Link, J. (1986) 'Kleines Begriffslexikon', *kultuRRevolution*, 11: 71.

Link, J. (1992) 'Die Analyse der symbolischen Komponenten realer Ereignisse. Ein Beitrag der Diskurstheorie zur Analyse neorassistischer Äusserungen', in S. Jäger and F. Januschek (eds), *Der Diskurs des Rassismus*. Oldenburg: Osnabrücker Beiträge zur Sprachtheorie 46, pp. 37–52.

Link, J. (1995) 'Diskurstheorie', in von W.F. Haug (ed.), *Historisch-kritisches Wörterbuch des Marxismus*, vol. 2. Hamburg: Argument, pp. 744–48.

Link, J. and Link-Heer, U. (1990) 'Diskurs/Interdiskurs und Literaturanalyse', *Zeitschrift für Linguistik und Literaturwissenschaft (LiLi)*, 77: 88–99.

Marcuse, H. (1980) *Ideen zu einer kritischen Theorie der Gesellschaft*. Frankfurt: Suhrkamp.

Martin, J. (1992) *English Text: System and Structure*. Amsterdam: Benjamins.

Martin, J. and Hasan, R. (eds) (1989) *Language Development: Learning Language, Learning Culture*. Norwood, NJ: Ablex.

Martín Rojo, L. and van Dijk, T.A. (1997) '"There was a problem, and it was solved!" Legitimating the Expulsion of "Illegal" Immigrants in Spanish Parliamentary Discourse', *Discourse and Society*, 8 (4), 523–67.

Martín Rojo, L. and Whittaker, R. (eds) (1998) *Poder-decir o el poder de los discursos*. Madrid: Arrecife.

Marx, K. and Engels, F. (1969) 'Die deutsche Ideologie', *Marx Engels Werke* (MEW) 3. Berlin: Dietz.

Matouschek, B., Wodak, R. and Januschek, F. (1995) *Notwendige Massnahmen gegen Fremde? Genese und Formen von rassistischen Diskursen der Differenz*. Vienna: Passagen Verlag.

Menke, C. and Seel, M. (1993) *Zur Verteidigung der Vernunft gegen ihre Liebhaber und Verächter*. Frankfurt: Suhrkamp.

Merton, R.K. (1967) *On Theoretical Sociology*. New York: Free Press.

Mey, J. (1985) *Whose Language?* Amsterdam: Benjamins.

Miller, J. and Glassner, B. (1997) 'The "inside" and the "outside": finding realities in interviews', in D. Silverman (ed.), *Qualitative Research. Theory, Method and Practice.* London: Sage, pp. 99–112.

Mitten, R. (1992) *The Politics of Antisemitic Prejudice. The Waldheim Phenomenon in Austria.* Boulder, CO: Westview Press.

Mitten, R. (1994) 'Jörg Haider, the anti-immigration petition and immigration policy in Austria', *Patterns of Prejudice*, 28 (2): 24–47.

Moscovici, S. (1981) 'On social representations', in J. Forgas (ed.), *Social Cognition. Perspectives on Everyday Understanding.* London: Academic Press, pp. 191–209.

Mouzelis, N. (1995) *Sociological Theory: What Went Wrong? Diagnoses and Remedies.* London: Routledge.

Muntigl, P., Weiss, G. and Wodak, R. (eds) (2000) *European Union Discourses on Un/employment. An interdisciplinary approach to employment policy-making and organizational change.* Amsterdam: Benjamins.

Ng, S.H. and Bradac, J.J. (1993) *Power in Language. Verbal Communication and Social Influence.* Newbury Park: Sage.

Nishida, K. (1958) *Intelligibility and the Philosophy of Nothingness.* Tokyo: Maruzen Co. Ltd.

Norris, S. (2000) 'Sites of engagement in children's discourse: watching a movie, playing on the computer, and eating hotdogs'. Paper presented at the Sociolinguistics Symposium 2000, Bristol.

Oevermann, U., Allert, T., Konau, E. and Krambeck, J. (1979) 'Die Methodologie einer "objektiven Hermeneutik" und ihre allgemeine forschungslogische Bedeutung in den Sozialwissenschaften', in H.-G. Soeffner (ed.), *Interpretative Verfahren in den Sozial- und Textwissenschaften.* Stuttgart: Metzler, pp. 352–434.

O'Neill, J. (1979) *Kritik und Erinnerung. Studien zur politischen und sinnlichen Emanzipation.* Frankfurt: Suhrkamp.

Parsons, T. and Shils, E. (eds) (1951) *Towards a General Theory of Action.* Cambridge, MA: Harvard University Press.

Pêcheux, M. (1982) *Language, Semantics and Ideology.* London: Macmillan.

Pedro, E.R. (ed.) (1997) *Discourse Analysis.* Lisbon: Colibri Editions.

Peräkylä, A. (1997) 'Reliability and validity in research based on transcripts', in D. Silverman (ed.), *Qualitative Research. Theory, Method and Practice.* London: Sage, pp. 201–20.

Perelman, C. (1976) *Juristische Logik als Argumentationstheorie.* Freiburg/Munich: Alber.

Perelman, C. (1980) *Das Reich der Rhetorik.* Munich: Beck.

Perelman, C. (1994) *Logik und Argumentation.* Weinheim: Beltz Athenäum.

Potter, J. (1997) 'Discourse analysis as a way of analysing naturally occuring data', in D. Silverman (ed.), *Qualitative Research. Theory, Method and Practice.* London: Sage, pp. 144–60.

Ragin, C.S. and Becker, H.S. (eds) (1992) *What is a Case? Exploring the Foundations of Social Inquiry.* Cambridge: Cambridge University Press.

Randolph, T. (2000) 'Mediated discourse analysis: the social actor as mediational means in agents' habitus'. Paper presented at the Sociolinguistics Symposium 2000, Bristol.

Reeves, F. (1989) *British Racial Discourse: A Study of British Political Discourse about Race and Related Matters.* Cambridge: Cambridge University Press.

Reisigl, M. (2000) 'Literarische Texte als heuristische Quellen und kunstfertige Herausforderung für die sprachwissenschaftliche Analyse gesprochener Sprache – Eine Fallstudie am Beispiel von Friedrich Glauser', in O. Panagl and W. Weiss (eds), *Noch einmal: Dichtung und Politik Vom Text zum politisch sozialen Kontext, und zurück.* Vienna: Böhlau, pp. 237–319.

Reisigl, M. (2001) 'Wie man eine Nation herbeiredet. Eine diskursanalytische

Untersuchung zur sprachlichen Konstruktion der österreichischen Identität in politischen Gedenkreden'. Unpublished thesis, University of Vienna.

Reisigl, M. and Wodak, R. (2000) '"Austria First". A discourse historical analysis of the Austrian Anti-foreigner petition in 1992 and 1993'. In M Reisigl and R. Wodak (eds), *The Semiotics of Racism*. Vienna: Passogen Verlag, pp. 269–304.

Reisigl, M. and Wodak, R. (eds) (2000) *The Semiotics of Racism*. Vienna: Passagen Verlag.

Reisigl, M. and Wodak, R. (2001) *Discourse and Discrimination. Rhetorics of Racism and Antisemitism*. London, New York: Routledge.

Ruesch, J. and Bateson, G. (1968 [1951]) *Communication: The Social Matrix of Psychiatry*. New York: W.W. Norton and Company.

Sacks, H. (1992) *Lectures on Conversation, Vols I and II*, edited by G. Jefferson. Oxford: Blackwell.

Sarcinelli, U. (1998) 'Legitimität', in O. Jarren et al. (eds), *Politische Kommunikation in der demokratischen Gesellschaft. Ein Handbuch*. Opladen: Westdeutscher Verlag, pp. 253–67.

Saville-Troike, M. (1989) *The Ethnography of Communication*. Oxford: Basil Blackwell.

Scharsach, H. (1992) *Haiders Kampf*. Vienna: Kremayr and Scheriau.

Scharsach, H. and Knuch, K. (2000) *Haider. Schatten über Europa*. Cologne: Kiepenheuer and Witsch.

Schegloff, E.A. (1998) 'Text and context paper', *Discourse and Society*, 3: 4–37.

Scollon, R. (1997) 'Handbills, tissues, and condoms: a site of engagement for the construction of identity in public discourse', *Journal of Sociolinguistics*, 1 (1): 39–61.

Scollon, R. (1998a) 'A second sphere: media, English and the modernizing consciousness in contemporary Chinese secondary school children'. Paper presented at the conference 'Images and issues: new communication research in Asia', City University of Hong Kong.

Scollon, R. (1998b) *Mediated Discourse as Social Interaction: A Study of News Discourse*. New York: Longman.

Scollon, R. (1999a) 'Official and unofficial discourses of national identity: questions raised by the case of contemporary Hong Kong', in R. Wodak and C. Ludwig (eds), *Challenges in a Changing World: Issues in Critical Discourse Analysis*. Vienna: Passagen Verlag, pp. 21–35.

Scollon, R. (1999b) 'Mediated discourse and social interaction', *Research on Language and Social Interaction*, 32 (1,2): 149–54.

Scollon, R. (2000a) 'Mediated discourse: an integrated theory of sociolinguistic action'. Paper presented at the Sociolinguistics Symposium 2000, Bristol.

Scollon, R. (2000b) 'Methodological interdiscursivity: an ethnographic understanding of unfinalizability', in S. Sarangi and M. Coulthard (eds), *Discourse and Social Life*. London: Longman, pp. 138–54.

Scollon, R. (2000c) 'On the ontogenesis of a social practice'. Paper given at Theory and Interdisciplinarity in Critical Discourse Analysis, Institute on Discourse, Identity and Politics, University of Vienna.

Scollon, R. (2001) *Mediated Discourse. The Nexus of Practice*. London: Routledge.

Scollon, R. and Scollon, S.B.K. (1979) *Linguistic Convergence: An Ethnography of Speaking at Fort Chipewyan, Alberta*. New York: Academic Press.

Scollon, R. and Scollon, S.W. (1997) 'Political, personal, and commercial discourses of national sovereignty: Hong Kong becomes China', in M. Lauristin (ed.), *Intercultural Communication and Changing National Identities*. Tartu: Tartu University Press, pp. 49–71.

Scollon, R. and Scollon, S.W. (forthcoming) *Intercultural Communication*, revised edition. Oxford: Blackwell.

Scollon, R. and Yung, V. (1996) 'The social location of reading: methodological issues in the study of reading as social practice'. Paper presented to the Centre for Language in Social Life, Macquarrie University, Sydney, Australia.

Scollon, R., Bhatia, V., Li, D. and Yung, V. (1999a) 'Blurred genres and fuzzy identities in Hong Kong public discourse: foundational ethnographic issues', *Applied Linguistics*, 20 (1): 22–43.

Scollon, R., Tsang, W.K., Li, D., Yung, V. and Jones, R. (1999b) 'Voice, appropriation, and discourse representation in a student writing task', *Linguistics and Education*, 9 (3): 227–50.

Scollon, R., Scollon, S. and Kirkpatrick, A. (2000) *Contrastive Discourse in Chinese and English: A Critical Appraisal*. Beijing: Foreign Languages Teaching and Research Press.

Scollon, S. (1995) 'Methodological assumptions in intercultural communication'. Paper presented at the Fifth International Conference on Cross-Cultural Communication: East and West, 15–19 August 1995, Heilongjiang University, Harbin, China.

Scollon, S. (1996) 'The commodification of the art of Taaigik Kyuhn (Taijiquan) in Hong Kong: a comparison of sahn wahn pang yau and organized classes'. Paper presented at the Conference on Consumer Culture in Hong Kong, Hong Kong University.

Scollon, S. (1998) 'Identity through the embodiment of authoritative gesture: the practice of taijiquan in Hong Kong', in D.R. Heisey and W. Gong (eds), *Communication and Culture: China and the World Entering the 21st Century*. Amsterdam: Rodopi Editions, pp. 181–204.

Scollon, S. (1999) 'Voice and authority: positioning in taijiquan by interviewers/ editors in contemporary China'. Paper presented at the annual meetings of the National Oral History Association, Anchorage.

Scollon, S. (2000a) 'Whose side are you on? Mediation of national identity through positioning in public space in real time during the Taiwan Missile Crisis'. Paper presented at the Sociolinguistics Symposium 2000, Bristol.

Scollon, S. (2000b) 'Pruning and grafting: The cultivation of identity through imagined genealogies'. Paper presented at the American Anthropological Association, Chicago.

Scollon, S. (2000c) 'Political and somatic alignment: habitus, ideology and social practice'. Paper given at the workshop on Theory and Interdisciplinarity in Critical Discourse Analysis, Institute on Discourse, Identity and Politics, University of Vienna.

Scollon, S. (2000d) 'Who do you think you are? Identity, cognition and pragmatics in a taijiquan group'. Paper presented at the seventh International Pragmatics Association Conference, Budapest.

Scollon, S.W. and Scollon, R. (2000) 'The recursive discursive construction of agency and action: positioning ourselves against neo-liberalism'. Paper presented at the third Conference for Sociocultural Research, Campinas, Brazil.

Silverman, D. (1993) *Interpreting Qualitative Data. Methods for Analysing Talk, Text and Interaction*. London: Sage.

Silverman, D. (ed.) (1997) *Qualitative Research. Theory, Method and Practice*. London: Sage.

Strauss, A.L. (1987) *Qualitative Analysis for Social Scientists*. Cambridge: Cambridge University Press.

Tannen, D. (1994) *Gender and Discourse*. Oxford: Oxford University Press.

Tannen, D., Schiffrin, D. and Hamilton, H. (eds) (2001) *Handbook of Discourse Analysis*. Oxford: Blackwell.

Teubert, W. (1997) 'Zum politisch-gesellschaftlichen Diskurs im Postsozialismus'. Unpublished manuscript, Mannheim.

Teubert, W. (1999) 'Zum Verlust von Pluralität im politisch-gesellschaftlichen Diskurs: Das Beispiel Besitzstände', in U. Kreft, H. Uske and S. Jäger (eds),

Kassensturz. Politische Hypotheken der Berliner Republik. Duisburg: DISS, pp. 29–48.

Thompson, J.B. (1988) *Critical Hermeneutics,* fourth edn. Cambridge: Cambridge University Press.

Thompson, J.B. (1990) *Ideology and Modern Culture.* Cambridge: Polity Press.

Titscher, S., Meyer, M., Wodak, R. and Vetter, E. (2000) *Methods of Text and Discourse Analysis.* London: Sage.

Toulmin, S. (1969) *The Uses of Argument.* Cambridge: Cambridge University Press.

van Dijk, T.A. (1977) *Text and Context: Exploration in the Semantics and Pragmatics of Discourse.* London: Longman.

van Dijk, T.A. (1980) *Macrostructures.* Hillsdale, NJ: Erlbaum.

van Dijk, T.A. (1981) *Studies in the Pragmatics of Discourse.* The Hague/Berlin: Mouton.

van Dijk, T.A. (1984) *Prejudice in Discourse: An Analysis of Ethnic Prejudice in Cognition and Conversation.* Amsterdam: Benjamins.

van Dijk, T.A. (ed.) (1985) *Handbook of Discourse Analysis* (4 vols). New York: Academic Press.

van Dijk, T.A. (1986) *Racism in the Press.* London: Arnold.

van Dijk, T.A. (1987) *Communicating Racism: Ethnic Prejudice in Thought and Talk.* Newbury Park, CA: Sage Publications, Inc.

van Dijk, T.A. (1990) 'Social cognition and discourse', in H. Giles and W.P. Robinson (eds), *Handbook of Language and Social Psychology.* Chichester: John Wiley and Sons, pp. 163–86.

van Dijk, T.A. (1991) *Racism and the Press.* London: Routledge.

van Dijk, T.A. (1993) *Elite Discourse and Racism.* Newbury Park: Sage.

van Dijk, T.A. (ed.) (1997) *Discourse Studies: A Multidisciplinary Introduction.* London: Sage Publications.

van Dijk, T.A. (1998) *Ideology: A Multidisciplinary Approach.* London: Sage Publications.

van Dijk, T.A. and Kintsch, W. (1983) *Strategies of Discourse Comprehension.* New York: Academic Press.

van Leeuwen, T. (1993a) 'Genre and field in critical discourse analysis', *Discourse and Society,* 4 (2): 193–223.

van Leeuwen, T. (1993b) 'Language and representation – the recontextualisation of participants, activities and reactions'. Unpublished thesis, University of Sydney.

van Leeuwen, T. (1995) 'Representing social action', *Discourse and Society,* 6 (1): 81–106.

van Leeuwen, T. (1996) 'The representation of social actors', in C.R. Caldas-Coulthard and M. Coulthard (eds), *Texts and Practices: Readings in Critical Discourse Analysis.* London: Routledge, pp. 32–70.

van Leeuwen, T. (1999) *Speech, Music, Sound.* London: Macmillan.

van Leeuwen, T. and Wodak, R. (1999) 'Legitimizing immigration control. A discourse–historical analysis', *Discourse Studies,* 1 (1): 83–118.

Volosinov, V.I. (1973 [1928]) *Marxism and the Philosophy of Language.* New York: Seminar Press.

Vygotsky, L.S. (1978) *Mind in Society: The Development of Higher Psychological Processes.* Cambridge, MA: Harvard University Press.

Wagner, W. (1994) *Alltagsdiskurs. Die Theorie sozialer Repräsentationen.* Göttingen: Hogrefe.

Waldenfels, B. (1991) 'Michel Foucault: Ordnung in Diskursen', in F. Ewald and B. Waldenfels (eds), *Spiele der Wahrheit. Michel Foucaults Denken.* Frankfurt: Suhrkamp, pp. 277–97.

Webb, E.J. (1966) *Unobtrusive Measures. Nonreactive Research in the Social Sciences.* Chicago: McNall.

Wengeler, M. (1997) 'Argumentation im Einwanderungsdiskurs. Ein Vergleich der Zeiträume 1970–1973 und 1980–1993', in M. Jung, M. Wengeler and K. Böke (eds), *Die Sprache des Migrationsdiskurses. Das Reden über 'Ausländer' in Medien, Politik und Alltag*. Opladen: WDV.

Wenger, E. (1998) *Communities of Practice: Learning, Meaning, and Identity*. Cambridge: Cambridge University Press.

Wertsch, J.V. (1991) *Voices of the Mind: A Sociocultural Approach to Mediated Action*. Cambridge, MA: Harvard University Press.

Wertsch, J.V. (1998) *Mind as Action*. New York: Oxford University Press.

Wertsch, J.V. (forthcoming) 'Vygotsky and Bakhtin on community', in U. Sätterlund-Larsson (ed.), *Socio-Cultural Theory and Methods: An Anthology*.

Widdowson, H.G. (1995) 'Discourse analysis: a critical view', *Language and Literature*, 4 (3): 157–72.

Williams, R. (1977) *Marxism and Literature*. Oxford: Oxford University Press.

Wodak, R. (1989) 'Introduction', in R. Wodak (ed.), *Language, Power and Ideology*. Amsterdam: Benjamins, pp. i–ix.

Wodak, R. (1996a) *Disorders of Discourse*. London and New York: Longman.

Wodak, R. (1996b) 'Critical linguistics and critical discourse analysis', in J. Verschueren (ed.), *Handbook of Pragmatics*. Amsterdam: Benjamins, pp. 207–210.

Wodak, R. (2000a) 'The rise of racism – an Austrian or a European phenomenon?', *Discourse and Society*, 11 (1): 5–6.

Wodak, R. (2000b) '"Wer echt, anständig und ordentlich ist bestimme ich!" – Wie Jörg Haider und die FPÖ die österreichische Vergangenheit, Gegenwart und Zukunft beurteilen', *Multimedia*, 20 (2): 10–11.

Wodak, R. (2000c) 'Does sociolinguistics need social theory? New perspectives on critical discourse analysis'. Keynote speech at SS 2000, Bristol, April 2000 (shortened and published in *Discourse & Society*, 2 (3): 123–147).

Wodak, R. (2001) 'Diskurs, Politik, Identität'. In F. Brix, H. Goebl and O. Panagl (eds), *Der Mensch und Seine Sprache(n)*. Vienna: Böhlau, pp. 80–102.

Wodak, R. and de Cillia, R. (1988) 'Sprache und Antisemitismus. Ausstellungskatalog', *Mitteilungen des Instituts für Wissenschaft und Kunst*, 3.

Wodak, R. and van Dijk, T.A. (eds) (2000) *Racism at the Top. Parliamentary Discourses on Ethnic Issues in Six European States*. Klagenfurt: Drava.

Wodak, R., de Cillia, R., Reisigl, M., Liebhart, K., Hofstätter, K. and Kargl, M. (1998) *Zur diskursiven Konstruktion nationaler Identität*. Frankfurt: Suhrkamp.

Wodak, R., de Cillia, R., Reisigl, M. and Liebhart, K. (1999) *The Discursive Construction of National Identity*. Edinburgh: Edinburgh University Press.

Wodak, R., Menz. F., Mitten, R. and Stern, F. (1994) *Sprachen der Vergangenheiten. Öffentliches Gedenken in österreichischen und deutschen Medien*. Frankfurt: Suhrkamp.

Wodak, R., Nowak, P., Pelikan, J., Gruber, H., de Cillia, R. and Mitten, R. (1990) *'Wir sind alle unschuldige Täter'. Diskurshistorische Studien zum Nachkriegsantisemitismus*. Frankfurt: Suhrkamp.

Yung, V.K.Y. (1996) 'A readership study of tertiary students in Hong Kong'. Paper presented at the International Conference on Communication and Culture: China and the world entering the 21st century, Peking University.

Yung, V.K.Y. (1997) 'The discourse of popular culture among tertiary students in Hong Kong'. Paper presented at the LACUS Forum, York University, Toronto.

Yung, V.K.Y. (2000) 'Focus groups as sites of engagement: a study of comparative conversational practices'. Paper presented at the Sociolinguistics Symposium 2000, Bristol.

Index